FIRST WOMEN OF HOLLYWOOD

First Women of Hollywood

Female Pioneers in the Early Motion Picture Business

Mary Mallory

Essex, Connecticut

An imprint of The Globe Pequot Publishing Group, Inc.
64 South Main Street
Essex, CT 06426
www.globepequot.com

Distributed by NATIONAL BOOK NETWORK

British Library Cataloguing in Publication Information available

Library of Congress Cataloging-in-Publication Data is available

ISBN 9781493089307 (cloth) | ISBN 9781493089314 (ebook)

∞™ The paper used in this publication meets the minimum requirements of American National
Standard for Information Sciences—Permanence of Paper for Printed Library Materials, ANSI/
NISO Z39.48-1992.

Contents

INTRODUCTION

It's the visible star whose twinkle catches the eye.
But the invisible star some distance behind it may
be a lot more important.

There are many invisible stars of serious
magnitude in the movie business. Just as some
of the visible stars get their ability to glitter from
invisible luminaries somewhere beyond, as the
screen stars that glitter before the public would be
entirely dark were it not for off-stage luminaries
which make the spotlight possible.

In many ways the stars behind the screen are
more important than the stars upon it.[1]

When the women directed the films, the other
directors, the men, were very cooperative. And the
actors didn't resent it at all because a woman was
directing. They took direction just the same as if it
were a man directing. Everyone cooperated.[2]

In no line of endeavor has a woman made so
emphatic an impress than in the amazing film
industry, which has created in its infant stage a
new and compelling art wherein the gentler sex
is now so active a factor that one may not name
a single vocation in either the artistic or business

side of its progress in which women are not con-
spicuously engaged. In the theaters, in the studios
and even in the exchanges where film productions
are marketed and released to exhibitors, the fair
sex is represented as in no other calling to which
women have harkened in the early years of the
twentieth century.[3]

Women were the superpower of the silent-film industry. Middle-
class women were the juggernaut at the box office, turning it into a financial behemoth, and women in front of and behind the camera enabled it
to produce enough movies to keep up with that exploding demand. Sadly,
over time, most of these women were forgotten.

In its earliest days, moving-picture-making resembled a modest
cottage industry, operating under the umbrella of Trusts. Small companies, organized mostly like theater troupes, where everyone pitched in to
complete tasks, cranked out one-reel films that played to mostly immigrant and lower-middle-class audiences. When the industry turned more
upscale, and exhibition improved to small legitimate theaters, it publicly
acknowledged women's participation and contributions in producing
films, lifting movies out of lower-brow entertainment into one more
suitable for middle-class audiences. Around 1909 newspapers inaugurated movie sections, fan and trade magazines were created to discuss
and publicize films, and studios regularly began announcing star names,
all contributing to movies' growing success.

The early motion picture industry exploded in the 1910s when
middle-class women became hooked on movies. As attendance skyrocketed, the burgeoning field needed more workers to produce enough
product to keep up with demand. Largely created by immigrants, the film
industry creatively and scientifically evolved over its early decades thanks
to the work of people outside the mainstream—immigrants, people of
color, women—partly as a result of elites denigrating the fledgling field.

As the industry transitioned from neophyte to powerhouse, young,
ambitious rebels energized and revitalized its output. At the same time,
American culture was evolving as women sought the right to vote and

work outside traditional fields, unions exploded in number, and immigrants contributed to flourishing business output.

When younger men enlisted or were drafted for World War I, many positions opened up that required filling, giving scores of women the freedom and opportunity to handle more challenging, diverse jobs. Most found they enjoyed the work, but many discovered themselves replaced by returning GIs after the war.

Women entered film production for several reasons: for excitement, desire, challenge, opportunity, and for some, just to survive. They wore many hats: some beautiful actresses in front of the camera, others in leadership positions, and many involved in the various production stages of making a motion picture. Many in leading positions mentored younger women and employed as many as they could to diversify the workforce and increase female participation. Some worked for a few years before marrying and leaving to start a family or deciding to move on to greener pastures. Others worked steadily for decades, while others struggled to hang on as they aged. Some just tried it out for a lark.

Much is known of those women who appeared in front of the camera or in important positions behind it, as the industry publicized them in entertainment and fan magazines as well as major newspapers. Other females in more obscure or less powerful jobs received little to no public boost for the often backbreaking work they performed. For certain positions like projectionist, accompanist, and the like, the actual first woman might never be known, since many women probably managed theaters, projected films, and provided musical accompaniment all across the country in small mom-and-pop–style theaters but received no recognition for their daily contributions.

Mostly written out of history, women provided an integral component for popularizing silent film and turning it into an economic powerhouse, paving the way for the Golden Age of Hollywood. Women often pioneered practices and established trends, leading several fields in its earliest days. They were integral in producing enough films to keep up with exploding popular demand in film's second decade. Men often resented their presence, power, and success, however, and as the studio system of massive factories and industrialization took hold, women found themselves out of favor and replaced.

This book is an attempt to right that wrong, recognizing the pioneering, powerful women who made lasting impacts on cinema, and reintroducing to the public many who made important contributions in their own right, wonderful role models demonstrating perseverance, initiative, and risk-taking in pursuing their dreams to the fullest. These pioneers all opened the door to future generations of women looking to break into the industry themselves.

ACTRESSES

Tsuru Aoki portrait by Nelson Evans, circa 1916. *Mary Mallory*

Tsuru Aoki, First Asian Star

THOUGH LONG IN THE SHADOW OF HER BETTER-KNOWN HUSBAND, Tsuru Aoki achieved as great a fame as Sessue Hayakawa and as much renown for her acting. Born in Japan though raised in the United States, the beautiful Aoki functioned as a crossroads between the East and West, blending together the best attributes of both. Her life was a paradox: brought to this country as a child, her image revolved around her American assimilation and identity, but she rarely received an opportunity to perform as such onscreen. Growing up surrounded by art, she brought artistic expression to the screen herself. Tired of the usage of yellowface, she sought to actually represent her culture onscreen, giving it dignity and respect. Aoki was many things but especially a groundbreaker for Asian performers.

Born September 9, 1892, in Harata, Japan, the daughter of a poor Japanese fisherman and his wife, she was raised by her actor-performer aunt Sadayakko Kawakami, the "Ellen Terry of Japan," and uncle, Otijiro (Otto) Kawakami, the "Henry Irving of Japan."[1] The Kawakamis organized the Imperial Theatre of Japan, introducing Shakespeare plays to the country. From early in her life, Aoki was surrounded by art and artifice, preparing her for life on and off the film screen.

In 1899, the Theatre Company and Aoki sailed for the United States to perform on tour on their way to Europe and the World Exposition in Paris.[2] Aoki performed onstage with the troupe early on the West Coast but ran into trouble in San Francisco, where city officials declared her underage for performing. One reported, "Little Tsurru [sic] the juvenile member of the company has been left behind in the hands of J. Aoki, an artist of this city. She will complete her education under his care."[3]

Aoki, actually artist Hyosai Aoki, moved with the young girl to Pasadena, changing her last name to Aoki, raising her as his own. He introduced her to the arts, opening an artistic vein in her, allowing her to study dancing and acting.[4] During these years she also attended St. Margaret's Hall in San Mateo, California, where she was a classmate to future screenwriter Frances Marion.[5]

When the artist Aoki died in 1912, young Aoki turned toward her love of acting to survive, joining Los Angeles stock companies to train and grow, and studying with the Egan Dramatic School and the Scovell Juvenile Stock Company. She tracked down Louise Scher, who her father had asked to act as foster mother in case of his death. Aoki moved in with Scher and her family while figuring out her next move.[6] By 1913 she was acting and adapting plays for a Japanese company at Egan Dramatic School in Los Angeles, where she soon met a fellow pupil and performer Sessue Hayakawa, who was quickly attracted to the beautiful and ambitious girl.[7]

In a strange bit of luck, comedian Fred Mace discovered the warm Aoki and signed her to a contract with his company to costar with him in *Mimosa's Sweetheart*, as a prim young Japanese woman whom Mace is attempting to woo. Her acting impressed the cast, and she was called "exceptionally clever."[8] The bright and industrious young woman stated she hoped to form her own company and make artistic films in Japan to show to US audiences, to try, as the only Asian female star in film, to bring more understanding of Japanese to the American people.

Aoki soon appeared in *The Oath of Tsura San*, where she transformed from geisha girl into action hero. From this point forward, Aoki found herself almost typecast as an obedient, self-sacrificing Japanese maiden full of honor and value. Her next film, *O Mimi San*, saw her essay a very Madame Butterfly–like character opposite a former schoolmate from the Egan Dramatic School, Sessue Hayakawa. The two made a formidable team, with excellent chemistry and timing. Looking for authenticity and believability in his films, New York Motion Picture Company producer Thomas H. Ince had signed her and her Japanese company and trusted her instincts regarding the intense Hayakawa.[9]

Though he believed in authenticity onscreen, Ince had no problem with crafting elaborate false biographies à la Theda Bara to help promote films. Before the feature *The Wrath of the Gods*, Ince had released a false biography of Aoki, claiming that she was a native of the island of Sakura, almost destroyed by volcano on January 13, 1914, with most of her relatives killed in the eruption.[10] Aoki gave a restrained, thoughtful performance, helping to somewhat rein in Hayakawa's overacting.

Over the next several years, Aoki would star in such films as *Love's Sacrifice*, *A Tragedy of the Orient*, *Alien Souls*, and *The Curse of Caste* as a honorable young Japanese woman often sacrificing herself in place of her great love. She and Hayakawa, whom she married on May 1, 1914, after falling in love during the making of *The Typhoon*, also played Native Americans in *The Last of the Line* and *The Death Mask*. While Hayakawa soon starred in *The Cheat* for Cecil B. DeMille and gained superstardom, Aoki remained content to take on challenging roles and stay below the radar, taking the subservient role in their marriage, perhaps because her husband desired it.

When Hayakawa's career took off at Paramount, Aoki subsumed her own ambitions to support him in his features there and later at his own company, Haworth Pictures. Whatever her film, Aoki garnered excellent reviews, noted for her believability and sensitivity, whether playing traditional Asian roles or those of assimilation and acceptance. Though a fine artist, the actress remained stuck in Asian roles, with the industry failing to allow her to portray average American women, seeming to play to society stereotypes, sacrificing herself in some way for men, whether Asian or white.

Critics praised her acting, with the *Motion Picture News* stating, "Miss Aoki, besides possessing a face which seems to meet perfectly the screen's exacting requirements, understands restraint so well that her impersonation of the ill-fated wife ceases to be acting at all, and is transformed in the spectator's mind, to life itself."[11] *The Billboard* exclaimed, "Miss Aoki left no doubt in the minds of those who witnessed her debut that she is destined to become one of filmdom's most popular leading women."[12] The *El Paso Herald* wrote, "It is dangerous to make comparisons, but the work of this little artist in this beautiful picture in point of style bears a striking resemblance to Mary Pickford's. Both are appealing in their simplicity and emotion rather than resorting to exaggerated methods."[13] Aoki sold her performances through her expressive eyes, simply underplaying her parts with a pleasing naturalness that charmed audiences.

Many noted Aoki's focus, discipline, sincerity, charm, and intelligence. While she was happy to gain such praise, Aoki always worried that people wouldn't like her, perhaps because of never feeling quite accepted because of her background. In many ways, her self-effacing attitude was an attempt to blend in and be at one with others, especially at a time of growing resentment against Asians in America.

Hayakawa and Aoki lived as any young couple in America would, wearing typical dress and residing in a simple bungalow with a dog while enjoying pleasures like reading, sports, and taking drives. As Hayakawa grew more successful, they purchased Argyle Castle and ever more elaborate sports cars, while throwing some of Hollywood's most entertaining and popular parties. The couple took part in bond drives and war rallies just like other Hollywood stars did, with Aoki also appearing at Red Cross events, fund drives, pageants, and at women's events at places like the Hollywood Studio Club, all while taking dance lessons from Ruth St. Denis, piano lessons from Godorowsky, and singing lessons, as well as horseback riding and playing golf.

Publicity stories, on the other hand, noted the blending of the two cultures, pointing out how their home contained both Japanese and English decoration, and that Aoki sometimes wore her colorful kimonos off-camera as well. The press always subtly noted their otherness, pointing out that Aoki was the more American of the two with her flawless American accent and knowledge of American ways. A story in the 1920 *Picture Play* magazine stated, "You would never be at all convinced that Tsuru Aoki were Japanese if your acquaintance was restricted to over-the-phone conversations."[14] The couple walked a fine line trying to bridge both cultures and please both.

Hayakawa and Aoki continued working well together, especially costarring opposite each other in his Haworth Productions. Most of the films provided the opportunity for giving Asian characters dignity and

A set at Inceville during production of *The Wrath of the Gods* (1914) with Tsuru Aoki at right. *Marc Wanamaker/Bison Archives*

agency, unlike what happened in most studio films of the time. Offscreen, Aoki spent time ensuring authenticity of costumes, hair, and cultural depictions.

Aoki signed a three-picture deal with Universal to once again star in films, noting she yearned to play comedy again because she was tired of drama and always being killed off in films. While she earned great reviews from critics, growing resentment against Asians, Japanese in particular, rankled. After her last film, the actress announced her retirement, perhaps in grief over the change in American attitudes, and perhaps because Hayakawa forced her to abandon starring roles on her own and devote herself to him. She became known as Mrs. Hayakawa. Trying to escape growing anti-immigrant sentiment, the couple traveled to Japan and later Europe to distance themselves from hateful times. Aoki appeared in one more American film in 1960.

Talented in both acting onscreen and charming people off, Aoki attempted to bridge cultural divides during her time as a cinema star, proud of her Asian heritage and hoping to educate Americans about it. Mostly stuck in stereotypical roles throughout her career, she deftly brought sensitivity and expressiveness to her performances, whether as sacrificial heroines or the few comedic scamps she played. Self-effacing and private, she lived a life of peace and contentment, remaining true to her values and a role model for all.

UNDERWOOD & UNDERWOOD
STUDIOS. N. Y.

Theda Bara portrait as a vamp with a raven by Underwood & Underwood. *Angie Schneider*

Theda Bara, First Vamp

IN THE EARLIEST DAYS OF THE CINEMA, FEMALE CHARACTERS WERE mostly portrayed as young and innocent, reflecting the patriarchal view of women. Persevering, loyal, dedicated, women were depicted as contented wives and mothers, or aspiring to be. By 1912 female representation on screen grew more animated, more risk-taking, perhaps tying in with the growing action-oriented serial craze featuring headstrong young women, and perhaps also with the rising suffrage movement fighting to get women the right to vote. In 1915 Fox Film Corporation introduced audiences to the vamp character, one who would lead men to destruction. A film-created celebrity, Theda Bara grew famous portraying the first vamp onscreen, giving her power and strength while adding softening touches. Though finding fame as a vamp, Bara was nothing like the woman she portrayed onscreen.

Born Theodosia Goodman, on July 29, 1885, in Cincinnati, Ohio, the daughter of a tailor and his wife, Bara was raised a good Jewish girl looking out for others. The local newspaper commented on the "beautiful little six-year-old" delivering a donation to help a local family and then "taking all the sunshine of the day" when she left.[1] She brought in a donation for Christmas baskets in December, leading the paper to call her "the same little sunbeam."[2]

A delightful child, Bara enjoyed reading and studying music, performing in a piano recital at the age of eleven.[3] As a teenager, her dreams turned to the stage. By 1905 the family was living in Rochester, New York, before Bara studied drama in New York City while working as an actress, perhaps because of a financial reversal in the family.[4] She appeared onstage in New York and traveled with a stock company before scouring casting offices looking for work at what would then have been the advanced age of thirty.

Though she first appeared as an extra in the 1914 film *The Stain*, Bara found superstardom in her second film and first starring role for Fox, *A Fool There Was*. Based on the Rudyard Kipling poem of the same name, the film featured the quiet, retiring actress as a Spanish siren of doom, whose overwhelming sensual presence lured men to their destruction. What led to the film's popularity was the studio's creative buildup of their unknown star, employing fantastic hyperbole to create an exotic woman of history. Press releases claimed that the dramatic actress was the daughter of an artist and an Arabian princess, with her name an anagram for "Arab Death." To add to the sensationalism, they luridly posed her with snakes and skulls in photographs released to the public.

Thanks to the film's overwhelming impact on culture and Bara's dramatic portrayal, she shot to celebrity as the screen's first vamp. Folks around the country inquired about her background, naively believing in the original story. Others, perhaps angry about women raising voices and marching to declare their right to vote, looked on the portrayal of an independent, passionate woman in search of her desires onscreen as a threat. Even a British magazine wrote that "it was due more to Theda Bara than to any other siren of the screen that people on this side of the Atlantic came to know the modern meaning of the word 'Vamp.'"[5]

Perhaps to correct the record, some information about Bara's real background was published after the release of *A Fool There Was*, acknowledging her American birth as Theodosia Goodman and theater background, while still claiming she was studying abroad when she took the stage name Bara before coming back to the States.[6] Mocking the apocryphal for all its worth, a facetious unnamed columnist wrote, "Temperamental Parisienne who robs timid and unattractive wives of their cantaloupe-headed husbands is real arch-torpedo of domesticity and may in reality be plain Cincinnati girl. . . . This pretty woman has become the symbol against which every woman's fist is raised, the terror of the flat-housewife, the Ishmaelite of femininity. The fact that Theda Bara is a home-buster only in working hours, and in other hours is a gentle, slightly melancholy, even timid creature, will, of course, not be believed by the women."[7]

A story in early 1916 from an Atchison, Kansas, newspaper revealed Bara's actual background from former schoolgirl friend Sara Salzer, who called her a "very proper young person," raised of a good Jewish family. Salzer revealed that "back in Cincinnati the old school friends of Theodosia Goodman in talking of her fame, say the silent drama is her salvation as her speaking voice comes right through her nose, with a decided twang."[8]

Waiting sometime after the film's release, Bara opened up to young Delight Evans of *Screenland*, revealing her true nature, decidedly different from what she played onscreen. An introvert, she preferred to quietly remain at home if not going out for dinner or the theater. Evans found her "a consummate actress; but it is such a pity that she must make up for the role. She had a part to play that afternoon; and she played it much more cleverly than she did Cleopatra. . . . A clever actress in her high-school days, Theodosia Goodman later developed a somewhat extraordinary aptitude for portraying vamps, ancient, medieval, and modern."[9]

Bara starred in seven films for Fox in 1915, many playing off her "vamp" persona, with such titles as *The Devil's Daughter*, *Sin*, *Destruction*, *Siren of Hell*, and *The Serpent*. She starred in eight films in 1916, meaty ones offering more range, like *East Lynne*, *Under Two Flags*, *Her Double Life*, and *Romeo and Juliet*.

In 1917 Bara traveled west to the California studio to star in its historic opus *Cleopatra*, which surpassed all box office expectations. Featuring massive sets, a cast of thousands, and exotic, skin-baring costumes, the film raked in profits at the box office, with many critics considering it Bara's best work; one stated that she made *Cleopatra* "a sensual voluptuary of the most luring type who conquers only by her seductiveness." Her alluring performance and come-hither stares hearkened back to that of *A Fool There Was*.

The actress made another seven films for Fox in 1919 before the studio canceled her contract, and her film career was basically over. She married older, refined director Charles Brabin in 1921 and retired from

Theda Bara pictured on *Theda Bara, I'll Keep Away from You* sheet music during vamp period, 1916. *Mary Mallory*

the screen, though she made two short films in the late 1920s, trying to revive her career.

By 1921 the embroidered lies about her name bothered Bara, and she opened up, telling a magazine, "But I have read so many lies about myself that I hardly know the truth any more. My manager and my press agent have treated me like a freak in a circus side-show."[10] She was ready to exit the fame train.

Truly selling a performance, Theda Bara, the quiet Jewish girl from Cincinnati, created the screen's first spiderlike "vamp," ensnaring men in her web of allure and danger, causing their destruction. Perhaps she became such a public sensation because of women's conflicting views at the time of their roles—that of independent, action-oriented women making their own decisions or that of more conservative, homebound women, following men's dictates that "good" women remained at home as wives and mothers, content with their lot.

Clara Bow portrait with a smoldering look, circa 1928. *Marc Wanamaker/Bison Archives*

Clara Bow, First Sex Symbol

THE IMAGE OF SILENT HOLLYWOOD'S LEADING LADIES EVOLVED QUICKLY from its beginnings. Focusing on the innocent young girl characters of Mary Pickford and the Gish sisters, it morphed into action-oriented, assertive serial heroines like Helen Holmes and Ruth Roland, then man-eating vamps like Theda Bara, the flirty flappers like Colleen More, and finally, the sexual flare of the late 1920s "It" girl, Clara Bow. The screen's first true sex symbol, Bow exuded a sensuous, infectious spirit that charmed audiences and moviegoers, sexy and innocent all at the same time. Born into poverty in Brooklyn, the playful young ingenue wowed audiences in the late 1920s as she became one of Paramount and Hollywood's top icons.

Born July 25, 1905, in Brooklyn, New York, Clara Bow lived a Dickensian childhood full of poverty and despair. Bow found herself surrounded by tragedy at every turn, forced to care for a mother suffering from mental illness while living in decrepit hovels with an emotionally and sexually abusive father. Feeling out of place, alone, and extremely sensitive and self-conscious with a slight stammer, Bow yearned for escape, usually finding it in movies and fan magazines.

Bow found an escape route through an ad in a 1921 issue of *Motion Picture Magazine* promoting a Fame and Fortune contest, which the magazine called "The Magical Key to the Screen."[1] It awarded a part in a movie as first prize. Taking a chance, Bow delivered two terrible portraits to the contest office in person, with the manager writing, "Called in person—very pretty" at the bottom of the photos.[2] Called for a screen test along with other contestants, Bow watched and instinctively realized the importance of individuality. "The girl who spent hours imitating Mary Pickford sensed that to be special, she must be herself."[3]

Quick, instinctive, Bow improved rapidly in front of the camera, letting her guard down, going on to win her one-chance-in-a-million contest to escape poverty, appearing in a small part in the 1922 movie *Beyond the Rainbow*, totally cut upon release. Bow's intuitive grasp of the camera led director Elmer Clifton to continually expand her role in *Down to the Sea in Ships* the next year, developing her as an actress. Thanks to his role, Bow earned a spot as a WAMPAS (Western Association of Motion Picture Advertisers) Baby Star in 1924.

She struggled to find parts before gaining a role in *Enemies of Women* (1923). Bow found release in the movie from her abject despair of home life, shining vivaciously onscreen while crying within. As she wrote later, "In the picture I danced on a table. All the time I hadda be laughin', rompin', displayin' joy of life. . . . I'd cry my eyes out when I left my mama in the mornin'—and then go dance on a table."[4] *Motion Picture Magazine*'s story on Bow winning the contest caught this contradiction, featuring a photo of the vulnerable winner while writing, "She is full of confidence, determination, and ambition. She is endowed with a mentality beyond her years. She has a genuine spark of the divine fire."[5]

From the first, her portraits revealed a wistful, lost little girl seeking refuge and a place to call home. In front of the cameras, however, the desperate teenager displayed great charisma, personality, and potent sensuality, drawing audiences' gaze. Looking for protection, her film benefactors would more often exploit her and her career rather than nurture the talented star.

After just a few films, the Los Angeles–based Preferred Pictures signed her to a contract, bringing her west after a swarm of scandals besmirched the film capital. Undergoing a brutal test with new boss B. P. (Benjamin Percival) Schulberg, Bow passed with flying colors. Agent Maxine Alton exclaimed, "She was an emotional machine," volubly expressing a range of emotions with ease.[6] Preferred starred her in their own films besides loaning her out for others for a nice payback. Lent to First National for *Black Oxen*, Bow impressed director Frank Lloyd by merely walking through the door, as she later reminisced: "A big smile came over his face and he looked tickled to death."[7] Interviewed by the press, Lloyd stated, "Bow is the personification of the ideal aristocratic flapper, mischievous, pretty, aggressive, quick-tempered and deeply sentimental."[8] Her career as the screen's ultimate flapper queen was born—somewhat ironic, because all the mad exuberance at life covered the disillusioned, sad little girl hiding underneath.

Bow achieved her first lead in *Poisoned Paradise* early in 1924, playing a charming though tough-minded flapper, starting to find her stride onscreen. Loaned out to Universal, she starred in the 1924 prohibition tale *Wine*, drawing high praises from *Los Angeles Times* writer Alma Whittaker: "She radiates sex appeal tempered with an impish sense of humor. . . . She hennas her blond hair so that it will photograph dark in the pictures. . . . Her social decorum is of that natural, good-natured, pleasantly informal kind. . . . She can act on or off the screen—takes a joyous delight in accepting a challenge to vamp any selected male—the more unpromising specimen the better. When the hapless victim is scared into speechlessness, she gurgles with naughty delight and tries another."[9]

Preferred kept her busy during this time; she acted in eight pictures in 1924 and fourteen in 1925, learning her craft while making the studio lots of money on the loan-outs. Audiences grew for her films, entranced by her effervescent screen personality, with her last Preferred Picture, *The Plastic Age*, released in 1926, her most popular ever. As actress Louise Brooks wrote years later, "[Bow] became a star without nobody's help."[10] About to face bankruptcy in the fall of 1925, Schulberg landed the position of associate producer at Paramount Pictures, bringing Bow as his ultimate playing card.

More confident in herself and her acting talents, Bow wowed with her pictures at Paramount, a wonderful contradiction of flirty, take-no-prisoners young women hiding the vulnerable, naive parts of their psyches underneath, all seething with sexy vitality. Her spontaneity, personality, and flashy eyes let emotions play across her face, charming audiences. Director Victor Fleming captured her intuitive performances: "Touch her, and she responded with genius."[11] Bow played a wide range of roles, from tough tomboys and confident shop girls to flirty flappers, all combining moxie and sensitivity.

Bow came into her own at Paramount, owning every film she starred in. *Photoplay* wrote, "When she is on the screen, nothing else matters. When she is off, the same is true."[12] In the 1926 film *Dancing Mothers*, she played "Kittens," a selfish, saucy flapper reduced to despairing vulnerability after recognizing her mother as her love rival. Bow's vivacious, saucy manner onscreen led novelist Elinor Glyn to call her the "It" girl, one of several nicknames Bow had claimed, but the moniker fit. Paramount produced the film *It* in 1927 to capitalize on her fame, garnering rave reviews for Bow as the poor but plucky shopgirl Betty Spence who steals the heart of her boss Cyrus Waltham (Antonio Moreno). Bow ranked as one of Paramount's top stars with her passionate, sexy onscreen performances but once again found herself exploited by studio bosses, who raked in big bucks while paying her middle-rung rates.

Offscreen, Bow lived as wildly as many of her characters, partying, dancing, and never standing still. A total nonconformist, she lived for the moment, passionately enjoying each one. While this fueled lively onscreen performances, it also engendered negative reviews in the press, leading to many difficulties. She cycled through emotions onscreen while cycling through money and men offscreen, while looking for a place to call home.

Though uneasy with the new sound medium, Bow remained "box office queen" through several sound performances in *The Wild Party*, *Dangerous Curves*, and *The Saturday Night Kid*. Her nervousness over sound recording grew in intensity, requiring retakes for *The Wild Party* as her eyes wandered to look at the overhead mike. As Bow pined in an interview, "I can't buck progress. I have to do the best I can."[13] Her nervousness and stress grew, perhaps exacerbated by latent mental issues inherited from her mother. Bow continued working through 1931, still popular at the box office but seeing picture revenues drop as new stars arose, but her emotional health cracked due to overwork, scandals, and celebrity.

After spending time in a sanatorium, Bow retreated to boyfriend Rex Bell's ranch in Nevada to recuperate, marrying him in December that year. Feeling better, she signed a contract with Fox Film Corporation in 1932 for a two-picture deal for *Call Her Savage* and *Hoop-La*. Released in 1932, *Call Her Savage* revealed Clara at her sexy, passionate best, a scandalous wildcat who upends convention while defeating all manner of destruction thrown her way. An over-the-top melodrama with plenty of pre-Code sexual scandal and innuendo, *Call Her Savage* allowed Bow to play a real woman and burn up the screen with sexual intensity and desire. She came alive onscreen, but life behind the cameras was torture for her. After making *Hoop-La* in 1934, her last film, Bow retired from public life to be a wife and mother until mental instability once again came her way.

Bow wowed the moviegoing public in the 1920s with her effervescent, natural, and spirited onscreen persona, which masked the hopeless despair and vulnerability underneath. Her innocent yet sensual flair onscreen ushered in more physical and explicit depictions of sexuality in the decades to come, yet they never topped her electric performances. Bow ran wild as Hollywood's first sex symbol, a complicated blend of wild eroticism and charming naivete.

Marie Eline identified as the "Tanhauser Kid" [*sic*] on *Tattle Tale* sheet music, 1914. *Mary Mallory*

Marie Eline, First Child Star

In the first decade of American cinema, children often starred in and "stole" films. Many acted onscreen only a few times and many just as extras. Only a few composed a regular part of studios' acting stables at this time, like Biograph's Gladys Egan and Jack Pickford, Essanay's Baby Lillian Walker, and Thanhouser's Marie Eline. Sometimes called "Child Bernhardt of the Silent Drama,"[1] Marie Eline joined the Thanhouser Company in 1910 and, thanks to her popularity, became the first female child star of the screen and the first to be advertised as such. Her popularity and stardom would lead to the crowning of such child superstars as Jackie Coogan, Baby Peggy, and Shirley Temple.

Born February 27, 1905, in Milwaukee, Wisconsin,[2] little Marie Eline took to the stage as a tiny tot to help support the family. She began her career appearing in *The Bridge* starring Guy Bates Post in 1908, appeared in 1909 with star Fanny Ward in *Van Allen's Wife*, and starred in singer-songwriters' Nora Bayes and Jack Norworth's *The Jolly Bachelor* in 1910 as "captain of the kiddies."[3] Marie Eline gained further credits in *La Belle Rouse* and *The Fatal Wedding.*[4]

Many Thanhouser movies revolved around her character, whether she played a boy—a common practice at the time—or a girl. She received mostly excellent notices for her work, such as this for *David Copperfield* in 1911: "The child actress known as 'The Thanhouser Kid' is to be heartily commended for her work in this production: for a child of her years she is a marvel—her conception of the part she plays is remarkable."[5] Others claimed that she possessed the invaluable gift of true genius.[6] So popular was she that the studio began sending her to theaters around New

York City to perform and to promote their films as audiences fell in love with her.

The Thanhouser Company recognized the great advertising hook of the cute Marie Eline. Dubbing her "The Thanhouser Kid," they publicized her by nickname in many ads and press releases in order to attract female and family audiences, often placing her photo first among all their stars. Using a bit of hyperbole, the studio often promoted Marie Eline as "the greatest child actress in the world" in advertisements in 1910,[7] often the only actor credited. Quick on the draw, Thanhouser was the first studio to promote their child performers, with *Moving Picture News* reporting "'The Thanhouser Kid,' I believe, set the pace, and Biograph, Vitagraph, Rex, when it got to noting, and other firms took the hint and fell in line for the promoting of the little ones before the camera."[8] Marie Eline was so famous that major music publisher Jerome H. Remick & Company commissioned one of their staff composers to draft the song "The Thanhouser Kid," which they published as sheet music illustrated with her photo.

In 1913 Marie Eline took to the vaudeville stage, even world-famous Proctor's, in a limited engagement through the graces of the Thanhouser Company, playing off her fame in clean entertainment for women and children. While she sometimes promoted films, like *The Changeling*, in which she played two identical children, most of the time she appeared on the vaudeville stage with her own act, performing character songs and dances and impersonating others.[9] Marie Eline would continually update her act, switching out songs and occasionally teaming with her sister and others.

Marie Eline aged out of playing "The Thanhouser Kid" at the age of eleven in late 1913. C. G. Hite of Princess Films, based in New Rochelle and released by Mutual Films, hired her in December 1913 as a featured player under her real name, Marie Eline, to play opposite actors like Muriel Ostriche and Boyd Marshall.[10] While no titles appear to have actually been produced, Marie Eline did earn the further potential to shoot film roles.

World Film Corporation hired her in 1914 to appear in its feature film *Uncle Tom's Cabin* in the prime role of Little Eva.[11] The original

1852 story by author Harriet Beecher Stowe was a huge hit that galvanized the antislavery movement; the film continued to screen for local audiences across the country over the next ten years, mostly promoted on Marie Eline's name. As her child star cuteness faded away, Marie Eline found it more difficult to gain roles as she became a teenager. Indefatigable, she soldiered on.

Marie Eline and ten-year-old Eugene Blessin performed a comedy skit called "Springtime" in 1915 as part of a vaudeville act in which she played three different parts while making "lightning changes of costume."[12] One review called her sketch "charmingly carried off," where the children "act with a freedom and naturalness most delightful as it is most unexpected in an act of this kind."[13] Often these performances were advertised for local children, and parents could drop off their kids for supervision by theater staff. By 1916 she turned to vaudeville full-time after Mutual canceled her contract, creating her "Marie Eline and Company" troupe soon thereafter. Her last film roles came in 1919,when she and actor Neal Burns starred in a series of two-reel shorts for Capitol Comedies released through Christie Comedies.

With no residuals or film roles coming their way, Marie Eline and her sister Grace crisscrossed the country in vaudeville attempting to make ends meet, playing up Marie's background as the "Thanhouser Kid." In late 1926, the sisters joined forces as a comedy act on the vaudeville stage after Marie appeared in *Rose Marie* in 1926. Over the next several years, they toured the country wowing audiences with their performances. In a stage show preceding the screening of Clara Bow's film *The Wild Party* in Indianapolis in 1929, the sisters, billed as the "Queens of Comedy," stole the show and "create much enthusiasm in the audience" as one newspaper stated.[14] Besides developing their own act, the sisters spent their free time drafting short stories about events surrounding their stage and film careers, which they hoped to compile into a book.[15] The sisters performed together through 1932.

Though only a film actress for a few short years as a young child, Marie Eline charmed audiences with her confident, self-assured performances, both male and female, which helped sell Thanhouser Films and gained her fame. The first child performer nicknamed by her studio and the first kid actor promoted, Marie Eline thus became the first female child star, setting the stage for several superstar child performers who followed her into the movies.

Myrtle Gonzalez facsimile autographed fan portrait, circa 1916. *Mary Mallory*

Myrtle Gonzalez, First Hispanic Star

VASTLY OUTNUMBERED IN THE EARLY DAYS OF CINEMA, HISPANIC actors faced obstacles like stereotyping and prejudice while trying to make it in in the industry and become stars. Only a few broke through the clutter to rise to the top. Making an indelible impression with her dazzling smile, determination, and positive attitude, Los Angeles native Myrtle Gonzalez gained the moniker "Nature Girl" as she became cinema's first Hispanic female star.

Born September 28, 1891, in Los Angeles, Gonzalez grew up in the Catholic church, a haven for her Los Angeles–born father Manuel and her Irish American mother Lillian, employing her talents in praise. Like her mother, she practiced her God-given musical talents performing in religious services and various entertainment programs. Gonzalez and her baby sister Stella studied music under their mother, learning how to sing soulfully while also selling a song. In 1898, Gonzalez first performed for a Sacred Heart Church benefit, with her comic dance so pleasing audiences she won the prize for most popular little girl.[1] Over the next ten years, Gonzalez gained fame and attention singing, dancing, and reciting for fairs, benefits, recitals, and productions.

Celebrating her Hispanic heritage, Gonzalez often performed at the Cura Hidalgo Club, including at its Mexican Independence Day galas. An exclusive club for prominent Latino Angelenos led by her father, the Cura Hidalgo Club recognized Hispanic holidays and customs at a time when the main population of the city did not. Gonzalez demonstrated multiple music skills in 1905, singing, dancing, and playing violin obbligato, and gaining publicity when a local newspaper included her smiling photo with a story.[2] The more Gonzalez performed, the more popular she became, growing her audience beyond the church.

Gonzalez continued working on her music, learning new instruments and gaining experience giving recitations and oration, appearing before patriotic and civic groups. In the 1906 Liberal Alliance performance staged by her mother at Chutes Park, Gonzalez and a trio of young children received a special ovation and their photo in the newspaper representing California, with the girl carrying the state flag. Organized by her father, by Paul de Longpre, and by others in 1905, the organization's aim was "to promote a spirit of unity and good fellowship among the citizens" of Los Angeles, "and especially to foster a desire for public gatherings of a cosmopolitan nature."[3]

In September 1907, sixteen-year-old Myrtle was featured both in prose and photograph in the *Los Angeles Times*, extolling both her burgeoning success in music along with her stunning beauty. The paper declared her "the most beautiful girl in the Spanish-American colony, whom the artists rave over . . . quite famous among local beauty lovers for her rare type of features." The paper went on to describe her gray eyes, long, curling lashes, and dewy white skin, noting that a well-known local artist likened her photographic appearance "to one of Raphael's Madonnas."[4] While objectifying, the story's acknowledgment of her photogenic qualities would aid her rise in films. Growing into a star, Gonzalez, a charismatic diva, dazzled audiences in operatic and stage performances across the city. She wowed audiences as the Angel of Compassion in a massive performance of the Passion Play.[5] Newspapers praised her beauty and performances, making her a minor celebrity in the city.

Finding time to romance through her busy performance schedule, Gonzlez married J. Parks Jones at the old Plaza Church in summer 1910 and gave birth to a son just a year later. The young couple separated in 1912, perhaps not temperamentally suited to each other, particularly if Gonzalez desired an entertainment career. Newspapers noted a contentious hearing for divorce, with Jones claiming she demonstrated temperamental behavior while Myrtle reported emotional and physical abuse from Jones. Looking to financially support herself and her toddler son, Gonzalez approached studio managers, lobbying for a career.

Something in Gonzalez's passionate spirit and vulnerable eyes touched Vitagraph Studios' Western Manager Director Rollin S. Sturgeon, leading him to sign her to a contract. Starting as an ingenue and quickly rising to juvenile western leading lady, often in what the trades called "Spanish" (Hispanic) parts. Gonzalez took to cowgirl roles, learning to ride a horse, wade creeks, and become physically active. She appeared in more melodramatic parts opposite male stars like William Duncan and Jack Mower and demonstrated nice chemistry with future director William Desmond Taylor in five films, revealing growing acting skills. Proud of her Hispanic heritage, Gonzalez promoted it while becoming the first Latino female star in films.

Promoting herself in the trades, Gonzalez accentuated her "Spanish aristocracy" in Los Angeles and embroidered her résumé, claiming she worked with the Belasco stock company in Los Angeles, with local motion picture exhibitors recommending she launch a career in moving pictures. She also claimed that she "took advantage of securing an athletic training, learning to swim, ride and play gymnasium games,"[6] an ironic statement, since she told newspapers in 1907 that she possessed no athletic talent or gene and never participated in any physical activity besides dancing. She was truthful, however, in her love of cars and fashion, driving sporty models and acting as mechanic while also designing parts of her wardrobe. She loved breaking norms and taking action, a young woman looking for adventure in often cloistered times.

Gonzalez received fine notices for her action roles. *Motion Picture News* called them "an admirable vehicle for Myrtle Gonzalez. As the wild, free girl of the back woods, she gets a taste of society that doesn't appeal . . . Gonzalez appears to fascinating advantage."[7] A Japanese film magazine called her the "Virgin White Lily of the Screen" and said she was "typifying the vigorous out-of-door type of heroine."[8] She gained some of her strongest praise for one of her last Vitagraph films, *Chalice of Courage* in 1915.

Though gaining a fine reputation in films for her charming personality, Gonzalez continued singing and dancing around Los Angeles. Her religious faith led her to charitable acts, raising money for churches and social organizations in recitals, benefits, and vaudeville shows, the love of the stage in her blood as well. Her onstage performing more finely developed her expressive skills, leading her to be more vulnerable and open. At the same time she enjoyed her celebrity, having the opportunity to ride in a flower bedecked car in Pasadena's Tournament of Roses Parade.[9]

In the fall of 1915, Gonzalez moved over to Universal, where she made a variety of movies, many with director Lynn Reynolds for his nature films like *The Girl of Lost Lake*, *The Secret of the Swamp*, and *The End of the Rainbow*. The city girl learned to perform her own stunts on diverse and sometimes dangerous locations like Mount Wilson, Big Bear, Santa Cruz, Catalina, Truckee, and even the redwood forests, becoming an action-adventure queen. While in Truckee, they performed with three feet of snow on the ground. Gonzalez fell ill, with a doctor reporting that high attitudes led to an enlargement of her heart.[10] In 1916 she was reported ill before a trade noted that she arose from her sickbed after the production was shut down for two weeks, to complete the last scenes.[11] Trades reported in the summer of 1917 that Gonzalez had resigned from Universal, perhaps for further recuperation.

During her time working at Universal, Gonzalez met assistant director Allen Watt. Over time their relationship blossomed, and on December 8, 1917, the couple married in an impromptu ceremony at her parents' South Los Angeles home. Her health issues worsened in 1918, keeping Gonzalez away from the screen. On October 23 of that year, Gonzalez passed away after suffering for four days from influenza, which caused her heart to fail. Just twenty-seven, she left her husband, seven-year-old son, parents, and siblings.

The first Hispanic woman to become a star in Hollywood, Gonzalez rose from ingenue in two-reel shorts to star of feature films, diversifying from Hispanic roles to action-adventure heroines. Just reaching stardom at the time of her death, the charismatic Gonzalez opened the door through which many other talented, beautiful Hispanic women would follow.

Elsie Janis portrait by Hoover Art Co., circa 1917. *Mary Mallory*

Elsie Janis, First Person to Visit the Troops

WORLD WAR I OFFICIALLY BROKE OUT JULY 28, 1914, CAUSED BY POLITical aggression, imperialism, and finally the assassination of Archduke Franz Ferdinand, heir to the Austro-Hungarian Empire in June. Over the next four years, a bloody conflagration consumed the world, with Allies France, the United Kingdom, Russia, Canada, and the United States fighting Central Powers Austro-Hungary, Germany, the Ottoman Empire, and others to bring peace to a challenged world.

Thanks to the use of moving pictures, the population learned news about the exploding chaos overseas and also how to contribute much needed support for the Allied cause. While films entertained weary, shattered troops stationed across the sea, effervescent vaudeville stage star Elsie Janis provided a healthier antidote: live appearances in front of the troops at the front. Long before comedian Bob Hope traveled the globe visiting American GIs during World War II, witty songstress Janis offered a ray of sunshine as the first American performer touring camps and hospitals, entertaining troops at the front.

Born in Columbus, Ohio, March 16, 1889 as Elsie Bierbower, the bubbly, doe-eyed Janis stole laughs and hearts with her impish personality and sweet singing voice from a young age. From her first performance onstage at the age of eight, she dazzled stage audiences, gaining the nickname "Little Elsie."[1] Janis stole the show with impish impersonations of celebrities, humorous caricatures of everyday folks, and warbling comic character songs sometimes in her own separate act and sometimes in small parts in touring shows. President William McKinley and later President Theodore Roosevelt invited the energetic scene stealer to perform for them at the White House.

In acknowledgment of her huge popularity, Janis graduated to headliner in 1905 when she replaced original star Anna Held in the successful Florenz Ziegfeld Jr. production of the huge musical comedy sensation *The Little Duchess*. She wowed audiences in 1906 with her Broadway debut in the new stage hit *The Vanderbilt Cup*, with *The Billboard* calling her "the brilliant and almost startling young comedienne."[2] Historian David S. Shields acknowledged her million-dollar personality in *Still*, his book on early still photography, stating she was a "consummate talent, an impressionist of clairvoyant ability, a song lyricist who combined wit and sentiment, an actress of immense dynamism, a vibrant solo dancer, and a singer who could project to the gallery."[3]

Once she became a star, Janis regularly performed in England and France, wowing audiences there as well, with her skits in the musical revue *The Passing Show*, "scoring the biggest hit yet registered over here by an American woman."[4] She was still performing there when war broke out, and ended up performing for British troops recuperating in hospitals, realizing the importance of a smiling face and lighthearted entertainment. Janis continued performing for injured troops whenever back in England in 1916 and 1917.

After the United States entered the war on April 6, 1917, Janis became determined to entertain the American Sammies as she had the British. She began promoting the purchase of Liberty Loan Bonds and touring US bases. Returning to London and Paris to perform in revues in 1918, Janis threw herself wholeheartedly into the war effort, performing at hospitals and camps, all on her own dime. As she related in newspapers, "Soldiers are the most appreciative audiences in the world."[5]

After arriving in France in February 1918, Janis devoted herself to troop performances, with newspapers reporting that she was "the first American musical comedy star to go to France to help furnish amusement for the American Expeditionary Forces."[6] Chauffeured around the country in a Packard limousine with her mother and pianist to YMCA camps near the front, Janis performed at everything from boxing rings to pickup trucks to airplane hangars. Dedicated to her task, Janis appeared multiple times a day, even during a bombardment and air raid at the conclusion of a Memorial Day show.[7] For the first time, overseas troops received morale-boosting entertainment during a war, with Janis the most important star to make the rounds. General John Pershing named her an honorary general for the American Expeditionary Force, thereby gaining her the nickname, "The Sweetheart of the A.E.F."

In her book, Janis wrote that she "felt useful for the first time in her life" after visiting and performing at the Neuilly-American Hospital.[8] The work was heartbreaking; often the troops she visited had such severe injuries that she was one of the last people to see them alive. She kept on smiling and joking through the pain. Men often joined her in singing some of their favorite songs or adding comic asides of their own.

Doctors were delighted with Janis's visits: "Surgeons welcomed her, believing the effects on the patients would be good, which proved true."[9] She sang ragtime songs, impersonated the famous, and recited stories, starting with troops with superficial wounds and eventually infectious wards, singing through windows. "For the time being the men forgot their pain, chuckling and many joined the chorus."[10]

Pershing praised her service as uplifting and inspiring to the men. The military praised her work in YMCA ads in entertainment journals. "You have kept my men from thinking of tomorrow's battle; they will fight better because of tonight."[11] Playwright Alexander Woolcott spread the word about her outstanding service in a news dispatch in which he called her the "Playgirl of the Western Front." Riding into an Army camp on a cowcatcher surrounded by cheering troops, Janis jumped from the train to the stage, lifted her hands, and yelled, "Are we downhearted?" The happy troops yelled no.[12] "For like the rare officer who can inspire his men to very prodigies of valor, so the flashing Elsie is compact of that priceless thing which for lack of a less pedantic phrase we must call positive magnetism." He described her "barnstorming with a vengeance" with one costume and "some bad hotels, performing in mess halls, beaches, and through windows of infected wards. In all her years on the stage she has known no such tumultuous or thundering welcomes."[13]

The *Atlantic News Telegraph* repeated a *Stars and Stripes* story on August 10: "To an army which has these many months listened perforce to lectures to an army that has been overwhelmingly informed and edified, Elsie Janis is a distinct relief. She is an oasis of color and vivacity in a dreary desert of frock coated and white tied lecturers."[14] Thanking Janis for her loving support, generosity, and risk-taking, gunners named one of their giant artillery guns after her. In Metz, gunners named one of their cannons "Elsie Janis," as did troops in another part of France.

In February 1919, *Variety* recognized her superior contributions. "As far as show business is concerned, she is the outstanding heroine . . . she came at the right time, and did the right thing. She cannot be praised too highly for what she has done. Her fame and name are as well known with the boys as General Pershing's."[15] Janis continued her mirthful performances, more than six hundred, until returning to the United States in May 1919. Various squadrons awarded her honorary titles, others medals or commendations for her work in war zones bringing joy to troops.

Janis would star in a few films for Selznick Pictures upon her return, including *A Regular Girl*, about a society woman who goes undercover to France to serve as a nurse to American doughboys, a nod to all her brave performing at the front. She would pen scripts and even songs for Broadway shows and movies into the 1930s.

While Bob Hope is publicly acknowledged for all his entertainment to overseas troops, vivacious stage performer Elsie Janis remains mostly forgotten for actually beginning the practice decades earlier.

Evelyn Preer, "An Electric Salome," April 18, 1923, *Washington Times.*

Evelyn Preer, First African American Star

THE EARLY DECADES OF THE MOVING PICTURE INDUSTRY OFFERED promise to women, immigrants, and people of color since it operated outside the confines of mainline society and finance. African Americans found films a mostly welcome place. Actors like Madame Sul Te Wan and others demonstrated screen charisma, while preeminent vaudeville performer Bert Williams rose to film prominence as well.

African American filmmakers began producing motion pictures in the midteens by and for other African Americans, looking to legitimize and normalize their everyday lives. Among these early pioneers, producer-director Oscar Micheaux created milestone films, many starring new discovery Evelyn Preer. Effervescent and charismatic, Preer served as Micheaux's muse, appearing in more than ten of his films and becoming the first true African American female film star and celebrity.

Born July 26, 1896, in postbellum Vicksburg, Mississippi, as Evelyn Jarvis, young Evelyn Preer imagined a freer, more successful existence outside the state. After her father died, her mother moved them to Chicago looking for a better life and more opportunities for freedom and advancement.[1] Gaining an education and openness to new ideas freed Preer's creativity, leading her toward the stage and the movies. During high school, she fell in love with performing as a member of the Lady Amateur Minstrels and later performed with Charley Johnson's vaudeville team on the Orpheum circuit.[2] She was beautiful and intelligent, with her vivacious personality and light caramel-colored complexion helping draw crowds to donate to her mother's pleas to build a church.

Writer Oscar Micheaux connected with her intellectually and emotionally, recognizing her moral strength, casting her as the lead in his inaugural film *The Homesteader* in 1919, based on his own novel about his difficult circumstances as the only Black rancher in the Dakotas. Preer displayed great dramatic range and vulnerability in the domestic tragedy of power and pain unfortunately afflicted on her and others in the fight for equality and rights. The film announced Micheaux as the premiere African American director of the period, a multi-talent who produced, directed, and wrote his own films and established Preer as a pioneering star and role model for Black women who worked to uplift her race.

They both achieved even greater renown for his landmark second picture *Within Our Gates* (1920), which depicted racial and sexual violence under white supremacy, which her character Sylvia overcomes. Preer starred in over ten of the director's landmark films, all documenting the difficult experiences of African Americans as they strove to better their lives and society around them. Most of her roles in these films featured her traumatized characters caught in violent and often troubling psychological situations, struggling to overcome prejudice, segregation, and oppression. African American newspapers called her the "Colored Queen of the Cinema"[3] for her outstanding performances as both heroine and villain.

Preer alternated her time between starring in Micheaux films and performing lead roles with major Negro theater companies, as they were called at the time, like the Ethiopian Art Theater, Avenue Players, and Lafayette Players, all bringing professional, legitimate theater featuring African Americans to others of their race. She wowed audiences with both her dramatic range and her expressive singing. Preer made her debut on the legitimate stage in the musical comedy *Canary Cottage* in 1920 in Chicago, featuring songs written by Oliver Morosco and music by Earl Carroll, demonstrating her versatility as a performer.

Preer achieved high marks portraying the title role in Oscar Wilde's tragic play *Salome* for the Negro Art Theatre Company's traveling production in 1923, as the first African American woman to play the role onstage. The *Broad Ax* called her "a brilliant star of the first magnitude."[4] White newspapers praised her work as well, with the *Washington Times* calling her "an electric Salome"[5] and another "an artist."[6] Preer served as the star of many of these Avenue theater productions, designed to demonstrate the range and talents of African American performers. These excellent performances drew major white stars eager to see her onstage in every major city in which she appeared.

Even famed Broadway producer David Belasco admired her work, signing Preer to a contract in 1925 to play a featured role in his production of *Lulu Belle,* featuring a mixed cast and starring Lenore Ulric and Henry Hull. Preer captured the imagination again with her charismatic performance as a nightclub showgirl, understudying Ulric in the lead role.

Victor Records signed Preer to a contract in 1926 to record popular songs of the day. The discs sold well, showing her rich contralto voice and the wide range of her talents with such songs as "It Takes a Good Woman." Always looking for new opportunities and greater name recognition, Preer rotated between recording, the stage, film, and cabaret shows, often performing with the Lafayette Players in Chicago and Los Angeles or in popular musical cabaret shows accompanied by such performers as Duke Ellington.

Preer adored the movies and the opportunities they offered African Americans. She revealed in an interview, "I am crazy about motion pictures. I think there is a good future for colored people in pictures, but I think they will get their best chance from white directors who realize we have talent and will employ us just as they will other talent."[7] She hoped to usher in this promised future.

Thanks to her success drawing crowds for Micheaux's independent productions as well as fine notices appearing onstage, major white film companies approached her about appearing in their product in the late 1920s. Longtime Christie Comedies' producer Al Christie created the all African American comedy short *The Melancholy Dame* in 1928 to highlight Preer's work and, thanks to its success, produced two more. The short received good reviews, with some singling out Preer, whom they called "a real find for the talkers."[8] Her work impressed major studio producers as well, landing her roles in the prison picture *The Big House,* the Paramount film *Husband's Holiday,* and the Joseph von Sternberg–Marlene Dietrich spectacle *Blonde Venus.* Though they were not major character roles, they introduced her to white audiences, opening up possibilities for larger roles.

Just as her career seemed poised to rise in white circles in 1932, Preer developed pneumonia and died at Los Angeles's General Hospital, leaving behind her husband and five-month-old daughter. She was only thirty-two.

The premiere African American actress of her time, Evelyn Preer stole the spotlight wherever she appeared. Her starring roles in Micheaux's early melodramas wowed audiences, turning her into not only a bankable star but also the first African American female celebrity to dominate headlines, offering greater opportunity for those who followed her.

Lilian St. Cyr/Red Wing in the screen cast identification for *The Squaw Man* (Lasky Feature Play Co., 1914). *Marc Wanamaker/Bison Archives*

Lilian St. Cyr/Red Wing, First Native American Star

AMERICAN CINEMA HAS FEATURED NATIVE AMERICANS ONSCREEN from its beginnings, but not always positively. Native peoples were often stereotyped in demeaning or villainous ways, with nonnatives many times appearing in "redface" as these characters. From the first decade of America's early cinema, Lilian St. Cyr and her husband James Young Deer attempted to give their people the sympathy, dignity, and respect they deserved in films they themselves brought to the screen, starring St. Cyr as "Princess Red Wing" in the lead role. First appearing on film in 1908, St. Cyr achieved fame as the first Native American star, one giving her people agency and control of their onscreen narrative.

Born on the Winnebago Reservation, February 13, 1884, Lilian Margaret St. Cyr found herself caught between two worlds trying to bridge Native American and Caucasian cultures. As a teenager, she attended Indian boarding schools in Pennsylvania that provided only menial job training and attempted to drain Native American beliefs and attitudes from their students in an ill-advised attempt to homogenize them. Graduates left feeling disrespected and lost, never fully accepted by either culture. St. Cyr found herself caught in these attitudes. White society considered her an Indian, while many Native Americans found her too white in her dress, speech, and attitudes.

Feeling out of place on the Reservation in Nebraska, St. Cyr moved to Washington, DC, where she served as the maid to Kansas senator Chester L. Long and family. The young woman fell in love and married local resident James Younger Johnson, the son of mixed-race parents and successful African American business leaders. Soon after the couple joined Wild West shows, Johnson adopted the stage name "James Young Deer" and St. Cyr "Princess Red Wing" to provide positive role models of Native Americans at a time in which the federal government stripped them of property rights, land, and even their religion.[1]

Newly christened, Red Wing and Young Deer began working as a Native American couple, first in Wild West shows and then entertainment venues like New York's Hippodrome Theatre and Gotham Club.[2] They won small parts as Native Americans in a Kalem one-reeler called *White Squaw* in 1908 and in some Lubin one-reelers. The couple played a large part in Vitagraph's *Red Wing's Gratitude* (1909), which one trade called "graphically and interestingly told by some of the star members of the Vitagraph Company, the leading roles being sustained by real Indians, a novel departure in picture making. . . . This is a notable Indian picture in many important particulars."[3]

They also advised filmmakers on Native American customs, attitudes, dress, and speech, setting themselves up as experts. Renowned Biograph director D. W. Griffith also hired Johnson and St. Cyr as actors and advisers for *The Mended Lute* and *The Indian Runner's Romance* in 1909.[4] Later that year the couple joined the New York Motion Picture Company to shoot Westerns and "Indian pictures" under the name the "Red Wing series" in Hollywood as "perfect types of their race."[5] These early films garnered mostly positive reviews, with *Moving Picture World* calling *The Red Girl's Romance* "a slashing story, possessing all the imagined elements which make the West a land of romance and poetic misconceptions."[6]

Not long after, the couple joined Pathé Freres in New Jersey, eventually forming their own production unit and seeing Johnson named director and general manager of the West Coast Studio. Over the next few years, Johnson wrote and directed the short films starring St. Cyr. They positively portrayed Native Americans while focusing on her character, giving them agency. St. Cyr performed daring stunts riding bareback, jumping on and off horses, and rolling down hills, trying to save the day. Unfortunately she usually sacrificed herself for the white couple or leader who befriended or helped her, never usually getting a happy ending herself. Besides acting, St. Cyr worked to ensure the authenticity of Native

American portrayals in costume, customs, and speech. The early one- and two-reelers gained large praise from white critics for their look at western stories containing "native" actors, authentic locations, and strong visuals. Many reviewers praised her work, calling her the "foremost Indian performer" and the most famous.

St. Cyr separated from Young Deer and later divorced him, as she tired of Johnson's fooling around with younger women, reckless spending, and overbearing attitude, and she took control of her own life and career. She found her greatest success in the 1914 release of the Cecil B. DeMille–directed *The Squaw Man*. She played Nat-U-Ritch, the Native American wife of Jim Wynnegate (Dustin Farnum), an Englishman falsely accused of a crime who comes to America and ends up out West as a cowboy, whom she rescues from disaster.

St. Cyr's character took control of the story and action before sacrificing herself in order that Jim could more easily take their child back to England and end up together with his long-lost white love. As Waggoner writes in her book, Nat-U-Ritch embodies the stereotype of the Indian princess helper and tragic victim, "but on a deeper level her character falls victim to love, racism, and Manifest Destiny."[7] Most critics praised the film and St. Cyr's acting. *The Star Tribune* called her "a real American in every sense of the word."[8] Playwright Royle praised her work as "a revelation, she has many splendid moments in the play, which she handles with exquisite feeling."[9]

Though receiving great notices, Red Wing's film career was quickly coming to a close as Americans began tiring of these stereotypical westerns and she began aging out of more romantic leads. After appearing with Tom Mix in *In the Last Days of the Thundering Herd* (1914) and the 1915 film *Fighting Bob*, she played her last role, as the main character's mother in the original 1916 version of *Ramona*. In 1915 St. Cyr also appeared in John Stephen McGroarty's famous *Mission Play* to lend some much needed authenticity to the production.

St. Cyr retired from the screen and returned to Nebraska for family connection and comfort without finding a suitable career path. Trained in housekeeping at the Indian schools, she was forced to apply for domestic work in 1918 to survive. By the early 1920s, St. Cyr began appearing at theaters, schools, and libraries across the United States as Princess Red Wing, performing Native American songs, dances, and sayings, explaining differences in dress and language among the various tribes and demonstrating their impact on American history. Her aim was to correct misconceptions and bring dignity and respect to Native Americans who were often ridiculed in popular culture. She would spend her remaining decades demonstrating the similarities between the oppressive dominant culture and the powerless indigenous one, working to gain her people respect.

The first Native American woman to star in moving pictures, St. Cyr sought to bring authenticity and truth to her roles, whether in her portrayals or in the accoutrements of the story and role. She was the first actress to promote Native American respect and dignity, and one of the first to fight for Native American rights and reparations.

Gloria Swanson, First Fashion Icon

TINY IN HEIGHT THOUGH LARGE IN TALENT, GLORIA SWANSON REMADE herself as times changed, always ahead of the curve. Simple shopgirl, flirty bathing beauty, lavishly dressed society matron, she refashioned and remade herself to please audiences and address the times as she became one of the world's biggest film celebrities in the 1920s. All her roles reflected her incredible drive and intellect to tailor her persona and the industry as times changed, finally evolving into independent producer and businesswoman through shrewdness and smarts. Swanson negotiated her career moves through her divine fashion sense, crafting a dazzling screen career as one of the world's most famous glamour queens.

Born March 27, 1899, in Chicago as Gloria May Josephine Svensson, petite Swanson spent her self-possessed childhood dreaming of the glamorous life, a driven introvert already planning on making it big. Alone in her room she practiced acting and singing, preparing for a life onstage. Extremely self-confident, she knew she was destined for great things. Stylish at a young age, with a mother who fashioned her with bows, hats, and one-of-a-kind dresses, she was already standing out from the crowd.[1]

During her aunt's visit to Chicago in 1914 and through her aunt's connections, Swanson stepped onto the Essanay Studio lot to watch filming and walked herself into a dream. Dressed fashionably à la dancer Irene Castle, Swanson was noticed by a casting director, who asked the pretty girl to return the next day.[2] Finding her niche, Swanson worked her way up from bits and extras into a regular employee, eventually vamping her way into sophisticated drama. Film historian DeWitt Bodeen described *The Romance of an American Duchess* as "the film in which the future Swanson of glamorous authority and potent star-chemistry first manifested itself. . . . In some scenes she glows from the screen so incandescent that she almost throws the rather trivial little romantic drama off-balance."[3] Swanson starred in one- and two-reel shorts within weeks.

Within months, the ambitious Swanson corralled former Essanay actor Wallace Beery into marrying her, on her seventeenth birthday, and moving west to Los Angeles, determined to become a wife and make it in the movies. During her visit to the Sennett lot a week after marrying, studio chief Mack Sennett spotted Swanson quickly and interviewed her, with the young woman mentioning working at Chicago's Essanay and that she was ambitious. He said, "She had a cute nose and beautiful eyes. . . . I went overboard. 'Gloria I think you have a good chance to succeed in this business if you're willing to work hard and learn, and start from scratch.'"[4]

Joining Sennett in 1916, Swanson first gained success as a Sennett Bathing Beauty before finding her niche and nice chemistry opposite slightly built actor Bobby Vernon, making nine romantic comedies with him. Charming and funny, the series was very popular, especially the 1916 short *The Danger Girl*. Spotlighting Swanson's charm and reckless driving skills, the film showcased her beauty and star quality.[5] She was soon joined by the Sennett Studio dog, Teddy, and the twosome found their films becoming a comedy sensation thanks to the antics of the huge, lovable pet.

Tired of Sennett and dreaming of becoming a real actress, Swanson left for Triangle Film Corporation, finally getting the chance to work in romantic dramas offering a higher class of refinement. It also brought her into contact with Peggy Hamilton, the studio costume designer and future Hollywood fashion influencer, who served as her first fashion mentor.[6] After learning more about working in front of the camera, appearing natural onscreen, and dealing with studio insiders, Swanson departed the financially failing studio for what would become superstardom.

Joining Paramount to work with director Cecil B. DeMille finally allowed Swanson the life of glamour and style which she so passionately desired. To look the part, she visited makeup stylist Max Factor, who updated her makeup and hair into a more modern sleek look, perfect for the high society dramas produced by master showman DeMille. As historian Jeanine Basinger wrote, "DeMille . . . found the Swanson definition. . . . He turned her into a symbol of a particular new kind of American woman; sophisticated, soignee, and definitely not a virgin . . . she was out in the world, ready for something to happen . . . doing pretty much whatever she felt."[7]

Surrounded by glamour and upscale settings, Swanson found her destiny, wearing lavish costumes in period dramas, essaying strong, action-oriented women, and stealing scenes with her beauty and dramatic flair. Her image as one of the world's greatest fashion icons was born in a scene from DeMille's *Male and Female*, wearing a heavily beaded pearl and sequined lamé gown with a train and enormous white-peacock-feathered, bejeweled headdress, in which she laid down fearlessly in front of real lions.[8] She also later simulated a nude bath in a sunken tub, revealing her daring.

Swanson met her fashion sister in DeMille costume designer Clare West, who would sketch lush velvet, silk, and chiffon gowns festooned with beads, pearls, ostrich feathers, furs, and long trains that draped her body sensually, turning Swanson into the world's most famous clothes horse onscreen. Swanson continued the part offscreen as well, styled by such fashion mavens as Paul Poiret, House of Worth, and other Paris fashion houses. She recognized her bread and butter and emphasized it, to huge box office success.

After becoming a major star thanks to DeMille, Swanson was transferred over to main studio Famous Players-Lasky. Though unhappy, Swanson continued her winning ways, this time working with the likes of writer Elinor Glyn and director Allan Dwan, turning out romantic comedies, period dramas, and shopgirl fantasies. From this point forward, Swanson's costumes were always fashion statements, over-the-top creations changed multiple times within pictures. helping her become Hollywood's top paid star and leader of many world Best-Dressed lists for years.

Over the next few years, she appeared opposite Rudolph Valentino in the time-traveling romance *Beyond the Rocks*; as Paris music hall performer Zaza; shopgirl to fashion model in *Manhandled*; and, in the historical romance *Madame Sans-Gene*, as a laundress in Paris who becomes a duchess. Each featured stunning costumes, drawing the praises of millions of happy female fans. One of the best-known celebrities in the world at the age of twenty-six, Swanson dreamed of independent success while at the same time pondering how to maintain her enormous popularity.

Swanson signed with United Artists in 1925 to take control of her career and serve as her own boss. This time she pursued parts that offered more meat, that offered chance for growth along with stylish costumes. She stunned Hollywood with her adaptation of Somerset Maugham's short story, "Miss Thompson," playing an earthy prostitute who falls for a marine and undergoes harassment by a minister before reuniting with her love. The star shepherded the red hot *Sadie Thompson* script through Hays Code censors by focusing more on comedy and carefree elements, making it another hit.

Spending beyond her means both as a producer and star, Swanson turned to older financier Joseph P. Kennedy to manage her finances and investments, and the two quickly became an item. He seemed the protector she always yearned for but unfortunately turned wolf, using the actress as a piggy bank to finance her films and lavish lifestyle. Kennedy convinced her to hire the extravagant director Erich von Stroheim for what became the notoriously troubled *Queen Kelly*, a financial debacle that barely saw the light of day. Swanson demonstrated a fine command of sound and excellent singing in *The Trespasser* and earned high box office returns, wiping out the loss of *Queen Kelly*. Though she would make a few more films during the 1930s, her career was never the same. Her films were not bringing in enough money to finance her overspending.

Sunset Boulevard returned Swanson to screens as faded silent-actress Norma Desmond, haunted by ghosts of Hollywood's past and attempting to make a comeback. Walking the line between daring and self-parody, Swanson gave a performance for the ages in a potent cautionary take on the dangers of Hollywood and celebrity. Swanson loved making the film, later stating, "I wept when it was over for I was so happy during the making of it. I was so unhappy when we finished. . . . The whole experience was magical."[9] Like a phoenix, Swanson rose from the ashes, making one of Hollywood's greatest comebacks. Though she failed to win the Academy Award for Best Actress, she reestablished herself as one of Hollywood's greats.

Smart in many ways, Swanson established many firsts, among them, adopting a healthy lifestyle. One of the first stars to become a vegetarian, she spoke out against food additives and advocated for healthy eating, later promoting organic food. Employing her fashion history, the actress licensed clothing under her name and established a cosmetics line. Swanson was one of the first to endorse products all to finance her lavish lifestyle.

A true star in every sense of the word, Gloria Swanson outshone virtually everyone with her megawatt personality, fashion sense, and business drive. Physically small but hugely ambitious, she turned herself into one of Hollywood's greatest film and fashion icons, dazzling audiences with daring acting and extravagant costumes.

Anna May Wong portrait, circa 1936. *Marc Wanamaker/Bison Archives*

Anna May Wong, First Chinese American Star

GROUNDBREAKING STAR OF AMERICAN FILM ANNA MAY WONG appeared in more than sixty films, gaining worldwide acclaim for her consummate acting and fashion sense, though she never achieved the possibility of obtaining a happy ending or taking control of her own destiny in the film characters she portrayed. Wong was the first Chinese American woman to star in movies, a role model for young women determined to follow their own moral codes and achieve success on equal terms.

Born January 3, 1905, Anna May Wong grew up the daughter of a traditional Chinese family that ran a successful laundry in downtown Los Angeles's Chinatown. The second of eight children born under the birth name Wong Liu Tsong, which means "Frosted Yellow Willows," she was given the American name Anna May by her parents, the children of immigrants. As a child, Wong felt drawn to the movies, a place offering escape and a chance to remake oneself, at a time when Chinese Americans suffered under the Chinese Exclusion Act of 1882, which denied them citizenship, the right to own property, or the right to marry whom they pleased.[1] She grew curious about the crews filming around Chinatown, silently observing the strange goings-on. Asking so many questions about what they were doing, she came to be known as the "Curious Chinese Child."[2]

Wong attended Chinese Mission School in downtown LA after experiencing bullying at the public school down the street. She worked in the laundry and took Chinese language lessons after school. When she felt out of place and lonely, Wong often skipped school to watch movies, imagining herself onscreen. Though her parents detested the medium and preferred she marry and have children, she yearned for the excitement and escapism the movies offered. After answering a casting call and being introduced to the assistant director, Wong landed her first role as an extra in the Alla Nazimova picture *The Red Lantern*,[3] finding her new home. She went on to land other extra and bit parts in such films as Lon Chaney's 1921 movie *Outside the Law*.

Dropping out of high school in 1921 to work in movies full-time, Wong earned a supporting role as Toy Ling's wife in the movie *Bits of Life*, going on to make a vow to work ten years to see if she could make it before giving up. She landed her first starring role in the 1922 two-strip Technicolor film *The Toll of the Sea* at the age of seventeen, playing a character based on Madame Butterfly, and played herself in the 1923 film *Mary of the Movies*. Thanks to her portrayal in *Toll of the Sea*, she was cast as the Mongol slave in the Douglas Fairbanks's blockbuster *The Thief of Bagdad* in 1924. Gaining great reviews and showing herself to be a consummate actress, Wong still found herself struggling against "yellow face," in which Caucasian actors donned makeup to play Asian roles, whenever she auditioned for lead parts.[4]

Facing the fact of discrimination and prejudice, Wong gave up expectations, telling *Motion Picture Magazine*, "I have always said it is better not to expect anything. Then you are not bitterly disappointed."[5] Fatalistic, she expected the worst. Most Chinese Americans in Los Angeles had already experienced discrimination over where they could live or what professions they might try. Wong also experienced the film industry denying her roles because of her ethnicity and due to anti-miscegenation laws.[6]

Paramount Pictures cast her in their 1924 *Peter Pan*, an adaptation of the famous James M. Barrie stage play, shot by Chinese American cinematographer James Wong Howe. Earning fourth billing, Wong played Indian maiden Tiger Lily, leading an attack on older sister Wendy and finding herself exiled to Never Never Land alongside the boy-men.[7] The actress appeared in several films over the next few years but failed to break through to full star status. In the 1927 MGM film *Mr. Wu*, Wong played the unmarried daughter of leader Wu, played by Lon Chaney, who vows to seek vengeance against the girl's British lover, who vows to return to Great Britain after she announces her pregnancy.

Looking for greater opportunity and choices, Wong left Hollywood for Europe in 1928. Europe served as a finishing school for her, introducing her to art, culture, learning other languages, and gaining poise and confidence while meeting literary and cultural elites throughout the Continent. It opened her to possibilities she failed to find at home: open romance, starring roles providing her characters with agency, independence. During her years there, Wong felt at home with talented African American performers like Josephine Baker and Paul Robeson, who found refuge and acceptance among European residents who worshipped them for their talents and welcomed them as guests. She performed to acclaim in such stage plays as *A Circle of Chalk* with Laurence Olivier and the German operetta *Tschun Tschi*.

During that time, Wong starred in several films, including her first talking film, *The Flame of Love*, the German-French coproduction *Concrete Butterfly*, and the 1929 English film *Piccadilly*, in which she starred as an English nightclub's scullery maid who goes on to become the headline attraction.

Returning to America in 1930, Wong appeared in the Broadway stage play *On the Spot*. During the production, her mother was hit by a car and died. Wong returned to Los Angeles, helping to care for and raise her youngest siblings until many of them moved to China in 1934.

Wong re-signed a contract with Paramount Pictures in 1931, hoping for better luck but still ending up cast in stereotypical roles. She starred opposite Sessue Hayakawa in the film *Daughter of the Dragon*, gaining a positive love interest, which was unusual for her career. Wong landed some of her best reviews in the Marlene Dietrich film *Shanghai Express* in 1932, directed by Josef von Sternberg.

Once again deploring the state of the roles she was given, Wong traveled back to Europe in 1934 and 1935, returning to the United States just as MGM announced they planned to produce an adaptation of Pearl S. Buck's Pulitzer Prize–winning novel *The Good Earth*. Wong passionately desired to star in the film as O Lan, the story's heroine. Though many lobbied for her to get the part, MGM instead cast Austrian actress Luise Rainer, devastating Wong.

In 1936 she traveled to China to spend time with family and see the country of her heritage, falling in love with the country and its people. Along the way she shot home movies and appeared in newsreels and other short films.

Wong returned to the United States, finding nothing had really changed much, though she continued starring in several Paramount films over the next several years. Still no change in her career until 1952, when she was cast as the first Chinese American to star in a TV show: *The Gallery of Madame Liu Tsong*. Since her death, Wong has been honored with a Barbie doll in her likeness as well as her image on an American quarter.

Recognized as one of the world's Best Dressed Women multiple times due to her elegance and sophistication, Anna May Wong felt stifled in America. While she gave consummate performances in films, she found little opportunity to gain a happy ending or exhibit true agency in her characters in the States. Though not the first Chinese American woman to appear in a film, she was the first to truly become a star, bringing grace and beauty to the screen.

FILMMAKERS

"Mother of Cinema" Alice Guy-Blaché portrait, circa 1912. *Marc Wanamaker/Bison Archives*

Alice Guy-Blaché, First Filmmaker

The "First Mother" of film, Alice Guy-Blaché virtually created what it meant to a filmmaker, conceiving a vision, telling stories, managing people, all in the service of producing a motion picture. Introduced to the newly created medium of moving pictures in 1895, she envisioned how to tell stories and thereby entertain an audience. The first person to actually conceive of and manage a film studio, while experimenting with new innovations, Guy-Blaché was the first pioneering and prolific studio filmmaker, not just the first female one. Her mark in developing the fledgling new medium echoes through time, revealing the strength and ingenuity of women.

Born July 1, 1873, in Sante-Mandé, Val-de-Marne, France, but transported by her parents to their homeland of Chile shortly thereafter, Guy-Blaché grew up as the youngest of five children. After an early peripatetic young childhood, she returned to France and was educated in convent schools.[1] Upon the death of Guy-Blaché's father in 1891, friends assisted her mother in becoming director of the Mutualité Maternelle, a charity assisting pregnant textile workers in times of need.[2] After her mother was forced to resign months later, Guy-Blaché studied typing and stenography, eventually becoming a secretary in a varnish factory to support herself and her mother.[3]

In 1894, Guy-Blaché landed a more prestigious position as secretary to the Comptoir Général de Photographie, a camera manufacturing company, as photography exploded in popularity as a burgeoning new method of capturing moments in life. When the company changed hands in 1895, taken over by Gustave Eiffel and Leon Gaumont, Guy-Blaché went over as well, becoming a valued employee as Gaumont expanded into experimentation with motion picture cameras.[4]

After becoming familiar with the filming process, she asked to become involved but only received permission on the condition she complete her secretarial work first. After observing the process, Guy-Blaché directed her first film in 1896, *La Fee aux Choux* (*The Fairy of the Cabbages*), incorporating her idea of telling a story, the first narrative film. Over the next ten years, Guy-Blaché innovated many practices, including supervising the tinting of motion picture frames, directing Gaumont's first chronophone (sound) films, first filming on location and hand-coloring film, all while writing, directing, and producing a wide variety of films in every genre.[5]

Guy-Blaché fell in love with fellow Gaumont colleague Herbert Blaché, marrying him in 1907. She accompanied him to the United States as he opened a Gaumont Chronophone franchise later that year. Unwilling to subsume her own ambitions, Guy-Blaché created her own film studio in Flushing, New York, later known as Solax, becoming the first female studio president, producer, and director in the United States. Within a few months of establishing the studio, Guy-Blaché had turned it into a top producing concern thanks to her business acumen. Not only did she manage all business of the studio, she also wrote and directed its films, becoming the first woman in America to produce, direct, and write films.[6]

In 1912 the producer constructed a new state-of-the-art Solax Studio in Fort Lee, New Jersey, after outgrowing her original facilities. Innovative in its design, it featured glass ceilings that admitted natural light, which facilitated more controlled filming.[7] Guy-Blaché's studio included spacious grounds, allowing for various types of filming, well-endowed studio departments—including a large special effects department—and a diverse staff. She continued producing well-reviewed, entertaining, and popular films, which many reviewers called "high art films."[8] She also presented the first film lecture at Columbia University.[9]

Trades even acknowledged her professional experience in film production, with *Moving Picture World* writing, "She inaugurated the presentation of little plays on the screen, some by that company some sixteen or seventeen years ago, operating the camera, writing or adapting the photodramas, setting the scenes and handling the actors."[10]

The industry turned to pioneer Guy-Blaché to describe women's work in film production in 1914, but the director instead employed it as an opportunity to encourage more women to become directors and producers, believing that they more perfectly suited the position than men. As she wrote,

> Not only is a woman as well fitted to stage a photo-drama as a man, but in many ways she has a distinct advantage over him because of her very nature and because much of the knowledge called for in the telling of story and the creation of the stage setting is absolutely within her province as a member of the gentler sex. . . . There is nothing connected with the stage of a motion picture that a woman cannot do as easily as a man, and there is no reason why she cannot master every technicality of the art.[11]

While Guy-Blaché had been succeeding spectacularly in creating motion pictures that both entertained audiences and produced profits, her husband's financial mismanagement damaged the company. The director was forced to seek out work directing for other companies including Popular Plays and Players and Metro Pictures. Thanks to her respected reputation and affiliation with major companies, she collaborated with leading stage actress Olga Petrova to produce films featuring forceful women characters, at a time when women dominated film audiences and occupied a large part of its workforce.[12] Petrova was impressed with Guy-Blaché: how detail-oriented, precise, and organized she was in leading cast and crew while also making business decisions.[13]

But bad financial conditions, her husband's ill management and dalliances, and Guy-Blaché's illness eventually led to the company's demise. The director was able to make a few films before she rejoined her husband in California, but she saw her career drain away. As Wall Street money turned studios into large film factories, Guy-Blaché and other women found themselves pushed out the door and written out of history.

She was forced to return to France and attempt to write, while fighting to resurrect her reputation.

Mostly forgotten until rediscovered a few decades ago, Alice Guy-Blaché has been recognized as one of the most important pioneers in cinema, producing hundreds of films throughout her career. She was truly the "mother" of cinema, innovating practices; leading studios on two continents with writing, directing, and producing; and boldly opening doors and laying a path for other assertive women to follow.

Zora Neale Hurston, First African American Filmmaker

THE EARLY MOVING PICTURE INDUSTRY OFFERED OPENNESS AND OPPOR-
tunity for filmmakers outside the mainstream: women, people of color,
and immigrants. It also experimented with storytelling methods and
depictions of real life. Academics and scientists began employing the
new medium to collect visual and sound data for ethnographic concerns,
providing a historic record on the daily life of a people. More renowned
as a novelist, Zora Neale Hurston documented the daily struggles of
Black sharecroppers in South Florida in the late 1920s, becoming the
first woman African American filmmaker and the first ethnographic
documentarian on this vanishing way of life.

Born in Eatonville, Florida, as one of eight children in an all-Black
town, Hurston struggled to escape poverty and ignorance in order to
make a better life for herself and later her people. She endured a hard
six years after the death of her mother, doing a variety of odd jobs in
order to earn money to attend college and gain an education at Howard
University.

Ambitious and determined, Hurston focused on becoming a writer
with an emphasis on rural African American heritage. She won a play-
writing contest in 1925, drawing the attention of the Harlem Renais-
sance writers. She also entered several plays in the Urban League's
Opportunity magazine play contest in 1925, earning a second-place
award and honorable mention,[1] getting them published, and buoying
her confidence. These works brought her together with poet Langston
Hughes, leading to a long collaboration and friendship. Her wins set her

permanently on the road to documenting and sharing the Black experience in her work, combining her anthropological education and personal background, focusing on African American heritage in virtually all of her projects going forward.

Hurston attended graduate school at Columbia University to study anthropology under famed professor Dr. Franz Boas. In order to pay bills, she landed a job as novelist Fannie Hurst's secretary, answering telephones, running errands, handling chores, and responding to correspondence.[2] She gained, perhaps, better knowledge by watching and helping Hurst, learning the life of a writer—how to handle and publicize oneself—and nurturing relationships with the cultural elite. This real-life education would prove fruitful throughout her life.

Deciding to put into practice all that she had learned, Hurston traveled back to the area of her family's early beginnings, spending over three years to experience and record the daily lives, culture, and folklore of rural people—first in Florida and then across the South and the Caribbean—a people and a culture mostly forgotten in contemporary African American society and on the verge of being lost. She lived with and among the people she studied, which allowed her subjects to open up and trust her. As she wrote, "I not only collected a great deal of material, but it started individuals coming to me privately to tell me stories."[3]

Carrying on in this vein, Hurston decided to take a literal, anthropological approach to recording and preserving African American heritage. To aid her writing and future presentations, Hurston filmed encounters with those she met, capturing native dances, recitations, and celebrations, saving them for posterity. Some of this historic documentary footage would eventually be released decades later, for example, *Children's Games* (1928), *Logging* (1928), and *Baptism* (1929).

Always looking for new ways to document African American laborers and their way of life, Hurston employed a variety of methods to transcribe and propagate this tragically overlooked area. The writer first participated in an African American version of a revived musical revue called *Fast and Furious*, produced in New York City in 1931 and featuring a large lineup of Black stars in comedy skits highlighted by songs of renowned popular composers Mack Gordon and Harry Revel.

In 1932 Hurston compiled and produced a show of Black work songs and spirituals in New York while taking her troupe on the road to perform at St. Louis's National Folklore Festival. She hoped to capture the dignity and respect these early pioneers deserved for helping build a nation that didn't always recognize the freedoms and opportunities of others. Hurston turned play director in 1934 with *Singing Steel* to continue her work mining the history of Black Americans' labor. A stage play set in a Black labor camp, it was, per one review, "packed with folklore, drama and dancing, brings to the public not only the song and drama of a Negro working day, but all the pathos, joy and innate feeling of freedom so characteristic of, and inherent in the worker."[4]

Taking a more in-depth, personal approach, Hurston wrote the novel *Mules and Men* in 1935 to authentically examine primitive African folklore and magic by recounting her earlier fieldwork in the area. The book examined her return to her family's longtime home in Florida after attending college in the North, collecting the folk tales overheard in the community, which "the tellers themselves recognized the stories as fables."[5] The book went further than recounting vintage tall tales and superstitions to capturing a dying way of life, which professor Boas called "an unusual contribution to our knowledge of the true inner life of the Negro."[6]

Though she attempted a career as a Hollywood screenwriter with Paramount Studios in 1941, Hurston became better acclaimed for her novels, *Jonah's Gourd Vines* (1934), *Moses, Man of the Mountain* (1938), and, especially, *Their Eyes Were Watching God* (1937), later adapted into a movie. She remained somewhat forgotten until author Alice Walker wrote the article, "In Search of Zora Neale Hurston," which *Ms.* magazine published in 1975.

Rediscovered decades after completion, Hurston's anthropological films not only documented a vanishing African American rural way of life but also revealed the makings of an observant and humanistic filmmaker. They ensure her renown as the first African American female filmmaker.

Beatriz Michelena portrait for California Motion Picture Corporation, circa 1915.
Mary Mallory

Beatriz Michelena, First Hispanic Filmmaker

SEVERAL HISPANIC AMERICAN STARS CAME TO PROMINENCE IN THE early decades of the moving picture industry. Al Ernest Garcia, Don Alvarado, Ramon Novarro, Myrtle Gonzalez, and Beatriz Michelena starred in early silent films, earning fame and renown for their acting. Former opera singer Beatriz Michelena won accolades after turning to movies in 1914 for the California Motion Picture Corporation and playing assertive, take-charge roles. Looking for more control over her work, the actress and her husband, George Middleton, formed their own company in 1917, making her the first Hispanic American woman to shape her own image and produce her own films.

Born February 22, 1890, in New York City to former Venezuelan leading opera tenor and teacher Fernando Michelena and his singer wife Frances Lenord, Beatriz Michelena and her younger sister Vera spent their childhood learning coloratura and operatic singing. Both Michelena sisters joined the Kirke La Shelle Comic Opera Company during its fourth season in 1902 as members of the sixty-person ensemble. The group toured the United States performing one-night stands with *Princess Chic*, which ads called "a feast of melody and mirth."[1] After a short time with the group, the siblings returned to New York to further develop their three-octave ranges and acting versatility. Michelena landed strong supporting and starring roles in New York operas, performed with Oliver Morosco's companies, and toured the country as star with the Shubert Organization's *Girl from Dixie*. At the age of sixteen, some called her "the youngest prima donna on the stage."[2]

The Michelena family traveled cross-country when Fernando Michelena landed a teaching job in cosmopolitan San Francisco, California, where he long ago had performed. While their father meticulously trained the sisters for a grand opera career, more lucrative opportunities singing popular music came their way. Beatriz Michelena sang flirtatious showgirl parts in three impresario Max Dill shows and stand-alone concerts, earning raves.

Michelena, "the most beautiful of the most numerous California women who have won fame in the world of song,"[3] appeared locally, singing popular tunes in community concerts, which led to greater visibility and thus opportunity with larger roles in operettas and musicals across the country. Michelena earned a large role in the San Francisco production of *The Kissing Girl*, sang for New York producer Martin Beck in popular vaudeville shows,[4] and obtained a plum supporting role as the Rosebud Princess in Morosco's 1913 Chicago presentation of *The Tik Tok Man of Oz*.[5]

In September 1913, the California Motion Picture Corporation announced its formation in San Rafael, California, under financier Herbert Payne and other prominent San Francisco investors to produce films starring the "popular prima donna on the Pacific Coast,"[6] Beatriz Michelena. They intended to produce stories set in locations unique to the Golden State and often adaptations of opera works to take advantage of the San Francisco songbird's background and dramatic performances. Michelena herself looked to broaden her acting skills while growing her celebrity by starring in the company's films, with her husband Middleton serving as her director.

Thanks to her pantomimic skills in selling operatic performances, the spunky, vivacious Michelena appeared well prepared for film acting and selling a story. She received excellent reviews for her inaugural film with the company's *Salomy Jane*, based on a romantic Bret Harte tale of the Gold Rush Days. Her assertive, strong performance enlivened the story of a tempestuous young woman of a gold mining camp righting wrongs and serving justice.

Michelena's sparkling personality jumped off the screen in stories featuring California's redwoods and the West, demonstrating her forceful presence. She succeeded in stage adaptations as well, whether playing a gypsy or a Salvation Army lass. With a few films under her belt, Michelena grew confident in film acting, telling *Movie Picture World*, "I enjoy every moment I spend working in the pictures."[7]

Looking to build her popularity, the striking beauty penned a series of astute syndicated stories in 1916 sharing behind-the-scenes movie anecdotes and tips on succeeding, especially for starstruck young women. Many focused on "photographic values" that charmed cameras and earned roles,[8] while also revealing that luck often played a major role. In particular, Michelena offered a potent observation on the importance of eyes to movie acting. "The eyes are the most important of a picture actress' features. In drama, where the voice is denied one, the eyes are the most nearly audible part of the face."[9] She continued her analysis and writing in 1917, with a pretty accurate second series examining the history and evolution of the movies from Eadweard Muybridge to Thomas Edison to D. W. Griffith. All the time she continued to sing, always working to improve her voice.

Michelena grew disillusioned with California Motion Picture Corporation after her ninth and last film *The Woman Who Dared*, the story of an opera singer in Rome. Waiting for repayment of money loaned to the company and other disagreements, she took flight. The couple abandoned the studio in late 1916, establishing their own company, Beatriz Michelena Motion Picture Company.[10] After California Motion Picture Corporation ceased operation, the couple also purchased the San Rafael studio for their own use.

Taking full independence for the first time, Michelena and Middleton vowed to produce film vehicles starring the dark-eyed star that were dime store novels come to life. Most of the studio staff from San Rafael followed them to their new studio, eager to work on similar movies that also revolved around western themes. Michelena brought tempestuous passion, determination, and strength to roles that made women the sheroes of their own stories, under the direction of her husband.

Over the next two years, the couple combined forces to produce films showcasing the self-possessed Michelena. Reading scripts, considering casting, planning costumes, the two completed production of multiple films at one time, with Michelena portraying a Native American, a dance-hall girl, and a cowgirl. This time they arranged better distribution through Robertson-Cole Productions but received mostly mixed reviews.

Just Squaw foreshadowed *The Searchers*, with Michelena playing a young woman kidnapped as a child and raised by Native Americans who is forced to choose between two lovers and her future way of life. *The Flame of Hellgate* starred Michelena "as the daredevil cow-girl of the west"[11] in a story about the cattle range. Quick on its heels came *Heart of Juanita*, promoted as starring Michelena, "a Human Dynamo of Emotion as Dance Queen in stimulating drama of California."[12]

By 1920 Michelena was suffering health issues, and the company struggled at the box office. They were forced to rent out space, trying to pay bills. Tired of the grind, Michelena retired from films, returning to the operatic stage. Over the next decade, the couple occasionally toured Europe, with Michelena once again singing arias.

Passing away in 1942 after a two-year illness, the fifty-two-year-old Michelena was mostly forgotten even by those in the Marin area. While her company produced only a few films during its few years of production, it established Michelena as the first female Hispanic filmmaker. The ambitious actress focused on strong, self-confident women characters, a role model for the many filmmakers that followed her.

Mary Pickford portrait by Albert Witzel, circa 1918. *Angie Schneider*

Mary Pickford, First Major Studio Founder, Actress-Producer

Recognized as one of the true greats of American cinema, Canadian-born Mary Pickford combined immense talent, savvy business acumen, and strong leadership skills to help make the film industry what it is today. Following her own dreams and determined ambitions, the human dynamo mentored women, nurtured senior film professionals, and defined the essence of great film acting. A multifaceted pioneer, Pickford achieved many firsts in Hollywood, from the highest salary to star approval to becoming the first woman to establish a major motion picture studio.

Born April 8, 1892, in Toronto, Canada, as Gladys Louise Smith, the future Mary Pickford learned courage and risk-taking from a young age. After her father abandoned her mother and two younger siblings Jack and Lottie, Pickford took control, landing stage work to help supplement her mother's threadbare salary as a dressmaker.[1] Over the next few years, as breadwinner, she worked for such stock troupes as Selkas's Gaiety Stock Company[2] and on Broadway in the play *In Convict Stripes*.[3] In 1907 the determined young woman officially adopted the name Mary Pickford when she joined the prestigious David Belasco theater troupe to appear in *The Warrens of Virginia*. Pickford felt she had earned a measure of respect working with the theater master.

Looking for extra money after her contract with Belasco ended, the young woman determinedly approached Biograph director D. W. Griffith on April 19, 1909.[4] She would become so popular she gained the nicknames the "Biograph Girl" and the "girl with the curls," during her

77

time at the studio, as she fell in love with movies.[5] Becoming one of the most recognizable and bankable stars, Pickford appeared on the inaugural cover of *Photoplay* magazine in 1912.

Over the next several years, Pickford moved between different studios, building name recognition and importance to up her salary with each move. In so doing, she gained better terms with each landing. During renegotiations with Paramount in 1916, Pickford received her own production company, with a voice in script approval, her character, and final cut; the last word on director, cast, and advertising; and reducing her output to only six films a year. The star would earn 50 percent of the profits, ensuring a minimum salary of over $1 million for a two-year period. Most importantly, her films would be distributed separately from everyone else's. Pickford had basically been serving as producer anyway, to ensure the quality of the productions.[6]

Mary's popularity continued to grow as her artistry continued. Audiences enjoyed her artistic performances, sold through her expressive eyes, which seem modern even today. While she had earned a wide variety of meaty roles of women of all age brackets and social classes at Biograph, she continued to successfully play young, action-oriented characters with moxie and spirit beyond the age of thirty. She fought injustice and depravity and won.

Continually disappointed at the shady practice of studios who sold inferior product on the backs of hers, sliced and diced her deals, and tried to run roughshod over her, Pickford got the last laugh. Along with Douglas Fairbanks, Charlie Chaplin, and director D. W. Griffith, she founded United Artists in 1919, the first major studio organized by such important industry players. Each star retained complete control of their productions while controlling the distribution and sometimes even the exhibition process as well. Not only would the founders enjoy the freedom to work creatively under their own supervision but they also owned the revenue of each piece of the pipeline, the ultimate dream of any filmmaker.

Not long after, Pickford married male superstar Douglas Fairbanks, a co-owner of United Artists, creating the world's first power couple. Thanks to their acumen and celebrity, the couple ruled as the King and

Queen of Hollywood, entertaining and ruling from their own Hollywood castle, Pickfair. During their honeymoon in Europe the couple was met by mobs of people, reflecting how popular they were all over the world.

In 1927 Pickford was the only woman to join with other industry leaders to form the Academy of Motion Picture Arts and Sciences. Organized to provide a seal of approval for technical issues, to educate members, and to present awards, it was also formed as an attempt to stop the unionization of film studios.

Generous with her time and money, Pickford supported those who had worked with her and who grew old, suffered from illness, or faced hard times. During World War I, she ardently sold war bonds at rallies Besides giving money to needy individuals, the generous actress helped found the Motion Picture Relief Fund (MPRF), which served as a branch of the Actors' Fund until 1924, providing much-needed funding to help support older members through hard times. Pickford always gave back, supporting those had who built the industry through their contributions and hard work. She would go on to help organize the Motion Picture Country House and Hospital, which when opened in 1942, providing housing and medical care for entertainment employees.[7]

Throughout her life, Pickford mentored others, especially women, on how to develop themselves and their own careers, gain experience, and promote themselves. She hired many women to work with her as well, especially friend Frances Marion, who served as one of Pickford's top screenwriters.

One of the most powerful people ever in Hollywood, Mary Pickford displayed gumption, smarts, and daring when forging her own unique path in creating a film career and industry during the early decades of cinema. She set high standards and practices, combining a sharp business mind with generous charitable giving to others. Pickford served as a multitalented filmmaker who established studios and the Academy of Motion Picture Arts and Sciences, all in the service of making films and building an industry. Her multipronged success offers a shining example on how to serve others while also succeeding yourself.

Marion E. Wong, First Chinese American Filmmaker

THOUGH THE CHINESE FIRST IMMIGRATED IN THE UNITED STATES IN 1848, to Sutter's Mill, California, hoping to get rich during the Gold Rush, they suffered greater indignities in its aftermath. Though many worked constructing the transcontinental railroad, laboring in mines, or serving as farmers, they found it difficult to find acceptance. In 1882 the US Congress passed the Chinese Exclusion Act, which forbade immigration from China for ten years and rendered immigrants ineligible for naturalization, which was later extended for another ten years in 1892 and then made permanent in 1902. Determined California native Marion E. Wong overcame these and other hardships when she produced the first film ever made in the United States by a Chinese American—man or woman—in 1917.

Born into a wealthy third-generation San Francisco family in 1895, Wong grew up in Oakland after the 1906 San Francisco earthquake destroyed her family's home. The Wong family relocated to the East Bay city to run their Edvin's Oriental Cafe in the heart of the city's theater district. Young Wong served as a waitress in the family business, where she encountered theatrical performers and became determined to enter the business as well.

Wong studied singing and dancing, appearing onstage for local lodges and dancing in tea rooms during the summer of 1916 before appearing in Sid Grauman's *Midnight Frisco* and *A Night at the World's Fair* at Stockton's Yosemite Theater, credited as "Princess Marion Wong, the Chinese Song Bird."[1] She appeared in the Will King vaudeville show

Help Wanted at Oakland's Columbia Theater in late 1916,[2] billed as the "Chinese prima donna."[3] But she played a larger role in Sid Grauman's *Midnight Frisco* in San Francisco.

After succeeding onstage, the magnetic Wong decided to conquer movies, though she had never made one. "She conceived the idea that she wanted to be a film actress, and when other people met her announced desires with indifference, she determined to form a company of her own."[4] She began writing a story of East meeting West and organizing the elements to do so. Wong formed the Mandarin Film Company in 1917 to produce films by and for Chinese Americans. She told friends from the beginning that the company's early films constituted experiments and a learning process for the films she ultimately hoped to make.[5]

Raising money from merchants in Oakland's Chinatown,[6] the resourceful young woman began seeking out actors, equipment, and a studio for her inaugural production, *The Curse of Quon Gwon*, with herself as director and producer. A modern Chinese fairy tale, the film revealed a curse struck against a Chinese American family because they "worshipped at the shine of western civilization."[7]

Wong constructed a small studio behind the family home, borrowed props from local stores, hired a local cameraman, perhaps from the nearby Essanay Film Manufacturing Company in Niles, and convinced family and friends to serve as her actors, besides essaying an important supporting role herself. A one woman dervish, Wong not only wrote the script, arranged financing, produced, and directed the movie but also designed its many costumes. Before filming even began, Wong arranged for the cast to rehearse the story under the guidance of "an old-time stage director of Chinese theaters in San Francisco"[8] before shooting in Oakland and even on location in China.

Upon completion, Wong reached out to local papers to publicize the film. She told one Oakland newspaper, "I had never seen any Chinese movies, so I decided to introduce them to the world. I first wrote the love story. Then I decided that people who are interested in my people and my country would like to see some of the customs and manners of China. So I added to the love drama many scenes depicting these things. I do hope it will be a success."[9]

Wong held a private screening in Oakland in May 1917 for local cast and crew before heading east to screen *The Curse of Quon Gwon* for trade magazines and to find distribution. *Moving Picture World* praised the multiple-reel production in a July 1917 review. Acknowledging its unique status as the first production by Chinese Americans in the United States, the review praised the rich look of the film and acknowledged shooting locations in California as well as China. "The scenery and settings, especially in the latter half, are particularly interesting and show some wonderful Chinese scenery as well as strong dramatic sets, all combined with excellent photography."[10]

No states' rights distributors stepped forward to release the film. Mandarin Film Company disbanded, investors lost money, and Wong, depressed and embarrassed, shelved the film. The family rarely discussed the movie or even projected it. She returned to the family restaurant business, opening the Singapore Hut restaurant in Richmond, California, where she sometimes performed in musical cabarets.[11]

In 2004, Wong family members provided *Hollywood Chinese* documentarian Arthur Dong with the two surviving reels of original 35mm nitrate negatives and a 16mm print of *The Curse of Quon Gwon*. The Academy Film Archive of the Academy of Motion Picture Arts and Sciences restored the film that same year. It was finally released on DVD in 2010, over ninety years after completion. What little survives of *The Curse of Quon Gwon* demonstrates that Wong possessed a remarkable innate talent for filmmaking.

DIRECTORS

Mabel Normand portrait by Fred Hartsook, circa 1916. *Mary Mallory*

Mabel Normand, First Comedy Director

One of Hollywood's pioneering comedy queens, the beautiful Mabel Normand revealed that beautiful women could slip on a banana peel or take a pie in the face and steal scenes with hilarious pratfalls. Her comic expressiveness and athleticism would lead the way for future comedy icon, Lucille Ball. Becoming a star on her own, she would go on to clown around with Charlie Chaplin's Little Tramp and make a series of potent comedy knockouts with rotund comedian Roscoe "Fatty" Arbuckle. Perhaps most importantly, she demonstrated that women could successfully direct comedies combining mayhem and wistful moments, the first in her field to do so.

Born November 10, 1892, in Staten Island, the beautiful, doe-eyed Normand loved drawing and considered being an illustrator, before striking out for fame by modeling for them. She employed her beauty as an early New York model for renowned illustrators J. C. Leyendecker, James Montgomery Flagg, and Charles Dana Gibson in advertisements and art. Gaining experience in front of a still camera, Normand posed for lantern slides, photo postcards, and commercial advertisements for products like Coca-Cola, learning to sell her personality and charm.

Actress Alice Joyce suggested Mabel try out moving pictures. Mabel recalled in a 1918 interview: "She tried to get me over to the Biograph, where D. W. Griffith was working at that time. I didn't want to go at first. I was fairly satisfied with $3 a day for posing with an extra $5 to $10 at the Fashion Camera Studio. Besides I wanted to be an illustrator. I could draw a little and kept my eyes and ears open to pick up everything I could in the artists' studios."[1]

Normand visited Biograph the next day. After a mix-up, she appeared in several one-reelers before the company decamped for California in early 1910. Normand then signed with Vitagraph, immediately winning fans with her spontaneous, spunky style in front of the camera, not afraid to look silly. She displayed great rapport with lead star John Bunny, stealing scenes with an impish sense of humor and lovely charisma.

Now popular, Normand returned to Biograph in 1911, appearing in the short *The Diving Girl* in August, a precursor to Mack Sennett and his Bathing Beauties. Mabel put her modeling skills to use, looking svelte in a revealing suit, and showcasing athletic skills. Under D. W. Griffith's eye she portrayed a variety of characters in dramatic stories, but her heart remained in comedy. At this point Normand developed a kinship with Mack Sennett, who recognized the brio in this simpatico comic. The two made a formidable team onscreen, playing energetically off each other, as sweet Mabel turned feisty and rebellious.

When Sennett incorporated the Keystone Film Company in 1912 and moved west, Normand came along as his female star. They made a comically slapstick team, by turns loving and feuding. He recognized her comic genius. "Mabel Normand is such a splendid success even more on account of her head than her looks. She is quick as a flash and just funny. She is naturally funny. She is funny to talk to and seems to think in sparks."[2]

Busily turning out slapstick and suggestive beach girl fare the first few months, the company hit stride with the short *Barney Oldfield's Race for a Life,* a comic spoof of melodramatic stage presentations. In the short, a dastardly Ford Sterling snatches Mabel and ties her to the train tracks, requiring a last-minute dash by race-car driver Oldfield to rescue her. Many of these early shorts parodied moving pictures and melodramas and were overlaid with a huge dash of comically maniacal mayhem. Normand also found the opportunity to display her peppy fearlessness and daring, flying as a passenger in an airplane in the 1912 short *A Dash through the Clouds.*

Making these shorts was often brutal, backbreaking, and strenuous. As Mabel later revealed:

I have had to dive and swim in rough ocean scenes. I have fought with bears, fallen out of rapidly moving automobile, jumped off of a second story roof into a flower bed and risked life, limb, and peace of mind in innumerable ways—and all to make people laugh. Some work days I have gone home and cried with ache in body and heart and at the very moment of my misery thousands of theatre-goers were rocking in their seats with laughter at some few scenes in which I had worked a few years before.[3]

Wanting some measure of control over the physicality and direction of her films, Normand began writing her scripts and later directing, in 1913, especially as Sennett focused more of his time on actually running the business. Trades reported that "Mabel Normand, leading woman with the Keystone, will hereafter direct every picture in which she appears."[4] In so doing, Normand would be the first woman to direct comedy films, as Alice Guy-Blaché and Lois Weber focused on more dramatic and esoteric ones.

Though few of the shorts she directed survived, most show the typical knockdown, drag-out style of the Keystone brand. Her film *Won in a Cupboard* does demonstrate a creative filmmaker employing technology and special effects to put the story across, employing close-ups and double exposure shots in bringing two hopeful romantics together. Her three films featuring Chaplin showcase great energy and use of longer takes to allow greater spontaneity. *Mabel's Strange Predicament* showcased Chaplin in his Tramp getup for the first time, though the British actor disagreed and rebelled against Normand's direction in *Making a Living*, already trying to take control of his image. In *Caught in a Cabaret*, Chaplin dominates the action inside a madcap cabaret scene filled with usual Keystone hijinks. She directed one more time with *Mabel's Nerve*, before stepping away from the camera. Perhaps she considered directing comedy too easy, since most Keystone shorts just let mayhem rip.

Later in 1914, she costarred with Chaplin and overacting actress Marie Dressler in Sennett's first feature-length film, *Tillie's Punctured Romance*. A story of romance for ill-begotten gains, Chaplin woos Dressler to steal her inheritance while still enamored of girlfriend

Normand, with comic mayhem ensuing. Normand gives a winning, understated performance while both Dressler and Chaplin engage in competitive mugging. The film earned huge box office receipts however.

In 1915 Normand starred opposite Arbuckle in a series of hilarious shorts, demonstrating both their wonderful chemistry and great comic timing. Usually playing middle-class romantic or married couples, the two share household misadventures or public outings with more dramatic shadings than the normal Keystone output. Normand displays vulnerability and anger as a neglected housewife in these stories of marriage and relationships, showcasing her emotional range and perhaps growing resentment and anger over her changing relationship with Sennett.

Normand suffered a concussion in October 1915 from unknown causes and required hospitalization. Trade accounts reported her seriously ill and possibly at the point of death from an accident that occurred during production of a film and rendered her unconscious.[5] Perhaps this illness foreshadowed future health issues from which she suffered.

Whatever actually happened, it resulted in a permanent break with Sennett. Normand, Arbuckle, and Al St. John filmed their next series of shorts in Fort Lee, New Jersey. Normand began focusing more on real acting and farce than appearing in knockabout slapstick, perhaps planning for her future, explaining the difference in the two acting styles in a newspaper interview: "Most pretty girls who go into comedy work are content to be merely pretty. The great difference is to put character into acting without either distorting your face or using comedy make-up . . . to make a farce heroine more than a doll, you must think out the situation yourself and above all you must pay great attention to every little detail in the scene. The little bits of business that seem insignificant are what make great comedy."[6]

Normand experienced a number of emotional and health setbacks for the next few years. Ready to move on, Sennett doubled Normand's salary and built her own studio for her off Fountain Avenue in East Hollywood in 1916, under the name the Mabel Normand Feature Film Company. Normand would star in the films and have direction and story approval, starting with her intended first film, *Mickey*. Facing all manner of erratic delays and director changes, *Mickey* was not completed until

1917. Sennett failed to release the film until 1918, and by that time, Normand had moved on to the Samuel Goldwyn Company. Though she completed over twenty-five films during her time there, her appearance grew ragged, leading to health concerns.

In 1922 she was the last (innocent) person to see her friend, director William Desmond Taylor, alive before his tragic murder, and her life was never the same, thanks to innuendo regarding their actual connection. She returned to Sennett to make *Suzanna* and *The Extra Girl*, both reflected Normand's charm and vulnerability and cleaned up at the box office. But trouble arose for her again, and she wandered from pillar to post for the next several years,

Normand brought impish delight into comic production, stealing scenes with her physical athleticism and effervescent comic flair, gaining the nickname "madcap Mabel" for her propensity to cut loose and dirty herself with knockabout humor. With an intuitive sense for different types of humor and how to sell them onscreen, she also recognized the powerful connection the relationships in these comic films had with moviegoing audiences. Her personal touch added emotional moments to the films she did direct, toning down the slapstick to focus on connections. Beautiful but tragic, Normand served as Hollywood's first comedy director, combining the physical with a personal touch.

Lois Weber portrait for Bosworth Studios, circa 1914. *Mary Mallory*

Lois Weber, First American-Born Director-Producer

ALICE GUY-BLACHÉ INAUGURATED WOMEN'S FILMMAKING IN THE United States after she constructed and led the New Jersey–based Solax Studios, the first woman to write, direct, and produce. She offered a shining light for others to follow, including her early student Lois Weber. Modeling herself after Guy-Blaché, Weber would serve as Universal Studios' top film director, while become Hollywood's leading woman director in early Hollywood, employing films to showcase cultural and societal issues. The multitalented filmmaker eventually wrote, directed, and starred in films simultaneously, the first American-born woman to do so. She gained importance as progressive issues were on the rise, with suffragists fighting for the right to vote, unions gaining in strength, and more women working, offering a potent example to young women about following their dreams.

Born June 13, 1879, as Florence Lois Weber in Allegheny, Pennsylvania, Weber studied piano and music as a child, hoping to become a grand opera singer. She studied singing in New York and became an accomplished accompanist and singer. While studying, she served the poor and unfortunate through song. To placate her upset family, Weber "devoted much of her spare time to church army work, giving entertainments at army cantonments, prisons, and hospitals."[1] She sang for such groups as the Young Men's Christian Association in New York, serving the Gospel as well,[2] and the Methodist Epworth League back in Pittsburgh, her hometown.[3] Weber employed her pianist skills by giving concerts across the country as a teenager, ending when she was seventeen after a key

93

came off in her hand at a concert, which undermined her courage. Unable to finish, she vowed never to appear on a concert stage again.[4]

Unsure what to do next, Weber's uncle, a theatrical producer in Chicago, gave her the lead in a musical comedy he was producing.[5] Once back in New York, she joined a stock company, gaining experience and better roles. During the show *Why Girls Leave Home*, she met actor/stage manager Phillips Smalley.[6] After a short courtship, they married.

Weber gained her first film experience at Gaumont's chronophone studio in Fort Lee, New Jersey, singing songs for producer Herbert Blaché for two years.[7] Watching Guy-Blaché direct some of these films, Weber began considering the elements of filmmaking and what constituted a good story.[8] Smalley joined the company, and the two began their film collaboration at Gaumont's before moving on to Reliance Pictures and then Edwin S. Porter's Rex Motion Picture Company, at a time when the industry was attempting to solidify middle-class women audiences and produce nonconfrontational, respectable programming.

After Rex merged with Universal Pictures in 1913, Carl Laemmle signed the duo to serve as the head of the filmmaking brand. The couple moved westward, with Weber becoming recognized as an auteur. During their time with Universal, Weber starred in most of the films while writing each screenplay and directing most of the films herself. She cemented her status as one of Hollywood's top creative filmmakers during the couple's short sojourn to Bosworth, Inc., in 1914, starting her move to more serious filmmaking.

Weber pioneered innovative practices, as in her 1913 one-reeler *Suspense*, in which split screen effects reveal multiple events, sometimes even three, occurring simultaneously. In 1914, Weber became the first American woman to direct, write, and star in the full-length 1914 feature film, *The Merchant of Venice*, an adaptation of William Shakespeare's classic play. By the midteens, she was making creative use of double exposures and other effects to tell her stories, focusing on reiterating subject matter and themes in powerful poetic images, including an almost-nude woman in *Hypocrites*. Weber and Smalley returned to Universal in 1916, with Weber becoming the dominant person in the filmmaking team.

She developed stars as well. The director gave women like Mary McLaren, Claire Windsor, and Billie Dove opportunities to demonstrate their acting chops in challenging and meaty parts. In fact, Weber mentored women, hiring and placing them in leading roles, like Lillian Greenberger her business manager, and shaping the writing skills of future screenwriters Jeanie MacPherson and Frances Marion. Future directors John Ford and Henry Hathaway began as her prop boys.

At this time, Weber moved toward more serious subject matter, focusing on social issues like religious hypocrisy, poverty and wage inequality, abortion and birth control, and poverty and the death penalty in such often controversial films as *Hypocrites* (1913), *Where Are My Children?* (1916), *The Hand That Rocks the Cradle* (1917), and *The People vs. John Doe* (1917). Weber also produced and directed her only action picture, *The Dumb Girl of Portici* (1916), an epic story of lust and revenge set in Italy,[9] Universal's top-grossing action film of the time. She hoped to effect political change by making films "that will have an influence for good on the public mind."[10]

Weber's films focused on strong, complex women who were unafraid to take stands or voice opinions. She earned high returns at the box office for her films, demonstrating a large audience was looking for serious subject matter on issues important to the country. *Photoplay* magazine called her, "Lois Weber, director, author, musician and anaesthetist to a suffering world."[11]

In 1917 she formed Lois Weber Productions, renting property to establish her own studio on Santa Monica Boulevard, Los Angeles, and taking on, for the first time, complete charge of the filmmaking process without interference. She called it "my 'Old Homestead.'"[12] Unlike for other women in independent production, Universal Pictures distributed her films, ensuring a full release schedule and quality marketing. When the studio considered her films too controversial in 1919, she started releasing through Paramount Pictures, turning her focus on women and the home, looking at the world in miniature. At a time when men were returning from World War I, people were recovering from the Spanish Flu epidemic, and the country was suffering from a recession, films turned more lighthearted and easygoing.

Weber focused on women off the screen as well. She was one of the founding members of the Hollywood Studio Club, giving a home to young single women attempting to break into movies. Besides donating money, she often gave lectures on the industry to residents, providing a positive role model of success in the grueling film business.[13] During World War I, she actively participated with the Red Cross, serving on government panels and speaking around the country on how women could contribute to the cause.

Wall Street financing turned moving picture studios into factory towns in the mid-1920s as it looked to dominate distribution and kill off independent production. This virtually wiped out women's roles in the industry, as business types pushed out women, looking instead for a more muscular, businesslike approach. At the same time, the press seemed to write women out of history, denigrating their creative importance—even that of Weber, the most important woman filmmaker in the 1910s. She turned director-for-hire, looking to stay active, making only two more films before her death.

A pioneering visionary of American filmmaking, Lois Weber employed motion pictures to reveal important social issues as she became one of the leading filmmakers of the 1910s. Looking to open the industry to more women, Weber served as a mentor to several—actors, writers, and especially women behind the scenes—giving them a leg up to bring a woman's perspective to film work.

WRITER

Gene Gauntier portrait for Kalem Film Manufacturing Co., 1912. *Marc Wanamaker/Bison Archives*

Gene Gauntier, First Screenwriter

STORIES TELL US WHO WE ARE AND WHO WE HOPE TO BECOME. THEY illuminate us about life and each other. Every form of entertainment is a story in one way or another. In the first decades of moving pictures, scripts didn't exist per se; they were more scenarios that were treatments or outlines than pure stories, highlighting the emotional high points of a piece. For the most part, writers weren't credited, but in 1907 Gene Gauntier received credit for writing the story for the 1907 Kalem Film Manufacturing Co.'s adaptation of Lew Wallace's great 1880 novel, *Ben Hur*, which led to the first Supreme Court case for plagiarism by a movie company in the United States. The first known female screenwriter, Gauntier served as one of the first and most important trailblazing women in silent film.

Born Genevieve Gauntier Liggett on August 26, 1885, in Kansas City, Missouri, to an upper middle-class family, young Gene Gauntier loved words. She took part in elocution contests while attending the Kansas City School of Oratory.[1] By 1897 she was publicly reciting Shakespeare and, in 1898, performing in local theatrical presentations in a variety of extra parts, including in an opera company's production of Gilbert and Sullivan's *The Pirates of Penzance*.[2] Once graduating from high school and oratory school, she joined a local acting company and then joined New York traveling stock companies in 1904. By 1905 she adopted the stage name "Gene Gauntier."[3]

Looking for new challenges, Gauntier entered moving pictures in 1906, when fellow stage performer Sidney Olcott helped get her in the door at the American Mutoscope and Biograph Company. Here she began her long work in writing stories for the screen, especially those favoring independent, strong-minded young women. As Gauntier wrote later about that day in June 1906, "I literally jumped into the moving pictures. And from that day to this I have been connected with them as actress, scenario writer, producer and critic. In these different capacities I watched the very birth-pangs of the industry. I helped to develop and guide it, I cried and laughed over it, and was part of it as it was part of me."[4] She served as actor and producer with the company, giving D. W. Griffith his first directing assignment. After completing the season, Gauntier returned to theatrical work in the offseason.

Gauntier starred in a few films for Biograph, learning the art of appearing in front of the camera before joining the new Motion Picture Patents Company member, the Kalem Film Manufacturing Co. with her actor-director friend Olcott in 1907. She watched company member George Marion draft scenarios, basically bare outlines or sketches, sometimes writing them on the backs of envelopes, for the company to shoot the next day. During the summer of that year, Marion stopped, asking Gauntier to take over.[5] Daily practice improved her skills, leading her to eventually write over three hundred stories, freely stealing ideas and plots from other writers at the time, as she became "the mainstay of the Kalem scenario department."[6] Gauntier sometimes wrote three short scenarios a day, receiving twenty dollars for each reel.

In October 1907, Marion approached Gauntier about adapting the popular novel *Ben Hur* since they could use the closed racetrack at Sheepshead Park, along with scenery, props, and costumes from the closed Pain's Fireworks Company show. After two long days, she turned in a script highlighting the sixteen top sequences of the book, including the great chariot race, which the company filmed in three days, turning out the biggest epic seen on screen at the time.[7]

Once released, the General Lew Wallace Estate and Harper and Brothers sued Kalem, the Motion Picture Patents company, and Gauntier for copyright infringement, since the company had not purchased the rights from the estate. After an almost three-year court battle, the Supreme Court settled copyright law permanently for entertainment, ruling that motion pictures companies must legally clear the right to adapt material for the screen or other uses.

A determined Gauntier continued her writing and acting for Kalem, expanding to producing and location approvals, among other roles as well, writing in later years that she "picked locations, supervised sets, passed on tests, co-directed with Sidney Olcott, cut and edited and wrote captions."[8] She began drafting stories of self-possessed, take-charge women which she often portrayed onscreen under the moniker the "Kalem Girl." Leading the way was her Confederate Spy series starting in 1909, in which she played Nan, a cross-dressing spy who saves the day, setting the stage for adventure-minded serial queens to come. Gauntier often produced the films and sometimes co-directed with the talented Olcott as well.

In 1910 Kalem became the first film producing company to shoot on location outside the United States when it filmed *The Lad from Old Ireland* (1910) on the old sod itself. Gauntier helped arrange travel and filming details for this and other shoots, including the three years the company shot around Killarney, Ireland, during the summers for what came to be known as the O'Kalem films. In 1912 she organized location shooting in the Holy Land for *From the Manger to the Cross*, the first feature-length film on the life of Christ.

Ready to control her own destiny, Gauntier and Olcott departed Kalem in December 1912 to organize the Gene Gauntier Feature Players Company. The longtime creative team continued their collaboration, with Irish-born Olcott serving as director-producer. Just over a year later, Olcott resigned from the company to start his own independent concern. Though Gauntier and her husband Jack Clark tried to continue on, they were forced to close the company, joining Universal Film Manufacturing Company in 1915 for a short time. Gauntier continued seeking out work and made an occasional picture, but her career was virtually over. She made her last film appearance in the 1921 picture *The Witch's Lure*.

In 1919 Gauntier turned dramatic editor and critic for the *Kansas City Post* for a time, keeping active by writing. The former actress traveled to Sweden in 1923 to visit her sister, before mostly spending her time living there or in Mexico. She turned to writing novels in 1929, first with *Cabbages and Harlequins*, a novel of touring companies and early Broadway, and would later write two more. For her hometown paper, she claimed in an interview for the book that she "was the first woman to direct a picture—first woman studio manager for the old Biograph Company in 1908."[9] Over the next few years, she would claim to the *Kansas City Star* that she was the ultimate trailblazing pioneer, the first woman to hold virtually every position in filmmaking.

Gene Gauntier left behind a colorful legacy as one of the female pioneers of the silver screen, establishing practices that solidified it as the top entertainment medium of the United States in the twentieth century.

PRODUCTION

NELLIE BLY BAKER

GR anit 1266   Temporary Phone 7-0060
Present Releases
"The Snob"—*Monta Bell*
"Cheaper to Marry"—*Bob Leonard*
Recently finished four weeks' engagement with Harry Langdon in his
first five reel feature, "His First Flame," and three weeks with Hunt
Stromberg in "Paint and Powder"—*Warner Bros.*
"Red Hot Tires," with Monte Blue

GLADYS MOORE

Emotional and Mother Roles
Grande-Dames
Complete Wardrobe
Leading Mother Role in "His Greatest Battle"
Series of Thos. Regan Prods.

590-689   TU cker 9766

AGNES STEELE

As "Widow Spudd" in "My Old Dutch"
Directed by Laurence Trimble-Universal
Also "Minnie, the Housekeeper" in "Rose of the World"
Directed by Harry Beaumont
Stage Experience 25 Years
FI tzroy 3615 or HO lly 4102

LOUISE SWIFT

Character and Society Parts

GL adstone 3914   HO lly 4102

Projectionist-turned-actress Nellie Bly Baker in the *1927 Standard Casting Directory*.

Nellie Bly Baker, First Projectionist

WOMEN INCREASINGLY ENTERED THE WORKFORCE IN THE 1910S. WHEN the United States entered World War I and men went off to war, business required women joining the workforce to keep everything going. Women worked in munitions plants, drove trucks, and even took on new positions in the motion picture industry. While mostly anonymous females served as projectionists in small mom-and-pop theaters across the country in its early days, none worked for film studios or major theaters. Nellie Bly Baker stepped in to serve as a downtown Los Angeles film projectionist beginning in 1917, becoming the first woman to project films professionally.

Born September 7, 1893, on the Canadian River near Coweta, Oklahoma, Nellie Bly Baker fell in love with the movies as a young girl and saw it as her ticket out of the state. Driven and ambitious, she graduated from Kendall College as well as a women's business college[1] before winning a screenwriting contest in which the script would be employed in making an episode of the serial *The Tulsa Girl*.[2]

Though it failed to win her a trip to Hollywood, the script inspired her to move on, landing a job as stenographer in attorney Al F. William's office in Columbus, Kansas.[3] She returned home to Tulsa to work in a real estate office before heading to California in July 1918 to work, first as a switchboard operator and then as a stenographer at the Charlie Chaplin Studio, and making a brief appearance in the short *How to Make Movies*.[4]

So many projectionists enlisted or were drafted into the war effort in the fall of 1918 that downtown Los Angeles film palaces recruited women to serve in their place, as did other large cities around the state.

Women were eager to sign up, looking for more opportunities and challenging work. To land a job, however, they had to undergo training and pass an examination to be licensed in order to join the union.

Remaining male projectionists protested against women entering their workforce but were overruled. To try to prevent their hiring, the men increased the difficulty of both the written and actual projecting tests, though most women still earned their licenses. The *Los Angeles Times* reported the men distributed a twenty-five-question examination when men normally answered only a few questions verbally, besides having the women demonstrate their expertise with a projector.[5]

On October 2, after weeks of training,[6] Baker earned the distinction of becoming "the first girl to receive her license as a full-fledged motion picture operator in Los Angeles." Miss Baker was the first of a class of fifteen girls learning to operate projecting machines to be given a license at a school headed by Leo Ryan, member of the Southern California Theatre Owners' Association. Another twenty-five girls were to follow them into training. Ryan, Baker's instructor, was proud of her achievement and had confidence in others as well: "Miss Baker is only the start. There are fifteen more waiting to get their licenses. The girls know electricity and they are artistic. They get plenty of sleep and they don't smoke in the operating booths. They've got a great future before them."[7] Just a few months later, one trade report revealed that many large downtown theaters on the West Coast employed women operators after Baker accomplished the feat of working at one of Los Angeles's largest theaters.[8]

Theater owners were ecstatic about women training to become operators, seeing it potentially breaking the union, which protested instructing women though it was occurring on orders of the US government. As the *Los Angeles Times* reported in October, "This is considered a decisive blow at the motion picture operators' union, which has fought against the issuing of licenses to women."[9]

Just months after World War I ended, however, Baker's time as a Los Angeles theater projectionist ended along with that of other women when American GIs returned from the war. She returned to the Chaplin Studio as secretary to the great comedian,[10] later appearing in *The Kid*.[11] While in preproduction on his 1923 dramedy *A Woman of Paris*,

Chaplin cast Baker as a masseuse, with *Motion Picture Classic* calling her performance in the film "a big hit."[12]

Many studios came calling with acting opportunities, but Chaplin declined them all, finally relenting and loaning her to First National to appear in the Constance Talmadge romantic comedy *The Gold Fish*.[13] When the comedian turned to a comedy set in the Yukon called *The Gold Rush* in 1924, he once again gave a small part to his secretary. Chaplin himself remarked, "She is a wonderful actress with a keen sense of humor,"[14] helping galvanize her career. What had appeared a lark seemed to offer a new career opportunity.

At that point, Baker left the studio to seek her fortune as an actress. She received some nice supporting roles in films, the aim of many young women flocking to Hollywood. Later that year, the former secretary found herself cast in a role originally intended for Louise Fazenda in the Marie Prevost romantic comedy *How to Educate a Wife*.[15] Hoping to land bigger and better roles, Baker bought herself an ad illustrated with her photo in the "Character Women" section of the *1925 Standard Casting Directory*, which did appear to raise her profile.[16] She even landed a small role in *Salvation Hunters*, Josef von Sternberg's first time writing and directing a film, which starred Georgia Hale and George K. Arthur. Writer-director Dorothy Davenport Reid cast Baker in perhaps her largest part, in her film *The Red Kimono*.

Baker struggled to break through and in 1926 found herself cast in small parts in Tiffany Productions, Inc., films *The First Night* and *That Model from Paris*. In 1927 Baker only worked in one film, the First National movie *Breakfast at Sunrise*, a "breezy Parisian comedy"[17] before landing a role in the 1929 film *Love and the Devil*. Her acting career was winding down as talking pictures arrived on the scene. Baker appeared in a sadly ironic story about heartbreak along the Great White Way of Broadway in a 1930 Billie Dove film entitled *The Painted Angel*, costarred in the 1931 MGM Philo Vance detective story *Cock Robin*, starring Basil Rathbone, and made her last appearance in 1934 in the Joan Crawford film *Sadie McKee*.

By the late 1930s, Baker married O'Brien and they moved to the Mono Lake area, running a popular vacation resort. Always good with people, she often represented the Inyo-Mono area at Sportsmen's Shows across the state. Happy in her life beyond Hollywood, Baker, by working for Chaplin and appearing in studio films, had achieved more than most young women who arrived in Hollywood looking for fame and fortune. She earned her greatest fame serving as Los Angeles's first female licensed projectionist, opening new possibilities for ambitious young women with initiative.

Katherine Russell Bleecker, First Documentarian

THE EARLY DECADES OF THE TWENTIETH CENTURY INTRODUCED MOV-
ing pictures to audiences. First considered a pure entertainment medium,
it was later recognized as a strong educational tool for schools as well
as social settings. Businesses employed motion pictures to document
and promote their businesses, while progressive organizations employed
them to reveal financial inequalities, discrimination, and social injustice.
Carving out new possibilities for women, ambitious, driven Katherine
Russell Bleecker turned her experience recording society home movies
into making serious documentaries on important issues, making her the
first female documentary filmmaker and camerawoman in the United
States before becoming an early version of Martha Stewart.

Born May 5, 1893, to an upper-middle-class family in New York,
Bleecker always looked for challenges and opportunities to better herself.
A devout photographer, she practiced to improve her skills, falling in love
with movies and then into a career in movies by accident: "I knew a man
who had written a scenario he could not sell. He wanted to produce it
with his friends as actors and actresses. I'd never seen a motion picture
camera, but photography had always been a hobby with me and I told
him I'd make the picture."[1] Determined to succeed, Bleecker trained for
a year with a major film company learning to operate a camera, write
scripts, and organize cast and crew, while also serving as an assistant stage
manager. Thinking outside the box, Bleecker boldly demonstrated intelligence and initiative in achieving her dreams and conquering new fields.

Creativity came naturally to Bleecker. She attended art school to study drawing but fell under the spell of movies. Already experienced with still photography, both shooting and processing it, moving pictures caught her fancy. "When the moving picture craze arrived I became interested with the rest. At first I thought I wanted to do studio work. Afterward I decided that inside work was not what I wanted after all. But the two years' experience I obtained has proved of priceless value to me now as you see I understand every department of the business thoroughly."[2]

Taking her original idea, Bleecker approached high-society friends about recording movies about their lives, a fancy way of killing time by shooting expensive home movies but much more exciting than putting on little theatrical productions. In effect, she was making the first "home videos" of her day, with people who out-Gatsbyed *The Great Gatsby.*

The driven young woman found success writing and producing "amateur movies" that featured both adults and children, devising stories around locations where she and her society friends congregated. Serving as almost a one-person crew, Bleecker wrote, cast, cranked, directed, edited, and produced the films, which she later screened for the upper-crust set at private parties. After successfully completing her first "amateur movie," Bleecker turned to others featuring local people, producing such films as *The Perils of Society* in Cleveland, *Smuggler's Revenge* at Canada's Thousand Island Yacht Club, and *Man and the Millionaire* in Pittsburgh, Pennsylvania, basically a fictional, 1910s version of *Keeping Up with the Kardashians* or *The Real Housewives* series.[3] She rehearsed her amateur cast as much as possible before turning the crank, hoping to save time and money.[4]

Talented as she was, Bleecker recognized that women would need to fight to prove their worth to men. "There is a great field in the line of directing motion pictures for women if they ever get the chance to 'break in.' I hardly think the time has come for women to take up the professional work. I know we could do it as well as the men, but the men do not know that yet. It will be in this field of endeavor as in every other work, men will not acknowledge we are their equals until we fight them every inch of the way and force them to see our worth."[5]

Some of her "society" movies raised money for charity or even the Red Cross, while others featured everything from cars to tugboats to yachts to airplanes. Bleecker's initiative and success led commercial organizations to hire her to produce films promoting themselves, commercial documentaries, or perhaps the first infomercials. The City of Asbury Park, New Jersey's Department of Public Affairs and Chamber of Commerce hired her to produce a film showing major landmarks and city departments, which would be shown to the public on Thanksgiving night.[6] She earned $5,000 making these films that second year, allowing her to set up a small studio in the Grand Central Terminal Building in New York City.[7]

Alexander Cleland, Secretary of the Joint Commission on Prison Reform in New York commissioned her just a month later to shoot serious documentary films showing the drudgery and degrading living conditions of prisoners at Dannemora, Auburn, and Sing Sing Prisons in order to improve the prisoners' lot and provide them with mental and physical opportunities to better their lives. While working at Sing Sing to "demonstrate antiquated methods of punishing transgressors," as she told the *New York Times* in 1915, she boldly filmed without a guard while convicts milled around her. She completed *Within Prison Walls*, *A Prison Without Walls*, and *A Day in Sing Sing* in 1915, all of which were employed to lobby for better prison conditions.[8] Talented Bleecker would also direct a commercial film entitled *Madame Spy*, starring Jack Mulhall, Claire Du Brey, and others, released early in 1918.

Carl Laemmle, Universal Studios chief and New York's Broadway Theatre owner, appointed Bleecker as operations manager for the theater. She was the first woman to serve in such a capacity in a major New York City film theater, replacing previous manager Walter Rosenberg over decreasing revenues. Unlike most theaters, its staff was also very "feminized," with female press agent Rose Shulsinger and many "usherettes." As she glibly informed journalists, "I'm going to prove that theatre managing is like housekeeping—a woman's job. I'm going to give patrons the same fare that I would give guests at my house—lots of solid dishes and a good, spicy dessert."[9] While at the theater, Bleecker also produced films for the American Red Cross.

Bleecker worked for more than a year in the position, even after marrying Willis Noel Meigs, a vice president of a window and door manufacturing concern, and going on to start a family. As her children grew, the inquisitive and proactive woman developed business ideas to assist upper-middle-class customers with their needs, a vintage Martha Stewart envisioning new businesses and culture.

Long before Amazon, Expedia, or Google came on the scene, the Postal Telegraph Company hired the social doyenne in 1931 to serve as the "Emily Post of the telegraph wires," providing service to harried consumers. The savvy Bleecker pitched the company on answering etiquette questions, offering fashion advice, reserving hotel rooms, or finding chaperones for young women via questions submitted by telegrams. "I started out with the idea of forming a shopping service, and the rest just developed. . . . I hoped to make it different from other such bureaus by confining the cost of the service to the expense of sending a telegram," as Bleecker described her idea to the United Press.[10]

The astute businesswoman and feminist also hoped to inspire other women to follow their own passions and to influence young children to recognize the intelligence and skills of their mothers. Bleecker told newspapers in August 1931, "It seems to be children are really benefitted when their mothers have interests outside the homes."[11]

Developing a career in what is now called personnel training, the sharp Bleecker trained Postal Telegraph delivery boys in etiquette to better serve the needs of those to whom they delivered telegrams or took orders in offices. She also soon sold Postal Telegraph on branding telegrams for special announcements: "orchidgrams."[12] By 1937, Bleecker taught classes in business and life etiquette at Hunter College, "the only university classes in the art of good manners,"[13] while also serving as the president of the New York League of Business and Professional Women. In 1938, she was named director of personnel with the Service Bureau, a problem-solving agency.[14]

Demonstrating leadership and creativity, Katherine Russell Bleecker boldly stepped forward to blaze new trails for women in developing their own businesses, managing film crews and theater staffs, and even cranking cameras and producing documentaries. The first female documentarian in the United States and also perhaps its first camerawoman, Bleecker aptly proved that women could handle anything—including managing men— and reap large rewards.

Helen Gibson in a scene from *The Hazards of Helen* serial, circa 1916. *Marc Wanamaker/Bison Archives*

Helen Gibson, First Stuntperson

In the early days of the fledgling moving picture industry, actors, male or female, mostly performed all their own stunts, no matter the danger. As movies became big business, however, prudent decision-makers recognized the importance of protecting their assets, the stars who sold the movies, and stunt work was born. During the height of the serial craze in the mid-1910s, most serial queens performed their own stunts. Helen Holmes, however, faced some extremely difficult situations in her railroad pictures, requiring someone else to perform her feats of derring-do. In 1915, Helen Gibson performed stunts on behalf of railroad serial queen Holmes, thereby becoming the first official stuntwoman.

Born Rose Wenger on August 27, 1892, in Cleveland, Ohio, to European immigrants, Gibson loved the outdoors as a kid, becoming a tomboy and trying to be the son her father desperately craved. She grew tough and fearless in confronting any challenge. Gibson fell in love with the thrill and danger of bucking broncos and speed after attending the Miller Brothers 101 Ranch Wild West Show (a live-action rodeo and presentation on the settling of the West) in Cleveland with a friend in 1909. Never having ridden a horse, she reported to their spring camp in Ponca City, Oklahoma to try out. After long sessions learning plain riding, Gibson joined the touring act. She enthusiastically participated in group equestrian cowgirl performances and developed tricks of her own.

Thanks to her daring equestrian skills, some newspapers called Gibson "one of the champion cowgirl bronco busters,"[1] riding everything from speeding horses to wild steers during the show. As part of the troupe, she was known as a "daredevil with a sense of humor,"[2] willing to try almost anything. One of her special stunts involved galloping full speed across the arena, kicking up dirt to snatch a small, white handkerchief lying on the ground, all without flying off the horse.[3] Over the next two years, she and hundreds of other cast and crew members barnstormed the country, performing in towns large and small.

At the end of 1911, rising film producer Thomas H. Ince hired the entire Miller Brothers act to shoot westerns for the New York Motion Picture Company in the canyons near his Pacific Palisades studio. Over the winter, Gibson and her colleagues shot action one-reelers for eight dollars each per week, using their own horses in western scenes. Kalem took a shine to her in 1912, hiring her at fifteen dollars a week. To augment her income, Gibson secured a second job selling concessions at the nearby Venice Pier.[4]

Gibson performed in films while also participating in rodeos, looking for that adrenaline rush of risk-taking. She costarred as Ruth Roland's sister in the 1912 Kalem short *Ranch Girls on a Rampage*, in which simple country girls visit the lively Venice Pier, disrupting ride patrons and holding up the miniature railroad before gladly returning home. When not working, she participated in local rodeos, performing a variety of fast, injury-defying stunts like standing and racing on a horse.

While training and developing new thrilling stunts and riding techniques in Oregon, Gibson met fellow rodeo and future Western film star Edmund "Hoot" Gibson, with whom she prepared to enter team events at some of the largest and most important rodeos. The two grew friendly, competing and winning events at these far-flung family entertainments, and married September 6, 1913, in Pendleton, Oregon.[5] With their rodeo winnings, the couple moved back to Los Angeles to look for movie work again.

The couple soon gained entrance to the movies, landing extra and doubling work at competing studios, Hoot at Edendale's Selig Studio and Helen at Glendale's Kalem branch. Near the end of 1914, Hoot began doubling at Kalem for actress Helen Holmes in an exciting new railroad serial/action melodrama called *The Hazards of Helen*. Built around Holmes's strong connection to railroads, the weekly two-reelers featured feminist and upright telegraph operator Holmes in daring risk-taking, stopping villains and rescuing victims, male and female, from imminent dangers.

When Holmes fell ill with pneumonia, Kalem hired the spunky Gibson as her temporary replacement for a couple of films. She successfully portrayed Holmes and performed serious stunt work in the shorts *A Test of Courage* and *A Mile a Minute* and played extra roles in two more before the company hired her to permanently replace the departing Holmes, who was leaving to start her own Signal Film Corporation with her new husband, J. P. McGowan. Gibson landed the starring role on one condition, that she change her first name from Rose to Helen. Thus Helen Gibson was born.[6] Kalem promoted her in the press as the perfect Holmes's replacement, due to "her absolute lack of fear, the absolute delight she seems to take in performing even the most hazardous of feats, together with her ability as an actress."[7]

Gibson performed a variety of death-defying stunts for Holmes, including driving a motorcycle full speed off a pier, running out of a burning building, and swinging aboard a moving train and then running across the top of the moving cars to the front. Over the next two years she increased the seriousness of stunts, including leaping from the roof of a station onto a moving train, driving a motorcycle through the open door of a traveling train, and riding a team of horses "standing woman" style to catch a rope dangling from a bridge to pull herself atop a moving train for *A Girl's Grit*.[8] Thanks to her derring-do, Gibson earned nicknames like "Girl with Nine Lives," and "Daredevil Helen." Gibson earned only $50 a week putting her life on the line for these stunts and, after two years, moved on to Universal, which paid her $125 a week to star in action-thrilling two-reelers.[9]

A series of setbacks in 1919 and 1920 put Gibson into free fall, forcing her back into a variety of dangerous jobs to earn money to survive. Universal terminated her contract in 1919, and Hoot Gibson divorced her in 1920 as his career skyrocketed. Not long after, she formed an independent production company but faced bankruptcy when money ran out before the completion of her film. She suffered appendicitis in 1921, which further curtailed her career.

A true survivor, Gibson basically started over, making personal appearances at rodeos and theaters and eventually joined Ringling Brothers-Barnum and Bailey Circus as part of their Wild West Show for three years. She brazenly performed more daredevil stunts and tricks to wow crowds until 1927, when she began regularly doubling for Hollywood stars like Marie Dressler, Marjorie Main, and Ethel Barrymore[10] as well as taking any stunt doubling, extra, or bit parts that came along in order to pay her bills, through 1954. She continued performing in rodeos and stampedes in the 1940s, even appearing with Trigger at one such show. Years of putting her body through such horrendous stress led to health concerns throughout her later life. Gibson's final film appearance came in 1961, when she appeared as an extra in the John Wayne western, *The Man Who Shot Liberty Valance*.

Trying to gain respect and recognition for the backbreaking work of stuntwomen, Gibson helped reconstitute the Riding and Stunt Girls of the Screen in 1937 after former board members resigned, serving as treasurer. She compiled a contact list for all members, which she submitted to all casting agents and studios in Hollywood, before the group disbanded.[11]

The first woman to officially perform stunts for another woman in Hollywood, Helen Gibson created many thrilling, seriously difficult action sequences in serials and westerns that amazed movie audiences then and even to this day. Even after bankruptcy and career reversals, the tough, hardscrabble Gibson remained an ardent stunt performer, risking her life to make other stars look spectacular onscreen. The Stuntmen's Hall of Fame recognized her outstanding work by inducting her posthumously into their society, celebrating Hollywood's first female stuntwoman.

Winifred Laurance, First Assistant Director

FIRST ASSISTANT DIRECTORS ARE THE SUPERGLUE OF A FILM PRODUC-tion, the liaison between director and crew in facilitating a smooth film production. They analyze scripts for necessary sets, locations, and casts, schedule shooting, coordinate between cast and crew, and attempt to keep everything running smoothly. Women have often managed one or more of these skills, but it appears that British-Russian-American Winifred Laurance actually was the first woman to actually serve in the position during the early sound period.

Laurance's life seems ripped from action-adventure novels or the movies. Born in Nagasaki, Japan, in 1903 to a English businessman father and Russian mother whose family possessed Asian shipping interests, Laurance obtained her early education in Tokyo and across the Orient. The family first fled Nagasaki to Shanghai, China, at the start of the Russo-Japanese War before immigrating to St. Petersburg, Russia, for her father's business, where she attended Russian schools and received tutoring from English teachers. With the outbreak of the Russian Revolution, the family fled, traveling Europe and Asia as Laurance attended boarding schools across Europe and absorbed multiple languages.[1] The family eventually set down roots in Paris, France.

Laurance found a work home at the First National Exchange for a few years in the mid-1920s thanks to her fluency in French, German, Russian, and English, before deciding to chase fortune in Hollywood.[2] Upon arrival in New York, the MGM Scenario Department hired her as interpreter for newly signed Russian director Victor Tourjansky and actress Nathalie Kovanko as they traveled westward to MGM in Hollywood in 1926.[3] Her time as an interpreter was cut short, however, when the studio and director failed to agree on filmmaking principles and Tourjansky's contract was terminated a few months later. Laurance's visa expired, forcing her to leave the United States for Calexico, Mexico, before walking back across the border. She became a naturalized citizen in 1937.

The young woman continued her script continuity work, working in that capacity for renowned director Ernst Lubitsch, Ludwig Berger, and others, where her cosmopolitan background and language fluency served her well.[4] Once employed, Laurance thrived, thanks to her self-confidence, organization, attention to detail, and international experience. Her foreign background benefited her throughout her career, leading to positions translating scripts, interpreting for actors and crew members, and working with diverse people from around the world. Laurance worked to bridge differences and create a spirit of cooperation with those she served.

The late 1920s and early 1930s were a fruitful time for Laurance, as film studios hired foreign language directors and actors and completed foreign language versions of their films for distribution overseas before the introduction of foreign language dubbing or subtitles. Most of these films were shot on the same sets as the English-language versions and using the same costumes but were filmed after the main production had completed their scenes for the day. Thanks to RKO, Laurance gained the distinction of working as Hollywood's first female assistant director when she was hired in that role to aid director Fred Zelnik with the German-language version of *The Case of Sergeant Grischa* in 1930.[5] While Laurance never again worked in that position, she demonstrated leadership and unflappability wherever she served.

During the 1930s, Laurance worked her way into interpreter or script translator, positions taking the foreign versions of scripts and translating them into English for work by Hollywood scriptwriters. At this point, she was going by the name Sascha Laurance. Actress Simone Simon signed her an "trouble avoider" in 1936 to assist her with English interviews.[6] Laurance translated the French novel *Equipage* into English for RKO later that year, from which Russian director Anatole Litvak had produced a French movie of the same name.[7] MGM hired Laurance in

1938 to translate the original French script of *Pepi Le Moko* into English before its adaptation into *Algiers*, starring Charles Boyer and Hedy Lamarr.[8]

At the age of forty, Laurance resigned her translating and story editor posts to serve in the WACS (Women's Army Corps) during World War II to thank a country that had accepted her as an immigrant in 1926 and later as a citizen after gaining naturalization papers in 1937.[9] Her application to join stated that she did so "because I want to be actively engaged in the service of a country which has accepted me and given me more than I can ever hope to repay."[10] Over the next two years, she strove to sign up new recruits to aid the war effort and provide service wherever needed.

After war's end, Laurance joined Twentieth Century-Fox as a continuity clerk, working on films with producer Sol M. Wurtzel before turning to Columbia Pictures for a short time. In the 1950s, she eventually focused on the new medium of television on such productions as *Requiem for a Heavyweight*. Laurance served as both translator and script supervisor on several TV productions, ensuring smooth communication and production between cast and crew. Just like in her early movie days, Laurance served as a conduit between English director Stanley Kubrick and French cinematographer Marcel Rebiere on the Omnibus television production of *Mr. Lincoln* in 1952.

While Winifred Laurance only gained one credit as assistant director in the early Hollywood studio system, she demonstrated leadership in coordinating and bringing multinational casts and crews together to ensure smooth and fluid productions wherever she worked. Like most of the women in the early studio days, Laurance made integral contributions to the filmmaking process that have been lost over time.

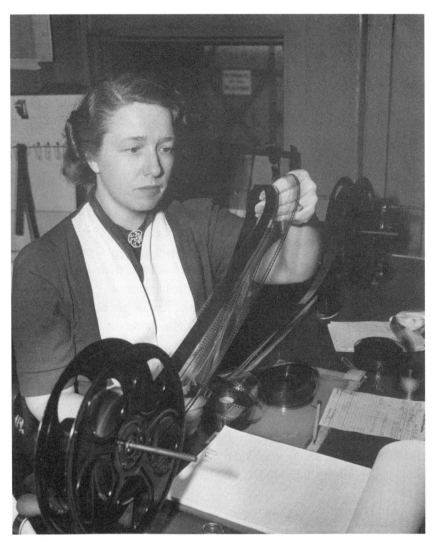

Viola Lawrence at her editing table at Columbia Pictures circa 1935. *Courtesy of Pollak Library, Cal State Fullerton*

Viola Lawrence, First Editor

In the first two decades of the moving picture industry, women dominated cutting rooms. Producers considered them more detail-oriented and precise in their work, which involved mechanically cutting negative to match sequentially shot positive film, cutting in titles, and trimming ends. By the mid-1910s, women began creatively editing films, and the field remained one of the few fields where women composed a large percentage of the entertainment workforce after Wall Street money financing established major studios in the early to mid-1920s. The first among many, Viola Mallory Lawrence became the first woman to edit a movie to tell a story creatively in 1912, and she would remain one of the top practitioners in her field throughout her career.

Born in 1894 in Brooklyn, New York, inquisitive Viola Mallory grew up in love with the fledgling moving picture industry. Childhood playmate Clara Smith introduced Mallory to her father, Albert E. Smith, cofounder of Vitagraph Pictures. At the age of eleven, she began working as a studio messenger after school. Just a year later, she stood on boxes holding cards being photographed as titles. Falling in love with cutting, she began cutting negatives to match positives. Apprenticing under Vitagraph editing chief Frank Lawrence, whom some early trade magazines considered the father of the field, she edited her first film, a three-reeler, in 1912, soon advancing to features.

Impressed with her work, Lawrence brought Mallory and two other assistants to Hollywood with him in 1917 after being named head of Universal's editing department. Poised and confident, the young woman worked with some of Universal's rising directors like Tod Browning and Erich von Stroheim, including von Stroheim's first directorial opportunity in 1919 on *Blind Husbands*. Mallory displayed calm unflappability in handling the new director on the film, with newspapers reporting that "the best titling and editing brains in the films have been turned loose"[1] on the movie. While working together, Mallory and the eleven-years-older Lawrence fell in love and married.

Within a few months, Lawrence, now Universal editor-in-chief, named Viola head of the cutting department. A 1919 story titled "Women Are Creating a New Field and Succeeding as Film Editors," noting that "woman's work in the world is jumping, leaping and gaining ground,"[2] profiled Lawrence and her editing work. Another story reiterated women's growing success in the field, stating, "Many of the larger studios have found that a woman could do this as well as a man . . . , and as a result of the shortage of man power during the recent war, scores of intelligent girls have been given a chance at this line of work."[3] *The Picture Show* featured her in a story called "Behind the Films: Woman's Part in Film-Making."[4]

Perhaps worried over possible nepotism, the young woman followed departing Universal producer-director Allen Holubar to First National in 1920 to serve as his personal editor for such films as *Man, Woman, Marriage* (1921). After his death in 1923, Columbia Pictures chief Harry Cohn hired Lawrence to serve as the fledgling studio's supervising editor before mogul Samuel Goldwyn lured her away in 1926 to serve as editor for his United Artists films. In 1929, she coedited Goldwyn's first sound film *Bulldog Drummond* with her husband Frank, one of his last editing jobs. Lawrence followed the dictum that editors provided "dramatic form, pace, and polish"[5] to movies, which the industry was quickly realizing.

Impressed with her talent, film superstar Gloria Swanson hired Lawrence to edit her second United Artists' talking picture *What a Widow!* (1930), bridging a trite, outdated story and musical numbers with sharp pacing and pruning. After that film's success, Swanson turned to her again in hopes of piecing together her wildly overbudget and unfinished silent film *Queen Kelly*, combining director von Stroheim's sophisticated but sometimes vulgar footage with sound and other new sequences from more conventional filmmakers. Whittling down mountains of film, devising scene bridges, and adding pace and polish, Lawrence shaped a releasable feature that played overseas in 1932.

Thanks to her smarts and savvy, Columbia's Harry Cohn brought Lawrence back to serve as studio editor that year, pleased with her affable and assertive qualities in dealing with difficult situations and personalities. Segueing between work on programmers and A pictures with the likes of John Ford, Frank Borzage, Dorothy Arzner, Edward G. Robinson, Joan Crawford, and Rita Hayworth, Lawrence remained cool and ruthless in the cutting room. Actress Ann Sheridan would later quip to the *Los Angeles Times* that Arzner and Lawrence "leave their femininity outside when they pick up their cutting shears."[6]

Lawrence's fast-paced editing complemented director Howard Hawks's masculine style of filmmaking in *Only Angels Have Wings* (1939), with *The Movies . . . and the People Who Make Them*'s review praising the film's "convincing, staccato dialogue and terse, taut scenes that move with speed and precision to create excitement and suspense."[7] Sharp-eyed and dependable, Lawrence would go on to edit Columbia's first color film *Cover Girl* (1944), its first 3D film *Man in the Dark* (1953), and its first Cinemascope picture *Three for the Show* (1955).

Lawrence achieved some of her best editing work during the gorgeously languid yet contentious production of Orson Welles's *The Lady from Shanghai* (1948). Dealing with a recalcitrant director who lacked a coherent story or vision, the cutter realized the film required close-ups and narration to understand character and motivation while also realizing the importance of speed at others. Close-ups were important to her; she believed that "actors do their best work in close-ups . . . the eyes to me are everything."[8] These provided emotional connection to viewers.

Lawrence's quick-cut, bold editing added pacing in the bravura hall of mirrors funhouse sequence, one of the most famous conclusions in film history. In response to a 1949 letter from critic Karol Reisz regarding the editing of the movie, Lawrence stated that "the cuts in this sequence were so short in many instances that fine grains had to be cut and a dupe negative made in order to make the double exposures possible."[9]

In 1950 Lawrence edited another of film noir's greatest films, *In a Lonely Place* (1950) starring Humphrey Bogart, an elegiac tone poem to

Hollywood and romance. Her second time working with iconoclastic director Nicholas Ray and third time cutting a Santana Productions film, she emphasized the characters' loneliness, connection, and despair in dramatic close-ups. This cutting added deep poignancy to the film.

Despite her immense gifts and contributions to cinema, Lawrence only earned two Oscar nominations for editing throughout her career and sadly has remained overlooked. The first woman to fully edit a film, Lawrence would be the only female to cut a film employing all forms of technology at the time—color, 3D, and Cinemascope—demonstrating her confidence and skill in learning and employing technology.

Nell Shipman portrait by Fred Hartsook, circa 1917. *Mary Mallory*

Nell Shipman, First Animal Trainer

ANIMALS HAVE OFTEN FIGURED AS IMPORTANT ELEMENTS IN FILMMAKing from its earliest days, either as entertainment, sensationalism, or documentary subjects. While many films captured them naturally cavorting, others sometimes employed harsh or cruel treatment to create the on-camera effect wanted. Unlike many in the entertainment industry, actress Nell Shipman revered animals, bringing a love of nature and animals to her writing and filmmaking.

While movies of the time often employed wire to trip running animals and often treated them harshly, Shipman abhorred these practices, working to provide healthy and safe living and working conditions for them. An early version of what could be called a "dog whisperer," she brought a gentle, loving touch and steadfast patience in training all types of wild animals without using force or raised voice. Thanks to these skills, Shipman became the first known woman animal trainer of the movies, rescuing, housing, and training animals for movie work.

Born as Helen Barham on October 25, 1892, in Victoria, British Columbia, to genteel British parents, Shipman demonstrated strong independence and ambition for a young woman of her time, especially after the family settled in Seattle, Washington, in 1904. The go-getter studied acting for several months before performing roles in touring stock companies that traversed the state and went up to Alaska beginning in 1907.[1] She later toured across the western United States, starring in a wide variety of roles for such leading stage producers as Oliver Morosco, Frederick Belasco, and George Baker, almost always receiving excellent reviews. The theater critic for Salem, Oregon's *Daily Capital Journal* called her "long a favorite among theatre goers of the country. Her work is complete in every detail and there is ample opportunity for her to display her emotional talents."[2]

Shipman also developed strong writing skills, updating plays and writing short stories during this time as well, always taking the initiative to better herself. After arriving in Southern California with husband Ernest Shipman in 1910, she wrote magazine articles and later scripts, which won two prizes in a 1912 photoplay contest, springboarding her career as a movie screenwriter.[3] Studios like Vitagraph and Kalem purchased her scripts and stories as she advertised herself as a "photoplay-wright" in trade ads.[4]

Shipman yearned for greater challenges and responsibility regarding her screen stories, and she found them. She landed a contract with Vitagraph Pictures, which set her on the road to becoming an action-adventure star performing her own stunts in scenic but dangerous locations. Director Rollin Sturgeon cast Shipman in the lead of the 1915 film *God's Country and the Woman*, which shot in Big Bear.[5]

A story of honor and survival, it began Shipman's long career starring as a feisty, independent young woman in her adaptations of action-filled, melodramatic Curwood stories set in the rugged wilds of Alaska. Shipman demonstrated her athleticism, skiing in snowshoes and traveling in sleds pulled by dog teams. *Moving Picture World* called her "as good an actress as she is a writer, which is saying much . . . her playing is marked by intelligence and sincerity."[6] Over the next several years, Shipman skipped from studio to studio, writing and starring in suspenseful, action-packed stories, often where she played a "shero," as *Wid's Review* called her part in the 1916 *Fires of Conscience*.[7]

Shipman loved animals of all types and possessed a natural rapport with them. Her concern for their treatment during filming grew out of watching, during the making of a Curwood movie, a wild bobcat first shocked by electricity to get it angry and then "doped" to calm it down, which killed the animal.[8] Gentle and calm herself, she resolved to connect and gain their trust through nonviolent and natural means. That allowed Shipman to train them herself to perform stunts and tricks required for filmmaking.

For the 1918 film *Baroo, Son of Kazan*, Shipman herself stepped forward to ensure that the five malamute dogs performed properly through gentle love and training. As newspapers reported, "These dogs worship Miss Shipman, and have done work for the screen that will create a standard for animals of the motion pictures that cannot be surpassed. Most of this work has been done under the direction of Miss Shipman, who for weeks has prepared the dogs for their work, and trained them until her slightest word is their law."[9] Her touch and look calmed animals, even those she rescued from inhumane conditions.

Cinematographer Joseph Walker recognized Shipman's special connection with dogs during the making of the 1919 film *Back to God's Country*, in which he served as assistant cameraman. During the filming of a major action scene with a vicious dog that became ferocious once unmuzzled, Shipman calmed both the canine and the staff threatening to beat it. Shipman yelled, "Keep the camera going, boys! Do you hear? No matter what happens, don't cut!" She rushed into the scene protesting the men's treatment of the dog, threw her arms around the enraged animal, everyone horrified and quiet. She began murmuring soothing and comforting words. The dog looked her in the eye, lowered his head and relaxed, allowing her to pet him. Nell told the men and everyone, "I had the feeling he wouldn't hurt me, that he'd understand. I—can't explain it."[10]

Looking for greater control of her work in films, Shipman organized her own independent production company Nell Shipman Productions, originally with her husband Ernest and later with Bert Van Tuyle,[11] in which she wrote, acted, directed, and produced. Starting with *The Girl from God's Country* in 1920, these "outdoor pictures" focused on feminist "sheroes," wild animals, and locations outside of Los Angeles, featuring the residents from her zoo, more than two hundred in all.[12] Shipman even took an assertive tone in the press against practices that hurt independent filmmakers. She bought full-page ads in trade journals like *Camera!* when exhibitors without her knowledge cut the film from eight to seven reels, leading to what she called "a stupid, meaningless affair that is a disgrace to its author, director, star, exchange and exhibitor . . . an earless, tailless, footless, lopsided freak."[13]

Though none acquired the big success of *Back to God's Country*, Shipman produced several films in the wild, shipping her animals north to a camp at Priest Lake, Idaho, to facilitate shooting. Facing financial problems, the filmmaker turned to one- and two-reelers focusing more on her animal menagerie, but she continued losing money and retired from the screen. Always a go-getter and industrious, Shipman returned to her writing after remarrying and giving birth to twins.

Shipman wrote action-filled plays, novels, and stories about assertive, strong-willed women and wild animals for a variety of national outlets, but she always looked for a way back into the motion picture industry. Paramount purchased her original script *The Eye of the Eagle* as a vehicle for Cary Grant, which the studio released in 1935 under the title *Wings in the Dark*, a story about competing aviators who fall in love through cross-country, action-fueled trips, but they failed to credit her onscreen. Shipman continued her writing and attempted to sell movie ideas to a variety of investors, eventually getting one small film made.

One of the first people in the entertainment industry to advocate for the safety and well-being of animals, Nell Shipman treated them humanely during filming as well as offscreen, an individual forerunner of the American Society for the Prevention of Cruelty to Animals. Shipman's reverence for animals through loving and gentle treatment demonstrated that they could be trained to perform stunts without incurring injury or harm, an upstanding example for generations to come.

DESIGN

Julia Heron, First Set Decorator

Producer David O. Selznick created the term "production designer" for the outstanding work accomplished by William Cameron Menzies in crafting the look and visual language that brought *Gone with the Wind* evocatively to life in 1939. The designer's drawings provided a blueprint in building sets, but it took an art director or set dresser to add the details that brought his design to fruition. Thanks to her flair and skill for filling out these details, Julia Heron worked in conjunction with some of the most renowned directors and production designers to become the first woman set decorator and dresser in the history of the movies.

Born in Montana in 1892, Heron and her family endured hardship after the death of her father. The Heron women, mother Lillian and daughters, moved westward to Los Angeles in 1910. All three took clerical jobs, with eighteen-year-old Heron working as a laundry book-keeper.[1] By 1917 Heron listed herself as "photoplayer" in the city directory. After struggling to find roles, she became a clerk in 1920, perhaps aided by her grandmother Nannie, who worked as a film cutter.

In 1921 Famous Players-Lasky hired Heron as the assistant to Earl Hodge, the lead studio art director and set dresser, and Heron learned quickly. Her strong attention to detail and calm self-confidence impressed the studio, who elevated her to a full-time set-dressing position in 1922 on the film *The Old Homestead*.[2] As a lead set dresser, she directed her crew of assistants in fulfilling the art requirements needed to bring interior sets truly alive, finding the right furniture, accessories, and decoration to accentuate the period or feeling of the movie. During her time at the Lasky Studio, Heron worked with top directors like James Cruze and Cecil B. DeMille, adding period detail and flair.

When DeMille set up his own independent studio at the RKO Pathé lot in 1926, he employed Heron as one of the studio's technical directors. She served as set dresser on *King of Kings*, his epic story on the life of Christ and perhaps was uncredited on other films during her short employment.[3]

Looking for the chance to work with renowned designer William Cameron Menzies, Heron joined United Artists in 1930 as head of the set-dressing department. In 1931 she served as Menzies's set dresser on the Douglas Fairbanks's talker, *Reaching for the Moon*, and would later work with him on two more pictures.[4]

The studio promoted Heron as an excellent "Jill-of-all-trades" with a stand-alone story in the pressbook for the Mary Pickford sound film *Secrets* in 1933 that exhibitors could employ in promoting the film. They praised her work: "Miss Heron is an authority on furniture of all countries and periods; objects d'art; appointments of every kind of home from humble to mansion; antiques; tapestries, rugs and other things that come under the category of set dressing."[5]

Twentieth Century Pictures also recognized Heron's talents for "perfection to the last detail"[6] with a story in its pressbook for the 1934 film *The Mighty Barnum*, praising her as the only woman working in this position at a major studio. Heron revealed the importance of research for getting details right in art direction, especially in eras where little information existed regarding furniture or interiors of the period. Sometimes that meant building furniture, sewing pillows or curtains, or even creating fake books. Heron remained on set during filming, ready to replace a prop or to fulfill an emergency request for additional decoration. As Heron later told a magazine, "The primary objective of any set decorator is to get anything required as reasonably as possible."[7] In fact, Heron would be one of the first people to recognize the cost savings by arranging tie-ins or product placements with companies in order to reduce actual production expenditures.

Returning back to the United Artists lot to work for both it and the Samuel Goldwyn Company in 1935, Heron found herself important enough for the studio to list her as Property Master in their studio listing for the *Film Daily Year Book of Motion Pictures*. Her work lit up the screen for such films as *The Hurricane*, *Wuthering Heights*, *Our Town*, *The Westerner*, and *Ball of Fire*, earning her praise. Writer Howard Barnes acknowledged her outstanding work, creating a believable urban slum and dead-end street for the powerful film *Dead End*, commenting, "It is because this set was so vivid that 'Dead End' has so much power. . . . It is a masterly job, distinguished for remarkable understatement when the temptation must have been great to pile on the squalor and misery of the district."[8]

After twelve years working at United Artists and the Goldwyn Studios, Heron joined the Alexander Korda company when he began producing in Hollywood in 1940 due to World War II restrictions in England. Working in collaboration with Korda's brother, production designer Vincent, and art director Lyle Wheeler, she "served as interior decorator on both *That Lady Hamilton* and the color film *The Jungle Book*, both of which earned Academy Award nominations for Art Direction–Interior Decoration.

When Korda returned to Europe, Heron joined Warner Bros. for a short time, working on such films as *Watch on the Rhine* and *Edge of Darkness*, and later at RKO, dressing *Casanova Brown* and *The Woman in the Window* before rejoining United Artists. While she decorated a few United Artists films like *The Diary of a Chambermaid*, Heron mostly dressed such Goldwyn classics as *The Best Years of Our Lives* and *The Bishop's Wife* in the 1940s.

Heron gave back to the industry for all it had given her during this time, serving multiple terms on the board of trustees for the Motion Picture Relief Fund, Inc. She contributed to the decorating of the Motion Picture Country Home for retired senior and disabled actors, donating her services in furniture design and books for the library, along with other industry leaders.[9]

Thanks to her respected film career, furniture companies as well as home decorating magazines and newspapers included Heron in stories regarding home and interior design during the 1940s. Pacific-Coast Buyers invited William Cameron Menzies, Travis Banton, Ray See, and Heron in 1941 to design furniture and accessories for display to furniture buyers in Los Angeles and Chicago during National Furniture

Marketing Week. The four professionals designed three rooms featuring "richly colored Chinese modern ensembles and three rooms of modernized traditional mahogany ensembles."[10]

In 1946, *American Home* magazine interviewed her about helpful home decorating pointers, since many found inspiration in movie sets for decorating their own homes. The magazine noted how her use of lamps to decorate the *Raffles* set led to their replacing chandeliers in popularity. They also reported Heron was the first to hang pictures in double pairs, to use lithographed wood in place of veneer, and to utilize cellophane accessories.[11]

During the 1950s, Universal International Studios employed Heron as a set dresser, assigning her to everything from Academy Award–winners to genre pictures. While there, she worked for such major directors as Anthony Mann, Henry Koster, and especially Douglas Sirk on all his romantic melodramas, adding rich detail to the magnificent sets. Heron received her only Oscar as part of the team nominated for Best Art Direction–Set Direction for a Color Film, for the Stanley Kubrick Roman slave drama *Spartacus*.

While Heron had occasionally dressed a few television episodes in the 1950s, she mostly focused on the medium during the 1960s, continuing her long string of professional work with major producers and directors. Most of her credits during this time came on such classic programs as *Alfred Hitchcock Presents*, *Leave It to Beaver*, *The Jack Benny Show*, and *The Alfred Hitchcock Hour*.

Julia Heron left a mark in a field dominated by men during most of her career, earning respect and admiration for her important contributions to screen classics. Her determination and longevity helped pave the way for more women to make their mark as Hollywood set dressers and decorators.

Elsa Lopez, First Art Director

LIKE MANY WOMEN WORKING IN THE EARLY SILENT-FILM INDUSTRY, whether in creative behind-the-scenes jobs or those more administrative, the intelligent, Paraguayan-born Elsa Lopez and others played an integral part in growing and shaping the medium. Lopez offered important creative contributions by designing sets for feature films as an art director at a time when few people of color or even women served in this capacity. Thanks to her pioneering work in this area, Lopez became one of the most important early Hispanic women in Hollywood.

Born in 1887, Elsa Solano Lopez followed traditional female paths before deciding to chase ambitions when moving to Hollywood. She arrived in Portland, Oregon, by 1910, marrying local clerk Justin Patrick O'Connor on October 29 later that year. Lopez gave birth to their son Patrick Justin O'Connor in 1912 and was happy to raise her son and maintain the household.

Perhaps hoping to make it in the growing field of the movies, the young family moved south to Los Angeles, California, by 1914. O'Connor served as a mercantile reporter while Lopez remained a traditional housewife and mother. She later served as an interpreter and newspaper reporter not long after the move.

Turning chances into opportunities, Lopez turned a 1916 meeting with D. W. Griffith into a job as Triangle Film Corporation's research director and title writer. Trade magazines praised her attention to detail as well as her connection to a foreign leader. Stories reported that she was born in Paraguay as the granddaughter of Francisco Solano Lopez, former president of the South American country, and that she was educated in Europe, spoke multiple languages, and was an international traveler.[1] Perhaps she remained quiet on her marriage, as stories made no mention of her husband, now Lasky executive Frank Woods's assistant.

Motion Picture News reported, "Miss Lopez holds down a job in which you would expect to find a scholarly old gentleman, who had spent his life delving in the musty recesses of libraries, but she is eminently qualified for her tasks and says she gets as much pleasure out of it as if she were posing before the camera or basking in the spotlight of fame. . . . She digs out historical incidents, customs of the time, or any and all embellishments that may serve further to adorn the characters with an air of realism and assembles them in such form that they will be readily available for costumer, carpenter and director."[2]

Her in-depth research provided atmosphere and details for lush sets, elaborate costumes, embellishments, and the life and culture of the story's people. This sometimes became difficult, especially when searching for information on, for example, eighth-century China, as mentioned in the *Saturday Evening Post* story, "The Alley of Flashing Spears."[3] For the filming of the Alma Rubens film *The Passion Flower*, Lopez examined Venice, Italy, and its sensuous carnival.[4] She conducted research for Thomas Ince in 1918, sometimes even visiting locations with cast and crew in order to provide information.[5]

Impressed with her work, Norma Talmadge convinced her husband Joseph Schenck to hire Lopez to serve as the Talmadge Studio research director in New York in 1919, with stories claiming they were impressed with her accuracy, attention to detail, and international background.[6] One newspaper called her a "Censor of Details," digging for information on everything from hair design and hairpins to furniture styles.[7] Lopez herself confidently promoted her background and her rightness for the job, stating, "I knew I could do it. . . . It is pioneering, but all women have something in them which longs to blaze new trials [*sic*].[8] Norma and her sister Constance supported women in their career ambitions, hiring and promoting many at their company. Their actions opened more possibilities and positions to women.

For Talmadge's *The New Moon*, Lopez examined the history and leaders of the Russian Revolution to analyze its causes, besides detailing the daily lives of the country's struggling people and its lavish elite.[9] Since

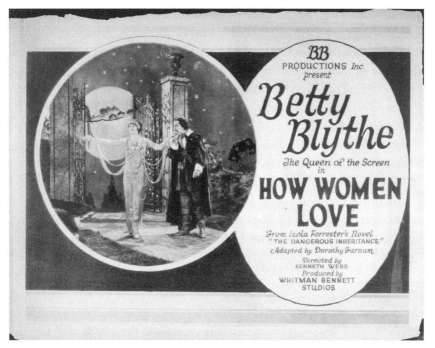

Lobby card for *How Women Love* (Whitman-Bennett Studios, 1922), art direction by Elsa Lopez. *Dwight Cleveland*

most of Talmadge pictures were period dramas, Lopez spent much time in libraries and books looking for period-specific details.

Within a year, however, the ambitious Lopez appears to have abandoned Norma Talmadge Pictures to provide more than just historical accuracy for films, looking to gain more industry clout and prestige as an art designer. In doing so, it appears she worked as the industry's first female art director. Late in 1922 producer Whitman Bennett announced that he had signed actress Betty Blythe for a series of society dramas for state release, with Lopez to provide "elaborate scenic dressings."

Over the next year, the talented woman designed sets as art director for such films as *Secrets of Paris*, *How Women Love*, *Fair Lady*, *His Wife's Husband*, *Idol of the Rich*, and *Modern Marriage*. *Secrets of Paris* required her to design the backstreets of Paris, from darkened paths, underground tunnels, and seedy cafés.[10] The studio went all out promoting itself, buying a full-page ad in *Motion Picture News* for the film *How Women Love*, listing factoids for each area of production. Under sets, they listed Lopez's previous work, and stated that for this film, "the sets will be as elaborate as any ever constructed by the Whitman Bennett Studios for First National or United."[11] Proud of the sets for *Fair Lady*, a full-page ad for the film reported, "A truly expensive picture THAT SHOWS THE MONEY unmistakably ON THE SCREEN where audiences can't fail to see it."[12] Even when Bennett reorganized his studio in 1923, Lopez remained as art director.

Perhaps by 1925, however, as studios turned into major factories and international conglomerates, Bennett could no longer afford to stay in business. It appears that Lopez took to the vaudeville stage at this point, signing with the Hackett and Delmar act through the Murray Phillips agency.[13]

Lopez mysteriously disappeared from newspapers and entertainment trades after 1925, and few details exist beyond that point. While her career as an art director lasted for only a few short years, Lopez designed sets for two of the most important female stars of the 1920s and demonstrated that women could both create striking sets for films while also managing staff and budgets.

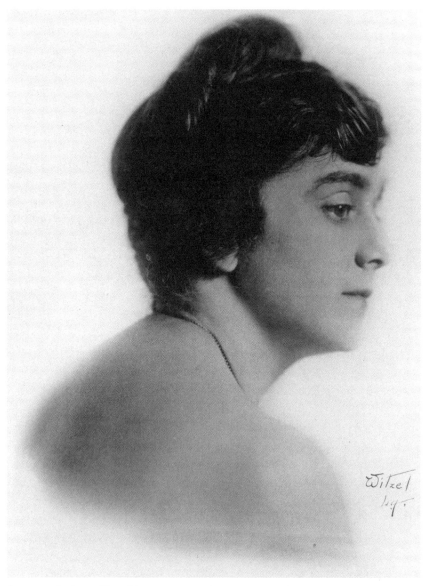

Costume designer Clare West portrait by Albert Witzel, 1916. *Mary Mallory*

Clare West, First Costume Designer

DURING THE EARLY DAYS OF THE MOTION PICTURE INDUSTRY, COMPA-nies created wardrobes as any legitimate theatrical company did. Actors often provided their own contemporary wardrobes; companies fashioned their own or rented/leased more elaborate designs from costume rental houses or theatrical companies. Some trades even claimed that "'any old thing' would do for gowning."[1] As the industry grew in stature, it looked to provide a rich consistency to costumes through the eyes of one per-son, one who could draft eye-catching, one-of-a-kind looks to dazzle audiences. In the mid-1910s, modiste Clare West appeared out of the shadows to become Hollywood's first credited costume designer, going on to establish Hollywood as a trendsetter in fashion.

Born January 30, 1879, in Missouri as the granddaughter of former governor Smith of Ohio,[2] West always loved clothes, first creating special outfits for her dolls. Her upscale family looked down on working women but after enough of her complaining, they acquiesced to her studying stenography. After graduating, she received an appointment to serve as a court reporter in a western state. "But I wanted to make clothes; I simply couldn't keep my hands off fabrics, and when I refashioned all my own things I'd fall to work on my friends. Sometimes they'd be rather startled when they'd come home and find me slashing into some new frock they had just bought, but in the end they would always admit that my remod-eling had improved it. And finally I decided to be a designer—it was the one thing I wanted to do."[3]

West slowly built a fashion career. She opened a millinery/dress-making shop in the Quad Cities area of Illinois in 1899.[4] Historian Allie Acker claims she attended college. Multiple trades report that she studied fashion design in Paris before opening the Maison Claire couture shop on Fifth Avenue in New York City.[5] As couturier to the ruling class, West's job was to create lush, out-of-this-world gowns elevating her clients to fashion queen status.

West herself burst onto the film-costuming scene with D. W. Griffith's historical epic *Intolerance*, requiring the costuming of hundreds in period dress over millennia. She revealed in an interview she spent two years doing "all the research work," working to get the details right. She took a break before designing the costumes for Theda Bara in the over-the-top *Cleopatra*.[6]

West's work delighted executives, who appointed her the first woman to lead a studio fashion department as head of Triangle's costume department.[7] During this period, West would draw costumes for director Allan Dwan for Douglas Fairbanks's films as well as Griffith motion pictures, moving between elaborate, scene-stealing works and more conservative, contemporary ones.

Impressed with her lush, extravagant design, Famous Players-Lasky Studios hired her in 1918 to create sensual, barely there clothing as lead costume designer for superstar director Cecil B. DeMille for his big-budget spectacles. The designer read scripts, consulted with the director on what he wanted, and talked with stars who would wear the exotic clothes. She first draped fabrics on a mannequin before creating watercolor sketches for DeMille's approval. *Picture Play* magazine called her "a painter in fabrics" for how she deftly illustrated the characters' status and moods with just a drape of cloth.[8]

While not always credited for her work, West's dazzling and often outlandish costumes of chiffons, silks, and velvets often drew high praise from critics as well as female moviegoers. West created spectacular new gowns with long, sweeping lines, body-hugging wrapping, and sparkling sequins and beading for such studio superstars as Gloria Swanson, Bebe Daniels, Mae Murray, and Agnes Ayres, while extras and bits wore stock costumes or altered pieces. Many compared her work to Paris couturier Paul Poiret. Her designs for *Forbidden Fruit* were declared the "most elaborate on the screen," soon topped in praise for her *The Affairs of Anatol* costumes.[9]

It took a village to produce all the lavish costumes for DeMille and other top directors. West told trades her workshop included sixty-eight employees—seamstresses, tailors, finishers, cutters, and flower makers—with Fern Frost managing finishing and Mildred Morris managing stock.[10] Two women headed Lasky's costume department; West as DeMille's lead designer and Ethel Chaffin heading the general costume department in "exaggerated modiste shops. A great deal of material of the first quality is always on hand, in the raw and made up."[11]

The Women Film Pioneer Project's biography states that director DeMille praised "her lavish hand," "as demonstrated by outfits such as the patent leather swimsuit that reflected nocturnal watery light in *Saturday Night* (1922), or the octopus dress and cape designed for Bebe Daniels in *The Affairs of Anatol* (1921)."[12] The Octopus Dress grabbed plenty of publicity for its tongue-in-cheek lusciousness.

West's job was to anticipate or even premiere fashion a year before Paris modistes during the almost yearlong process of producing and distributing a film, drawing admiring gasps from adoring female audiences. Within a few years, Hollywood costumes influenced New York and Paris designers, setting trends and pushing boundaries, with couturiers now copying film designs.

As West told reporters,

Sex psychology plays a tremendous part in fashion creating, because women dress to impress men first, other women second, and themselves third. In each instance, intense femininity is the keynote. For it is only by making fashions tremendously feminine that one can appeal to both men and women.

What the world today may be wearing does not influence the designer of screen fashions. Instinct and good taste much combine to say what will find favor a year from now. There are no other rules by which one can work. I believe the potential power of the motion picture upon feminine fashions is limitless.[13]

West drew costumes to fit her characters, not her stars' whims, per DeMille's edicts, influencing other women to follow their own style. As she revealed in a wire interview December 3, 1922, "'This dressing for the personality is perhaps the most important thing the screen has given the American women, a gift that is placing the motion picture at the head of a really American style influence as distinct from the French who have long held sway."[14]

By 1923, West reigned supreme as Hollywood costume designer. She appeared as herself in the lost film *Hollywood*, a behind-the-scenes story of a young girl attempting to break into the movies. She also traveled to Paris to find inspiration for the costumes in the second half—the modern sequence—of DeMille's *The Ten Commandments*.

That September, producer Joseph Schenck lured West to his new production company to design elaborate outfits for sisters Norma and Constance Talmadge and their First National productions.[15] She designed inspired hand-painted gowns and handkerchiefs for Norma's film *The Lady*, including an asymmetrical one-sleeve dress, daring for its time. West also created a diverse range of costumes for the Norma Talmadge film *Secrets*, from those depicting an energetic, stylish young woman to those depicting an older but wiser female. Schenck directed her to design a few pieces for the 1924 Buster Keaton film *Sherlock Jr.* and his film *The Navigator* as well.

Some reports indicate that West created thirty-four costumes for star Mae Murray for Erich von Stroheim's Metro-Goldwyn-Mayer film *The Merry Widow* in 1925. Other sources list her contributing runway outfits for a fashion show sequence in Paramount's film *The Dressmaker from Paris*, which also featured work from designers Howard Greer, Adrian, and Lucille.

West allowed Hamburger's Department Store in downtown Los Angeles to display three of her designs and their matching outfits from Barbara La Marr films in 1924, drawing crowds.[16] She also appeared in person at a 1925 fashion show employing some of her costumes at Buffum's Department Store. Soon thereafter, West resigned her position with Schenck, claiming she would open a downtown modiste shop.[17] While West appears to have designed for individuals after this point, her Hollywood career virtually disappeared, with newspapers rarely stating her name.

Clare West designed spectacular outfits and frocks that transformed wardrobe from simple everyday outfits into deep fashion statements, turning costume designers into trendsetters. It was thanks to her that costume design became an important element in telling motion pictures stories.

before, and for the same money, why shouldn't she be able to manage properties and build sets both economically and with artistic results?

"But I must have the same salary as I get for acting," answered Mrs. Whistler briskly.

Mr. Smith accepted the terms, but at the end of the first week, instead of receiving the same salary as she had been getting, she found she was receiving more. And that's all there is to the story, except that "Props" Whistler went shopping at once for a dozen pairs of overalls, and has been on the job ever since. When she's not overseeing properties she's out gardening on the lot or taking the place of an absent

"I'll earn a license," said Nellie Bly Baker —and she did.

Mrs. Margaret Whistler resigned her leading lady-ship to become head "property woman."

"hand" and hauling properties in herself. What's more, she seems to like it.

And there are the women who are now operating projection machines in the downtown theaters of some of the large cities on the coast—quite a respectably big number of them. A projection school has been started by the leading theater owners, and women are studying to become operators, passing examinations and receiving their licenses. After that the jobs come easy.

Yet it was only a few months ago that women operators were unheard of. Miss Nellie Bly Baker was the

Property master Margaret Whistler cutting wood and Nellie Bly Baker at the projector in the article "The Women Lend a Hand," *Picture Play* magazine, March 1919.

Margaret Whistler, First Property Master

The silent-film industry ran on women; they made huge contributions, often in more than one field. While she joined the film industry as an actress, Whistler possessed multiple gifts that could transfer to other jobs and responsibilities, including working with wild animals. When men went off to World War I, many positions required filling to keep movies flowing. Demonstrating her flexibility and leadership skills, Whistler stepped in to become the first female property master, building sets and props and managing staff.

Born Louise Margaret Pepper on July 31, 1888, in Louisville, Kentucky, Whistler grew up in Washington, DC, and attended the Notre Dame Academy there. Records don't show whether she married and gained the last name Whistler, but by the time she gained fame in the moving picture industry during the midteens, she called herself Margaret Whistler. The actress also claimed in a yearbook entry to have played on the stage, in vaudeville, in the circus across the United States and England, and with Bostock's Trained Animals at Coney Island, though these credits have not been verified. Whistler supposedly entered the movie business in 1911 with the Pennsylvania-based Lubin Film Company before joining Universal in 1912.[1] Universal featured her in films beginning in 1915, where she mostly played character parts, heavies, and second leads in films with stars like Cleo Madison, Lee Moran, and future great Lon Chaney.

Trade biographies also describe her talent for wardrobe and costume design. Her film costume design career began as early as 1915, as trade papers report she created frilly and feminine costumes for actress and director Cleo Madison's Universal films. Her writeup in the *Players'*

Directory promoted her talent for costume designing: "Besides being a talented actress, Miss Whistler is an authority on dress and very successful as a designer."[2]

Whistler's talents seemed to impress those she worked with, as trades mention that she designed offscreen wardrobes for some stars, and in 1916 she gained publicity for a hat she created.[3] She continued promoting her design talents in interviews or ads, as her parts grew smaller in size and she aged.

After the start of World War I when the studios saw younger men go off to service, women stepped in to fill certain positions. Whistler herself transitioned into working as both head of the costume and property departments at Vitagraph and serving as a "property woman," building and putting up sets, and is featured in *Picture Play* magazine cutting wood.[4] The talented woman deployed her creative skills and sharp eye in helping design, build, and put together sets and props. The magazine called her "the first property woman on the coast . . . , getting the position when the studio's property man was called up and no other property man could be found."[5] Whistler discovered she enjoyed the job, conceiving and building props, managing budgets, and supervising staff. For the first time, she was in charge and possessed a small amount of power.

Whistler also volunteered her time in the American Red Cross in Los Angeles, though in later biographies she would claim to have served as an ambulance driver overseas during the war. Later in 1918, Whistler headed both the wardrobe and property department at Vitagraph in East Hollywood before she was laid off when soldiers returned home after World War I.

Fox Film Corporation hired Whistler as head of its costume department in 1920, at a time when they were expanding into more historical spectacles. Whistler gained perhaps her greatest opportunity and highest achievement, "designing" costumes for Fox's over-the-top spectacle, *The Queen of Sheba*, starring Betty Blythe. Many of these can actually barely be called costumes, as photographs show some to be merely sheer lace, beads, and string, with many almost topless. One trade called her job designing costumes "some of which appear more rare than practical."[6] Newspaper stories credited her with designing twenty-six costume changes for Blythe, "dazzlingly beautiful, with headdress and hairdressing all its own." One of Blythe's gowns alone cost over $6,000 to complete because it consisted of 3,500 strings of white beads fastened to a girdle, which featured a peacock twenty-four inches high and twenty-nine inches tall with nine colors of beads. One woman spent sixty-eight working days to complete the gown.[7]

Whistler later designed costumes for a six-reel comedy, *Skirts* (1921), creating appropriate wardrobe for one thousand chorus girls, including little people. With seven changes of costumes required for the chorus, needleworkers labored in three eight-hour shifts to produce all the costumes.[8]

Designing wardrobe for such a massive spectacle would seem to cement a career, but instead it began a downward spiral for Whistler. Instead of staying at a major studio creating fantastic outfits for lavish dramas, the modiste found herself let go. When the original Fine Arts Studios was converted into a rental lot in 1922, Whistler was named head of the costume department, supervising the rental of costumes to outside producers.[9] While having little opportunity to create original costumes for productions, she was at least able to pull together outfits for pictures and offer creative output, coordinating outfits.

Just three months later, Whistler had moved on, heading the downtown-based Cinema Mercantile Company's costume department. Mostly renting out wardrobe once again, she did receive the opportunity to create comedy and gag costumes but little opportunity to fully employ her creative designing skills.[10]

In 1933 Whistler left or was forced out at the Cinema Mercantile Company, joining Columbia Pictures, where she worked in the mechanical department.[11] Over time, she was able to transfer back to costume work, her true joy, joining Columbia's wardrobe department as a designer in 1937. While she was no longer in charge of the department and perhaps not even a designer, she was once again employing her skills for fashion.

While she only served as a property master for a short time, Whistler revealed leadership and competence in the role, demonstrating that women could successfully manage staff and complete construction projects. She achieved perhaps her greatest accomplishment in designing some of the most exotic and revealing costumes in film history for *The Queen of Sheba*. Whistler revealed leadership and creativity in her diverse Hollywood roles, showing women's expertise in juggling multiple roles.

MAKEUP/HAIR

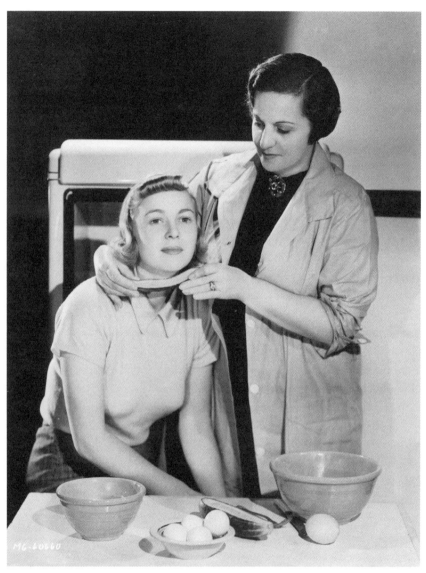

MGM Women's Makeup Head Lillian Rosine applies makeup to Cecilia Parker, circa 1932. *Mary Mallory*

Lillian Rosine, First Makeup Artist

FROM CINEMA'S VERY BEGINNINGS, MAKEUP HAS BEEN AN INTEGRAL component in creating characters and achieving beauty. Stars originally applied their own, employing many of the techniques they acquired from theatrical work. Mascara and liner highlighted eyes, the most important aspect of silent-film acting. Greasepaint and dark lipstick also enhanced a realistic look on camera during the early use of orthochromatic film, which possessed little color sensitivity. By the mid-1920s, makeup experts improved natural appearances onscreen with the introduction of color-sensitive panchromatic film, while also ensuring continuity throughout production. Hired as head of MGM's women's makeup department at the studio's creation, Lillian Rosine thus achieved fame as Hollywood's first female makeup designer.

Called the "Make-Up Doctor" or the "girl who 'makes' faces" in the press,[1] Rosine became a makeup specialist after a career singing and acting in films. Born in New Haven, Connecticut, in 1897 as Lillian Rosini, and later raised in Los Angeles, Rosine sang locally as a lyric soprano for the Los Angeles Chamber of Commerce, in vaudeville shows before movie presentations, and for community groups and relief organizations as a teen. She later taught music lessons while trying to make it in entertainment, employing both spellings of her last name.

Looking for something more steady, Rosine abandoned music for the movies. During the late 1910s and early 1920s, she appeared in a variety of roles for various studios, as Rosini never achieving stardom. While working on the 1917 Universal film *Hell Morgan's Girl*, the young woman grew impressed with actor Lon Chaney and his impressive use of makeup. He gave her her first makeup after advising her to enter the field.[2] Though it took several years, she gradually devoted her life to making others beautiful.

Rosine claimed to have found her entrance into the movies when she discovered a special preparation to apply silver and gold makeup to the body and have it last indefinitely.[3] She also developed her own special techniques for creating wrinkles and other aging features for the screen, all to enhance character.

Named the head of the women's makeup department at the studio's formation in 1924, Rosine beautified the stars and applied makeup under the lights in her studio on the second floor of the building housing the stars' dressing rooms. Her beauty office occupied an oblong room filled with natural light from windows lining one side under which a long table filled with mirrors of all shapes and sizes and makeup paraphernalia resided.[4] Besides applying makeup to play up highlights and accentuate each star's own personality, she often rushed to sets to apply castor oil through a dropper as a remedy for "Klieg eyes," caused by the overpowering lights required for shooting movies.[5] In effect, she doctored women in many ways.

In 1930 Rosine finally gained acknowledgment for her stature and skills. *Screenland Magazine* reported that "she created the first studio make-up department and has become one of the screen's leading authorities on the photographic values of powders and paints."[6] Rosine did more than just apply beauty treatments; she determined the best colors of makeup that would record as natural colors when panchromatic film was employed. She described creating vampire or seductive makeup for black-and-white film by using purple makeup by mixing blue and red greasepaint, which photographed a lovely pale on film.[7] She considered one of her most difficult jobs as creating makeup for Ruth Chatterton in *Madame X*, since the actress played the character at four different stages in her life, requiring Rosine to consider the habits, mannerisms, and moral character at each stage.[8]

Rosine beautified many MGM stars as "an artist whose canvas is the human body," including Myrna Loy, Rosalind Russell, Norma Shearer, Greta Garbo, Joan Crawford, Marion Davies, and Anita Page.[9] Tired of always buying hose, Page sometimes even called on Rosine to create makeup versions of them for certain events. She also palled around with some of the stars off camera. Rosine was one of the few people Viennese actress Lillian Rainer trusted, to whom she relayed confidences in her native German.[10]

When not working, Rosine often shared makeup tips with others, be it through features in magazines and newspapers or by attending women's clubs meetings. She advocated a very light use of cosmetics just to enhance natural beauty and denounced the use of panchromatic makeup or overapplication of any type. For Rosine, looking fresh and natural should be any woman's aim. She promoted a light use of makeup even on radio appearances on Los Angeles's KNX station in the late 1930s.[11]

MGM differentiated between men's and women's makeup at the studio through 1936. They acknowledged Rosine's importance by listing her in motion picture yearbooks as the "Women's Makeup Department Head" through 1936.[12] During that time, two men served as "Men's Makeup Department Head," Cecil Holland and later Jack Dawn. In 1937 the studio combined both departments into one, demoting Rosine and advancing Dawn to Head of Makeup. Though no longer department head, she continued providing professional makeup services to all MGM personnel.

By the 1940s, MGM occasionally lent Rosine out to other studios when certain stars requested it. She worked at United Artists in 1943 on the New York shoot for *Johnny Come Lately* with Jimmy Cagney. She continued her makeup trade at glamorous MGM until retiring in 1948 to spend time with her banker husband. Rosine spent the end of her days at the Motion Picture Country Home.[13]

Totally forgotten today, Lillian Rosine brought beauty to MGM stars as the head of its female makeup department by simply enhancing their regular features and downplaying their troublesome spots. Her simple lessons on applying makeup naturally assisted all women in looking their best.

Hattie Wilson Tabourne, First Hairdresser

EARLY MAKEUP PIONEERS LIKE THE WESTMORE FAMILY, MAX FACTOR, and Universal horror master Jack Pierce became famous for their prolific skills designing period-appropriate or character-driven makeup. Directors like Cecil B. DeMille, who brought lavish spectacle to the screen, required special makeup and coiffures to accentuate the eye-catching designs and render their female stars iconic and glamorous. Perhaps discovered by actress Julia Faye at an upscale downtown Los Angeles beauty salon, Hattie Wilson Tabourne was hired by Famous Players-Lasky in 1917 to design elaborate hairdos for such stars as Gloria Swanson, Bebe Daniels, and Rudolph Valentino, gaining fame in trade magazines and the press and a long-term contract from the studio, something unusual for screen hairdressers of the time. Not only did Tabourne serve as the first female hairdresser credited in film but she also became the first African American to serve in this position.

Little is known of Tabourne prior to 1897. Born in Nebraska in 1880, she and her family immigrated to California by 1890, where the Census lists them as living in Pasadena.[1] By the age of seventeen in 1897, she began working in a hairdressing salon to beautify women. She would meet and fall in love with married musician George Le Roy Taborn (later spelled Tabourn and Tabourne), giving birth to son Charles Le Roy Tabourne in Los Angeles in 1909. After he eventually divorced his wife, the two married on September 29, 1916, in Alameda, California.

Tabourne began her hairdressing journey at Weaver-Jackson Hair Company, "one of the most exclusive hair dressing establishments on the Pacific Coast,"[2] one that served some of the most important men and women of the area. She became renowned for designing and improving elaborate styles. The Frederickson Salon, known as the "celebrated hair cultivator," hired her away by 1908,[3] impressed with her talents. Several clients soon followed their favorite hairdresser to her new salon.

Wilson served as the main breadwinner to her polio-stricken son, due to her husband's absences when performing, and probably searched out any additional opportunities she could find. As early as 1916, Triangle Film Corporation and producer Thomas Ince employed her to design a hairstyle for star Dorothy Dalton in the film *The Flame of the Yukon*, called "The Yukon,"[4] which most likely led to other work for the studio.

Julia Faye later claimed she had discovered Tabourne and her wonderful hairdressing at a downtown salon and lured her into the entertainment business, where her work impressed Cecil B. DeMille.[5] Famous Players-Lasky hired her in 1919 to create elaborate hairdressing for their top stars,[6] which would include such celebrities as Rudolph Valentino, Nita Naldi, Gloria Swanson, Pola Negri, Betty Bronson, and Leatrice Joy. Tabourne strove for authenticity as well, researching books to create identical coiffures for the 1923 historical epic *The Covered Wagon*.[7] Stars loved her friendly and happy personality, as did the staff who worked under her leadership. Millions of men and women around the world admired and praised her work, without knowing that an African American designed the hairstyles projected onscreen.

Tabourne hated women's bobbed hair, which became popular in the early 1920s. Many of her elaborate hair designs were designed to hide it, making her "responsible for some of the unique coiffure effects that adorned the heads of movie stars."[8] Some of these exotic coiffures included braids, beaded headdresses, wrapped hair, flowers, and special ornaments.[9] As an assistant later revealed, "Her hands had some strange effect on hair. It seemed to shape itself miraculously under her touch. Waves, fringes, perilously frail-looking designs assumed permanence after she had touched them. Hattie loved hair."[10]

Upon her death from cancer surgery on March 30, 1925, newspapers proclaimed her "Filmland's most noted hairdresser."[11] Stars such as Lasky Studios, Cecil B. DeMille, Nita Naldi, Estelle Taylor, Betty Compson, and others sent flowers to her burial services at Evergreen Cemetery.[12] No other woman hairdresser at the time received such praise in the press, especially an African American one. Hattie Wilson Tabourne deserved all her accolades as the industry's first female hairdresser, slowly putting a foot in the door to allow other African Americans to follow her.

MUSIC

Edith Lang, First Composer-Accompanist

THOUGH SILENT FILMS LACKED A SYNCHRONIZED SOUNDTRACK, THEY were never silent. Music of some type always accompanied them in movie picture theaters to add energy and help provide emotional cues. In its earliest days, a single piano added musical voice, with theater or pipe organ coming soon thereafter. Some musicians improvised an entire score to the action they glimpsed onscreen, while others employed sheet music, popular songs, or perhaps even some type of musical score to accompany the movies. Some played themes compiled in cheat books to aid in pulling together music. Neighborhood houses often featured a small ensemble to play with the program, while movie palaces showcased full orchestras often playing fully composed scores commissioned for specific features.

Women accompanied silent films from its earliest days mostly anonymously, as small mom-and-pop–style theaters saw families or married couples manage most of the responsibilities in running and operating these houses. Major show palaces, however, employed men to lead their musical programs or provide a musical soundtrack. In 1916 young Edith Lang began accompanying films at her local playhouse, gaining renown not only for her playing but also for her cogent distillation of the act of silent-film accompanying, becoming the first important female accompanist of the time.

Born in Ohio, November 13, 1885, Lang possessed prodigious musical gifts as both organist and composer, which she employed to the fullest her whole life, perhaps both for the love of music and because she supported both herself and her mother most of her life. At the age of nine, she began playing the organ for her church. By 1905 she and her mother Clara resided in Rhode Island, with Lang serving as church organist. In 1910 they lived in Boston, with Lang continuing as a church organist while also teaching at Franklin Square House, an affordable Boston home for single women. Ambitious and driven, Lang sang church solos, accompanied vocalists in local concerts, and also played the organ for Watertown's Unitarian Church and the Watertown Choral Society, all while attending the New England Conservatory School of Music. Several of her compositions were performed at school presentations, a very rare occurrence.

Boston's Exeter Theatre hired Lang to provide accompaniment for their film programs in 1916, looking for someone experienced on the organ but well versed in all areas of music. She alternated with various male musicians on their Estey organ over the next several years, even while she taught at the Emerson Conservatory of Music. Lang also later played between programs and for movies at the Castle Square Theatre, earning more for accompanying movies than she did for performing serious organ concerts.

A music aficionado and student, Lang understood the importance of tempo and mood in telling a story. Her job was to undergird the emotions of a scene, not overwhelm them. She walked a fine line creating musical themes and interludes that hearkened to well-loved or specific pieces without falling into caricature or drawing attention away from the story. As she revealed in an 1920 interview, "You must never forget that you are not giving an organ or piano recital, but are furnishing theatrical music for a theatrical production and as such it must be able to carry people out of themselves or else your work lacks 'punch.' . . . The music must vitalize the action on the screen, but not absorb the attention of the spectator."[1]

Drawing on her musical and film experience, Lang began composing themes for the movies, playing off the themes and sounds of famous classical music pieces. In 1920 she completed *Prelude Religieux*, which the *Moving Picture News* called "of exceptional tonal beauty, and it can justly be said that it is a sequel to such famous compositions as Gounod's *Ave Maria*."[2]

Recognizing a need for explanation and distillation of musical accompaniment for the movies, Lang began a sideline in educating musicians and the public in articles as well as books. She joined forces with George West to write the book *Musical Accompaniment of Moving Pictures* for Boston Music Company in 1920, intended as a resource guide, or what they called a "'first-aid' manual for the beginner in the field of moving picture music."[3] It examined music in three parts: equipment, musical interpretation for different genres, and organs and organ techniques.

Many reviews at the time called it the pioneering textbook on accompanying silent films, generally praising it as an exception to most film books of the period. *The Billboard* magazine described it as dealing "with the problem of musical accompaniment for motion pictures in a comprehensive and practical matter."[4] London's *Daily Telegraph* commended the work, calling it, "a delightful little book, topical, expert, packed with common sense and humour, the ultimate word on being up to date on the subject."[5] Lang continued composing new books of silent-film works, including a *Thematic Catalog of Movie Music*, which she selected and described for the Oliver Ditson Company in 1923, though none achieved the renown as her first.[6]

The organist also recognized a need in educating the public and exhibitors about disruptive behavior at film theaters that annoyed other patrons. Lang penned articles for local papers as well as the trade journal the *American Organist*, offering tips as well as inspired stories on how to solve the problem. *The Billboard* reprinted one of her pieces demonstrating the best way to hush children into quietly enjoying film shows: have them sing. She recounted the story of a Boston movie theater that hired R. L. Harlow of Filene's Department Store's music program to musically train some of its unruly children into a choir which sang at the conclusion of Saturday matinees in exchange for a free movie ticket.[7]

Lang also suggested possessing a sense of humor as one of the primary assets for an accompanist, "for the musician must, at all times, feel the atmosphere and keep step with his audience."[8] Being relaxed and going with the flow allowed one to easily vamp and ad-lib when a film broke, audiences grew unruly, or miscellaneous mayhem occurred, in order "to control the show." She described changing the tempo or style of her music if the audience appeared restless, playing loud chords to overshadow those attempting to mock action onscreen, or even satirically jazzing off those attempting to rant at a film.

The musician, one of the best-known female organists on the East Coast, entertained and inspired audiences on Boston- and New York–area radio stations starting in 1924, on broadcasts carried across the country. These often helped promote the classical organ concerts she performed in major venues, including at Harvard and at the Library of Congress's chamber music auditorium in 1926, combining old masters like Bach and Mussorgsky, her own works, and major compositions by contemporary organ masters Louis Vierne and Charles Widor.

Hoping to increase the playing and number of women organists in the Boston area, Lang founded the Women Organ Players' Club in 1924. Her aim was "to bring church and movie musicians together to benefit their profession."[9] Women discussed organ interpretation, playing in front of different types of audiences, and how to attract younger players to their field. They hoped to increase pay for church organists, as many preferred playing for movie houses that offered $100 to $125 a week, or even $225 for featured soloists.[10] Just three years later, more than eighty-five members participated in the group.

Over the next four decades, Lang continued playing organ at churches, for concerts, and on occasional radio performances, always working to educate young students in the joy of music. The most renowned female silent-film accompanist of her day, Lang left behind a valuable legacy in her *Musical Introduction to Moving Pictures* book, one that educated thousands of players that came after her in the correct application of connecting music with silent film.

ANIMATION

Helena Smith Dayton, First Stop-Motion Animator

IN THE VERY EARLY DAYS OF THE MOVING PICTURE INDUSTRY, FILMMAKERS discovered that by stopping the camera, they could manipulate objects in short increments to suggest the idea of physical movement when played back at full speed. Popularized by pioneering French trick-film producer Georges Méliès in roving titles, stop-motion grew in use and popularity thanks to early American filmmakers like Edwin S. Porter, Wallace McCutcheon Sr., and J. Stuart Blackton. In 1917, artist Helena Smith Dayton produced three short films employing what she called "animated sculptures," becoming the first female stop-motion animator.

Born May 10, 1883, in Burke, New York, the young woman fell in love with words and the visual. She attended college for two years before marrying advertising sales manager Fred Erving Dayton in 1910. While he spent his time advertising automobiles and rubber, Dayton dedicated herself to the creative process. As early as 1906, newspapers printed her short stories revolving around young women's issues in the world, often written in the wry style of O. Henry. She later penned a series of fictional stories for syndicated papers.

As she matured as an artist, Dayton focused her attentions on sculpture in the mid-1910s. Jumping in by crafting malleable clay into small animals, Dayton sculpted small lifelike figures or "caracatypes"[1] representing some of the many people she observed in city life shilling newspapers, waiting tables, or dancing madly in cafés. An evocative sculptress and commercial artist, she turned expressive characters and situations into relatable caricatures, or what she called "toys for grown people."[2] Popular all over, she made $12,000 in one year.[3]

Dayton described herself as no artist, with no training, a "rank outsider."[4] The *New York Sun* called her instead "a detective trailing laughs with a lump of clay for a note book."[5] As Dayton walked the streets of New York, comical and relatable figures caught her eye, and she rushed to capture their likenesses as small maquettes and not full-size sculpture, making them more alive and seemingly in motion. In effect, these small "statuette cartoons" or Claymation led her toward film animation. The newspaper caught their energy, noting, "There is an astonishing amount of motion in the little figures. They look as if they had been caught with a camera instead of being patiently released from dead clay . . . they are all in the mode of the moment."[6]

Cartoons of all types grew increasingly popular during the 1910s. Newspaper cartoonists like Nell Brinkley, George Herriman, and George McManus became celebrities with their animated drawings before movies overshadowed them. Winsor McCay's *Gertie the Dinosaur* and Bray Studios grew out of art drawn on individual celluloid sheets photographed over a stationary background to create the feeling of movement. These popular shorts led to Willis O'Brien's stop-motion dinosaurs in *The Lost World* and Dayton's original concept, "animated sculptures."[7]

Newspapers acknowledged the longer and harder work in crafting sculpted stop-motion animation than in hand drawn animation. It required many individual sculpted little figures moved in small increments and photographed each time they moved before stitching each shot together frame by frame to make a complete movie. Under director Horace D. Ashton, Dayton created multiple individual figures for each movie, resculpting them for each movement for each of the sixteen frames for each foot of film, which the paper stated would be sixteen thousand movements for each figure in a thousand-foot reel.[8]

Her novelty appeared onscreen at New York's Strand Theatre March 18, 1917, featuring such characters as dancing girls, musicians in the orchestra pit, and high-end patrons.[9] *The Times* and other papers called Dayton's invention of animated sculptures special and unique. *Motography* called the results "amusing."[10] *The Billboard*'s review said, "She has a keen sense of humor, and all her work which will be shown on the screen is of a highly amusing nature."[11] At the same time, she created two small statues for display in the lobby, capturing popular hoofer George M. Cohan in two of his eccentric dance poses for his successful film *Broadway Jones*, an adaptation of his popular Broadway musical, which followed the screening of Dayton's short.[12]

The S. S. Film Company joined with Dayton and director J. Charles Davis Jr. to make a series of Claymation shorts, starting with an adaptation of William Shakespeare's *Romeo and Juliet*. While she crafted elegant figures for the cast members, the company produced historically correct miniature sets and costumes to add authenticity to the production.[13] *Moving Picture World*'s review praised the film, describing the story as a burlesque and the emotions perfectly captured by the characters. "Little need be said here of the wonderful talent of Helena Smith Dayton: her work speaks for itself. In the introduction to the picture we are privileged to watch her fingers fashion the form of Juliet from an apparently soulless lump of clay."[14]

That December Dayton created another little short, one of five scenes in the Argus Pictorial Number Three short about coral, with her section satirizing a banquet scene and called "Pride Goeth before a Fall."[15] Though all her films received excellent reviews, Dayton found the work tiring and resolved never to make another.

Wanting to make a difference in World War I, Dayton attended nurse training. In 1918 she accompanied other women trained by the Young Men's Christian Association (YMCA) overseas for actual service. She worked as director of the YMCA Canteen in Paris as well as the YMCA Canteen in London, not returning to the United States until August 1919.[16]

By the early 1920s, Dayton returned to writing, once again composing satiric pieces on women and society for newspapers and magazines. Dayton met Louise Benson Barratt, wife of the Shubert organization art director Watson Barratt at a Society of Illustrators meeting in 1923, becoming writing partners focusing on witty flappers and artists. The two women wrote the book for the Shubert musical revue *Artists and Models*, which grew out of a Society of Illustrators variety show. Dayton and Barratt wrote a few scenes for the revue, rehearsed the acts, helped choose the cast, and assisted in arranging the music, as they did with the 1924 revue.

In 1925 the two women collaborated on the New York City guidebook, *New York in Seven Days*, a chatty introduction to the city for tourists. The book pointed out top neighborhoods, museums, restaurants, and sites for those new to the city through a fictional story. Not a traditional guidebook, it was "the adventures of a young author and a 'feminine friend' from back home to whom he volunteers to show the town."[17] Over the next few years, the writing duo jumped between stage and books. They composed the three-act comedy *The Sweet Buy and Buy* in 1926, which actor James Gleason purchased to perform onstage, the comedy *Hot Water*, then later wrote the book *A Book of Entertainments and Theatricals*.

Though she only produced three short films, Dayton's innovative, inventive experiments in creating "animated sculptures" helped popularize telling stories through stop-motion animation or Claymation and rendered her the pioneering person in American stop-motion animation.

Great Cartoonist

Bessie Mae Kelley

Only woman cartoonist in the Moving Picture profession.

Hear! See!

Animator Bessie Mae Kelley posed at a drawing board in a newspaper photo from May 26, 1927. *Oxford Press.*

Bessie May Kelley, First Animator

LONG A STAPLE OF NEWSPAPER ILLUSTRATIONS TO SATIRIZE CURRENT events or spoof celebrities, animation grew even more popular after appearing on the big screen. Former newspaper illustrator turned Vitagraph Pictures cofounder J. Stuart Blackton introduced animation to the movies in the United States in 1900 with his short *The Enchanted Drawing* and then popularized it with his 1906 film *Humorous Phases of Funny Faces*, for which he drew caricatures that evolved into other comical features through stop-motion animation.

Winsor McCay's *Gertie the Dinosaur* premiered in 1914, followed later by Otto Messmer and Pat Sullivan's *Felix the Cat* and Max Fleischer's *Koko the Clown*, all building animation's popularity. At the same time, budding artist Bessie Mae Kelley both drew and directed such animated shorts as *Gasoline Alley* in 1918, making her the earliest known female animator.

Born in Pennsylvania but raised in Caribou, Maine, young Kelley fell in love with animation while studying at New York's Pratt Institute and was determined to break into the field.[1] Starting at the bottom as a lowly assistant sweeping floors and washing cels, Kelley rose to full animator.[2] Professional animators respected Kelley's work. Bray Studios employed her for seven years at both their New York and Chicago studios.

The young artist completed the finishing of such animated film shorts as Paul Terry's *Aesop's Fables* and Max and Dave Fleischer's *Out of the Inkwell* series and also animated and directed a few *Gasoline Alley* one-reelers.[3] In her free time, Kelley drew her own characters and completed such shorts as *Flower Fairies* (1921) and *A Merry Christmas* (1922) on the side.[4]

For Terry's *Aesop's Fables*, Kelley drew a little mouse couple originally known as Roderick and Gladys, later changed to Milton and Mary, popular characters with audiences.[5] Inspired after watching *Fables*, a young Walt Disney self-confidently followed his own ambitions and perhaps also found inspiration, later creating a mouse couple of his own.

Wanting to grow her name recognition while also informing audiences about the actual animation process, Kelley spoke to women's clubs, churches, education groups, universities, and even children's organizations around Pennsylvania and New England, where she had grown up. Like many performers of the time, Kelley traveled vaudeville and Chautauqua circuits to appear in front of local audiences to augment her earnings. As early as 1925, she appeared onstage demonstrating cartooning in Brattleboro, Vermont, billing herself as the "only woman animated cartoonist."[6]

Over the next several years, Kelley participated in several local Chautauqua association performances around the East Coast, appearing onstage drawing and demonstrating the cartooning process, revealing to audiences that it sometimes required nine hundred hours of work to complete one eight-minute film reel.[7] A night here, two or three days there, she described the painstaking process of creating an animated cartoon. In July 1927, she performed in Connecticut's six-day Chautauqua, in which multiple performers such as musicians, lecturers, and entertainers provided "Quality Programs for Everybody."[8] For this event, Kelley "entertained by explaining the method of producing animated cartoons, and by numerous freehand drawings in colored crayons, and by cartooning three of the young people of the audience."[9]

The artist proselytized on the budding field of cartooning and animation while at the same time offering inspiration to young women looking to join the workforce and make a difference in the world. Her fame spread as the media picked up on her self-styled billing, proclaiming her unique position as a female animator, with the *Barre Daily Times* announcing she was "the only lady drawing animated cartoons for the movies."[10] Most reviews praised her performances, one calling it "novel yet distinctly high grade, and remarkably entertaining."[11]

While touring through New England, animator Kelley met Emile Hirschy; she married him July 15, 1932 and, like many women of the period, retired from her animation career to become a stay-at-home wife. While her contributions remained unsung for decades, animation historian Mindy Johnson brought her out of the shadows to be recognized as America's first female animator.

M. J. Winkler

M. J. Winkler Takes Over New Cartoon Series

MISS MARGARET J. WINKLER, probably the pioneer woman distributor and a leader today in the Independent Short Subject field has received recognition from a source totally unexpected by her.

The Film Club of Boston, in existence since moving pictures first have been shown, issued a special invitation to Miss Winkler to make a speech before them. In her talk she told of the many hardships and difficulties she encountered in making "Felix," the cartoon cat, what it is today.

In addition to the "Felix" comics, Miss Winkler has taken over a series of combination cartoon and live character subjects known as "Alice Comedies" which are being made for her in Hollywood by Walt Disney; the Burton Holmes Travelogues; a series of two-reel kid pictures which are to be known as "Kid Kappers Komedies" and a further series of two-reel subjects based on the works of the nationally famed writer, Edgar A. Guest.

In a recent statement, Miss Winkler said that she could see a bright future in the short subject market.

"The courtesy and consideration shown me by all independent exchangemen with whom I have dealt have decided for me the fact that I will continue to distribute all my product in the state-right market and will continue to do so as long as my relations with my buyers are as pleasant as they have been and I hope this will continue for a long while," said Miss Winkler.

Independent to Release Five Reel Comedy in August

Though all arrangements were completed some time ago, Independent Pictures Corporation has just made announcement of the release by that concern in August of a five-reel burlesque comedy under the title "If Winter Goes." Raymond Griffith is the star and the picture is frankly "hokum" comedy. No attempt was made to produce anything but a straight laugh provoking five reeler replete with trick situations.

Jesse J. Goldburg, President of Independent Pictures, has made plans for a unique campaign to exploit "If Winter Goes."

Sees Opportunities For Independents

NEVER before in the history of the screen have States Rights productions had the brilliant opportunities now offered them, according to Irving M. Lesser, vice-president of and general manager of distribution for Principal Pictures Corporation.

"There will never be a monopoly in the motion picture field," says Mr. Lesser. "The reason for this is that it is, and always will be possible for anyone with brains and money to make a picture and then arrange for its distribution. The methods of distribution are (1) Through a regular releasing organization; (2) through the States Rights field.

"There is a steady improvement in the States Rights system. But there is still room for much more improvement. What we need among States Righters at present is a movement to give the producer an even break, or the same deal as he gets from one of the National releasing organizations.

"Such a movement is under way at present. And it soon will bear fruit. This is why I believe there are brilliant opportunities in the States Rights field.

"Our company has found the States Rights system an excellent sales medium because we follow this set policy in production: (1) Quality. This goes above everything. We aim at 100 per cent in quality of story, cast, production. (2) Liberal advertising. This is essential. If you have anything good you must let the public know it. (3) Fair dealing. Some people believe that motion pictures are a gamble pure and simple and go into them with that idea in view. Motion pictures are an investment that must be nurtured and watched and promoted. They are Big Business. And in all business you must have fair dealing or you are working without a foundation."

"For the present season Principal Pictures Corporation has five States Rights productions, which now are ready for release. They are:

"Daring Youth"—Presented by B. F. Zeidman, with Bebe Daniels, supported by Norman Kerry, Lee Moran, Lillian Langdon and Arthur Hoyt. Directed by William Beaudine.

"Listen Lester"—Produced and presented by Sacramento Pictures Corporation. Adapted from John Cort's famous stage success which had a phenomenal run on Broadway. In the cast are Louise Fazenda, Eva Novak, Harry Myers, George O'Hara, Alec Francis, Lee Moran and Dot Farley. This is a farce comedy directed by William A. Seiter.

"The Masked Dancer"—Produced and presented by Eastern Productions, Inc., with Helen Chadwick and Lowell Sherman. Also in the cast are Leslie Austen, Joseph King, Arthur Housman, Charles Craig, Mme. Andree, Dorothy Kingdon, Miss Alyce Mills and Helen Ward. It was directed by Burton King.

"Daughters of Pleasure"—Produced and presented by B. F. Zeidman. Starring Marie Prevost and Monte Blue, supported by Clara Bow, Wilfred Lucas and Edith Chapman. It presents a love story, dealing with modern social conditions and the 'idle rich,' and was directed by Wm. Beaudine.

"The Good Bad Boy"—Produced and presented by B. F. Zeidman, with Joe Butterworth and Mary Jane Irving. Brownie, the remarkable dog actor also is seen in the production. The story of a boy who tried to do the right thing but always got in wrong in the attempt, it was directed by Eddie Cline, who directed Jackie Coogan in "Circus Days."

Irving M. Lesser.

Animation distribution executive M. J. Winkler portrait in *Motion Picture News*, 1923.

M. J. Winkler, First Animation Distributor

In the early 1920s, legendary animation pioneers Otto Messmer, Max Fleischer, and Walt Disney found fame and fortune with energetic, self-confident characters now iconic in popular culture, all thanks to the savvy business acumen and innovative promotional practices of talented distributor and producer M. (Margaret) J. Winkler. Winkler's success as the first female distributor of animated short subjects shocked the industry, thanks to her nongendered name.

Unmasked in a 1922 trade magazine story titled "Distributor as a Woman Proves Surprise," Winkler acknowledged women's dreams of succeeding on their own terms: "I think this industry is full of wonderful possibilities for an ambitious woman, and there is no reason why she shouldn't be able to conduct business as well as the men."[1] Her business prowess and steady success earned Winkler praise and respect even from hardened industry professionals.

Born 1895 in Hungary, Winkler immigrated to the United States in 1904 with her family, who set down roots in the Bronx.[2] She entered the business world after leaving school, working as a typist and later becoming Harry M. Warner's private secretary at Warner's Features, in 1918.[3] Observant and a quick study, Winkler absorbed the complex, commercial nature of the business, attending film trade meetings and watching Warner's negotiating prowess.

Only chance led Winkler to distributing animated cartoons. Happy in her position, Winkler was aghast when Warner declined to release Otto Messmer's *Felix the Cat* cartoon. Throwing her hat in the ring, she took up the challenge to put the frisky cat in front of audiences, inspiring Messmer with her spunkiness. Determined to succeed in a field which often denigrated or underestimated women's contributions, the assertive young woman employed initials rather than her full name after establishing her own animation releasing company, M. J. Winkler Productions, in 1921.

Based in New York but with production offices in Los Angeles, Winkler's company specialized in marketing and exploiting high-end cartoons. The enterprising entrepreneur shrewdly recognized superior talent and their creations, confidently utilizing attention-grabbing advertising to sell them to wide audiences.

Otto Messmer and Pat Sullivan's frisky feline character Felix captured the public's fancy in 1921 thanks to Winkler's eye-popping novelty and smart distribution. First introduced in 1919 as an animal version of renowned comedian Charlie Chaplin,[4] the *Felix the Cat* series gained fame under Paramount Studios' distribution, but its popularity soared thanks to Winkler.

Employing flashy one-sheet posters, large trade magazine ads, advertising tie-ins and mass merchandising, and high-end theater bookings, she turned Felix into an iconic character not only in the United States but worldwide as well. The *Kentucky Post* declared that "the cartoon cat . . . was a nobody, until Miss Winkler got hold of him and put him over."[5]

Winkler signed brothers Max and Dave Fleischer to a distribution contract in 1922 after recognizing the box office potential of their comical fourth-wall breaking Koko the Clown in their *Out of the Inkwell* series. *Out of the Inkwell* combined live-action camerawork with drawn animation showing Fleischer engaged in comic mayhem with the acerbic clown. As with Felix the Cat, Winkler's assertive business practices, including ads that promoted the series and her own accomplishments in selling accentuated the brash moxie of Fleischer's Koko.

Slowly going bankrupt in Kansas City with his *Laugh-O-Gram* animated series, a green Walt Disney arrived in Los Angeles in 1923, looking to establish himself as an animation producer through better representation. Impressed with Winkler's success but unsure about working with a woman as distributor, Disney wrote Warner inquiring about her background. The executive praised her in his reply, stating that "she has done very well and I believe she is very responsible for anything she may undertake. . . . I don't think you need any hesitancy in having her handle your merchandise."[6]

A chastened Disney approached the talented executive for help in releasing his new animation series called the *Alice Comedies*, which blended live action of spunky Midwest transplant Alice Davis engaged in rambunctious activities with hand-drawn animated characters similar to those of Fleischer. Recognizing in him a kindred spirit of determination and risk-taking, Winkler signed the go-getter to a contract on October 16, 1923.[7]

Winkler's ads in the trades described the series as "kid comedies with Cartoons Co-ordinated in the Action, a Distinct Novelty."[8] She emphasized the unique aspect of the work in her Disney contract, emphasizing they must be produced in a "high-class manner . . . and satisfactory to the Distributor."[9] Trades and newspapers praised the series, highlighting its artistic elements and comic touches.

The savvy businesswoman officially incorporated her company under the name M. J. Winkler Productions, Inc., on October 27, 1923, just weeks after inking Disney to a contract.[10] Capitalized with $20,000, the company featured Winkler, her brother George, and Charles Mintz, her fiancé, as directors.[11] Winkler and Mintz married at the end of the year, the death knell for her burgeoning career. Traditional values–minded Mintz convinced his wife to loosen her business responsibilities and allow him to assume control. Three years later, Winkler officially retired from animation distribution, settling in as a stay-at-home mom.

Winkler's visionary insights and determination turned animation into a profitable business, making it an essential money-making component of movie exhibition for decades. She successfully kickstarted the career of legendary showman Disney a century ago while also developing Felix the Cat and Koko the Clown into household names. Her marketing and distribution prowess established animation as the highly creative and successful medium that it has become.

RESEARCH/PRESERVATION

Iris Barry, First Archivist

THE MOTION PICTURE INDUSTRY HAS MOSTLY FAILED TO PROTECT ITS assets for the majority of its history. Studios' flammable nitrate films were often all stored together, to be entirely lost in accidental conflagrations. Many filmmakers junked or destroyed prints as silent films gave way to sound, not realizing their worth for future technologies. Others grew tired of paying storage costs and just threw films away. Journalist Iris Barry recognized the value of preserving film history as early as the 1930s. Most of her life she championed the new artistic medium of the twentieth century, extolling it in the press, organizing film societies, and later establishing the Museum of Modern Art Film Library in 1935, the first film archive in the United States and world to preserve and screen its vintage history.

Born outside Birmingham, England, March 25,1895, as Iris Sylvia Symes,[1] she attended the movies every week, stating that the 1913 film *Les Misérables* "fixed my thirst for the movies."[2] She was accepted into Oxford University, but World War I disrupted her plans, leading her to become a typist at the Ministry of Munitions before later serving an assistant librarian at the School of Oriental Languages. While she worked, she wrote verse, submitting it under the name Iris Barry, which she began using professionally. Impressed with her work and forward thinking, poet Ezra Pound invited her to London and introduced her to Bloomsbury's literary elite. Writer Michael Binder has called her "an original, a New Woman writ large: outspoken, bohemian and intelligent."[3]

London's *Daily Mail*, England's highest circulation paper, hired Barry as film critic in 1925, allowing her to review and expound on movies for mass audiences. She also wrote more esoteric essays for *The*

Spectator beginning in 1923, analyzing film's impact on society. Barry mostly extolled popular films over esoteric ones, writing from the point of view of a dedicated cinemagoer and not as an academic, making her writing accessible to all. Her enthusiastic writing meant to inspire audiences to examine and think about movies. She wrote "the finest films are as lovely to the eye as they are moving the emotions."[4]

Drawn to intellectual discussions of film, Barry cofounded London's Film Society in 1925 with filmmaker Ivor Montagu and theater owner Sidney Bernstein as a place for filmmakers and literary society to watch, analyze, and celebrate movies young and old. It would serve as the progenitor for film societies around the world. Such cinema standouts as producer-directors Anthony Asquith and Michael Balcon, actors Ivor Novello and John Gielgud, and writers George Bernard Shaw and H. G. Wells were among its heady members. Taking it one step further, Barry wrote the book *Let's Go to the Pictures* in 1926 as her enthusiastic "championship of the kinema,"[5] hoping to entice intelligent readers and everyday filmgoers to attend and watch thoughtful, insightful, and beautiful films.

Fired from the *Daily Mail* for criticizing the work of novelist Elinor Glyn and appearing to champion American films over British ones, Barry moved to New York City in 1930 with her husband Alan Porter in the heart of the Great Depression. She found life tough in the major metropolis, trying to scrape by as a freelance writer and seeing her marriage dissolve. A fortuitous meeting at a cocktail party with architect Philip Johnson, director of the fledgling Museum of Modern Art's Architecture Department, led to Barry's hiring as organizer of the Museum's library.

Barry and second husband, Wall Street financier John E. "Dick" Abbott, promoted motion pictures, giving the medium respectability as an art form, taking it out of the realm of ephemeral detritus into one of cultural significance. As she wrote later, she and other cinephiles around the world "realized that probably we would never see again the films that had enchanted us and therefore that an effort was needed to preserve as much as one could of the films of the past."[6] Their arguments finally held sway over board members of MOMA, who sought out and won a grant from the Rockefeller Foundation to establish a film library in

1935. Abbott would serve as vice president and general manager of the library, with Barry acting as curator.

Justifying the archive's existence and the importance of film as historic artifact and also major social influence, Barry wrote, "The motion picture is unique in three important ways. First, it is the one medium of expression in which America has influenced the world. Second, it has had a marked influence on contemporary life. And third, it is such a young art that we can study it at first hand from its beginnings."[7] The archive would therefore collect movies and date their production period, better enabling their study and evolution as art form and cultural influencer, defining the organization and meaning of a film archive. The library would serve as a museum for film in its work: "Assemble a cross-section of films since 1889, edit them into a chronological and artistic sequence and exhibit them in a series of two-hour programs sponsored by colleges, museums and other cultural institutions throughout the nation."[8]

Looking to save important films from cinema's past, the couple visited Hollywood to cajole studios and major players like Douglas Fairbanks and Mary Pickford to donate money to their efforts as well as turn over important vintage prints to have some of their most important work preserved and highlighted. Pickford and Fairbanks, among others, did donate most of their film archives to the library to save them for posterity. Always a commercial business that viewed movies strictly as product, studios gave little money to provide upkeep but did give many vintage titles as they cleaned shelves to make room for newer merchandise.

Besides MOMA's own special screenings and retrospectives highlighting the serious appreciation of film as art, Barry saw educational outreach as one major component of the library, providing speakers and notes at screenings, allowing scholars to view movies, and facilitating the sharing of films and material with universities and various organizations around the world. Barry herself would teach popular history-of-film classes at Columbia University, thereby making films a legitimate subject worthy of study, showing their social impact on society and how they commented on the past while also revealing truths about the present.

As early as 1938, the Academy of Motion Picture Arts and Sciences honored the MOMA's Film Library and the work of Barry and Abbott with a special commendation, recognizing it "for its significant work in collecting films dating from 1895 to the present, and for the first time making available to the public the means of studying the historical and aesthetic development of the motion picture as one of the major arts."[9] Barry helped found the International Federation of Film Archives (FIAF) that year as well.

After the United States entered World War II, MOMA's Film Library helped create the *Why We Fight* film series that galvanized Americans in support of World War II and devised a propaganda campaign against Nazism in Latin America. Barry's screenings and programs returned after World War II, leading the march of film education onward. She helped the United Nations organize its own film programming in 1946 and served as the first American representative to the newly formed Cannes Film Festival in 1947. Barry eventually left MOMA in 1951, retiring to the South of France.

Without Iris Barry's persistence and dedication, the importance of studying and preserving American motion pictures might never have been kindled, and most of our early film heritage would be lost. Her influence led to the creation of major film archives across the United States and even the world, helping inaugurate the academic study of motion pictures and their influence on society.

Research librarian Elizabeth McGaffey portrait, circa 1932. *Courtesy of Margaret Herrick Library*

Elizabeth McGaffey, First Reference Librarian

RECOGNIZING THE NEED FOR A PERMANENT DEPARTMENT TO PROVIDE accurate historic details and catch anachronisms during filmmaking, Jesse L. Lasky Feature Play Company script reader Elizabeth McGaffey convinced studio executives to establish the first studio research department in 1914. Provided a measly dictionary, *National Geographic* magazine, and a public library card, McGaffey turned a mere afterthought into a prerequisite for any respectable film studio.

Born Elizabeth Brock, January 17, 1885, in Chicago, Illinois, the future librarian displayed a love for both performing and the written word as a young woman. She studied acting at the American Academy of Dramatic Arts in 1903 before appearing in a few Broadway shows and then becoming "an actress who had 'trod the boards' from Minnesota to Louisiana and from New York to California."[1] After marrying press agent Kenneth McGaffey in 1911, the couple moved to Chicago to join newspaper staffs.

In 1914, the Lasky Feature Play Company hired the McGaffeys to work at its Hollywood studio. Kenneth McGaffey joined the studio's publicity department, and Elizabeth worked as a script reader. Many around the studio began turning to her for assistance in recalling details of plays, books, furniture styles, and history, thanks to her "wide experience and excellent memory."[2] Intuitively understanding the need for quick access to historic information by hands-on filmmakers like Cecil B. DeMille, the driven McGaffey began organizing a giant reference library.

When stumped by difficult queries, she turned to local colleges, archives, San Marino's Huntington Library, and even the United States' Library of Congress. McGaffey's passion, organization, and attention to detail gained the department renown. Many of her indexing and organizational policies would later be copied by the Los Angeles Public Library, as well as other studios who began creating their own research departments.[3]

Recognizing the department's importance and exploding size, the Lasky studio moved it into its own building in 1920, officially naming McGaffey department head.[4] She traveled across country and overseas conducting research, meeting scholars, and acquiring new materials. Back in Hollywood, McGaffey applied her leadership skills to canvassing moving picture studios for donations to help construct the Hollywood Studio Club as a home for single young women attempting to break into the industry.[5]

Director DeMille, a stickler for details, respected McGaffey's talents for leaving no stone unturned conducting research, turning to her to discover the history and atmosphere of centuries past for his spectacles and melodramas. For his 1923 production of *The Ten Commandments*, McGaffey even studied illustrations in Henry Huntington's Gutenberg Bible at his San Marino library to ensure biblical accuracy.[6]

When DeMille established his own independent studio in 1925, he hired McGaffey to helm the research department.[7] Determined and unshakable, the stalwart leader and her department consulted more than 2,500 reference books when compiling a gigantic report for DeMille's biblical epic *King of Kings* in 1926.[8] McGaffey meticulously organized her research for each DeMille film, compiling a giant book filled with magazine and newspaper clippings, photos, brochures, letters, and ephemera to intimately describe each aspect of the story.[9]

McGaffey followed the mighty director to MGM in 1928, where she would employ any means necessary to answer his research requests. Before the making of *Dynamite* in 1929, the redoubtable McGaffey explored treacherous, dark mines to add color to the story of a miner and his dangerous profession. She even cruised about in dirigibles in 1930 to prepare for the production of *Madam Satan*, featuring an elaborate costume party aboard a blimp.

When DeMille departed MGM to return to the greener pastures of old home Paramount in 1932, McGaffey began networking. Her professionalism and research know-how in sleuthing for details impressed many, with one newspaper calling her the "walking encyclopedia of Hollywood."[10] RKO quickly hired her to helm their growing research department and shape it into the premier history archive of any studio.

As head of RKO's Research Department, McGaffey supervised more than twelve employees and managed over ten thousand books and periodical volumes, one million documents, maps, photographs, and various other ephemera. She and her staff hunted down facts providing specific background details and accuracy before films actually began production. Problems often arose during shooting because many filmmakers forgot this crucial step, leading her to quip, "The burning point today is to educate executives in the importance of research. We should have the script as soon as it's written so that we may be prepared for whatever is asked of us."[11]

Investigative procedures and organizational practices had evolved since McGaffey operated as a staff of one at Paramount, making detailed knowledge more easily available on virtually any subject. Successful filmmakers understood the necessity of this information in constructing exciting stories about little-known people or topics. "Research work has passed through many distinct stages since I first started seventeen years ago. When I started out the main concern of directors was architecture . . . costumes, however, came as the next phase. The third stage was devoted to details of all kinds. At present, our work embraces all of these things and goes further, delving into the habits and obscure customs peculiar to certain groups of people."[12]

Thanks to the respected work of talented leaders like McGaffey, the Academy of Motion Picture Arts and Sciences voted to add research directors as members in 1932, making them members of the technicians' branch under the art directors division. McGaffey herself was one of the first four women installed as members of the inaugural group, acknowledging her importance in the field.

The Academy turned to McGaffey for her expertise again in 1940 when librarian Margaret Herrick appointed her, other studio research heads, and Los Angeles city librarians to the advisory board for setting guiding principles for book acquisition by the growing Academy library. Already considered one of the top four libraries specializing in motion picture collections, the Academy hoped to establish it as the premiere film research institution in the country.[13]

McGaffey, a pillar in her field, continued working until her death in 1944. Having recognized a need in 1914, she assertively stepped forward to fill it. Her probing intelligence and visionary drive established the importance of research to all facets of filmmaking, giving the medium respect and admiration, then and now.

PUBLICITY

Magazine editor Delight Evans portrait, *Screenland* magazine, 1929. *Mary Mallory*

Delight Evans, First Fan Magazine Editor

CHARMING AND EFFERVESCENT, CORDELIA D. "DELIGHT" EVANS FELL in love with the movies and spent the rest of her life writing about it. She gained a reputation as one of the most important film reviewers and critics in the 1920s, becoming more famous as the youngest and only female editor of a fan magazine in 1926. Smart and down to earth, Evans delighted whomever she came in contact with.

Born in 1901 in Fort Wayne, Indiana, young Cordelia gained her nickname "Delight" at a very young age due to her high enthusiasm and energy. The precocious, curious child adored learning, spending her free time reading and watching movies, entranced by the dreamy, fresh medium. Evans later told *Screenland* magazine, after being named editor in 1929, "I'm a movie fan and always have been a movie fan. I know what we fans really want in the way of a magazine devoted to pictures. I know what I would like to see in a screen publication and I think I'm representative of the millions of movie-goers."[1]

A quick learner and overachiever, the young Evans frequently appeared in Fort Wayne newspapers for all her charity, educational, and service work, from good deeds at her church to outstanding work at school. Several reported how at the age of seven she began writing letters to successful novelists to learn their discipline and skills. By fifteen, she had been writing short stories and film reviews for several years, gaining fame around town for her dedication to the movies. She was also an eager fan and possessed a large collection of autographed photos from the many film personalities she wrote to.

Evans won a "Brains and Beauty" contest in *Photoplay* magazine, as reported in her local paper in 1915. Winners received the chance to make a screen test with New York–based World Film Corporation. Though she didn't get immediately discovered after her test, it whetted her ambition to work in the field she loved.[2]

Popular high school student Evans continued writing, gaining a regular outlet in the high school paper, *The Cauldron*, while also writing reviews and free verse, which she sent to *Photoplay* magazine, getting published multiple times in 1917.[3] One of the local papers reported that *Photoplay* had published the article "I Love Leading Men, Don't You?" and had run it in October 1917.[4] For her magazine article, Evans and her mother spent a week in Chicago in the middle of September touring film studios and interviewing stars like Douglas Fairbanks, as he made his way west for vacation.[5] Magazine articles in 1928 described how she began sending stories and verse to James Quirk at the magazine in 1916, with him inviting her to visit the office whenever in town, not realizing her young age.

For a few months she continued living in Fort Wayne and attending high school, but on December 1, Evans moved to Chicago to work at *Photoplay* as an assistant to Quirk. She would contribute her satiric free verse and other articles to both it and *Motion Picture Magazine*. The paper stated that "Miss Evans has an instinctively good choice of words and her language [is] fluent without being commonplace."[6] In fact, her breezy but astute comments would eventually lead her to both review and then later edit film magazines.

The young writer penned free verse with occasional features and interviews with such stars as Fairbanks, J. Warren Kerrigan, Mary McAllister, and others at the start, before beginning to write the column "Grand Crossing Impressions" in March 1918. She interviewed stars as they crossed the country and turning the interviews into effortless and easy verse.

Evans's pleasing smile, probing intelligence, and ebullient personality impressed all the stars who met her. Mary Pickford supposedly called her the "Delightful Delight Evans" in a spot-on pun. The Gish sisters considered her a friend. The mighty D. W. Griffith invited her to write titles, and her description of the novel *McTeague* led autocratic director Erich von Stroheim to purchase the novel and adapt it into the film *Greed*.[7]

Evans intuitively understood people and possessed a lyrical way with words, writing after an interview with Theda Bara in 1918, "She had a part to play that afternoon, and she played it much more cleverly than she played *Cleopatra*."[8] She pointed out Bara's cultivation of her special accent and how she played a part, even in publicizing a film, hiding the real Theodosia Goodman.[9]

The go-getter began branching out as well, writing occasional features with more artistic personalities such as actress Tsen Mei, travelogue producer Burton Holmes, novelist Elinor Glyn, Kay Laurell, actor Frank Borzage, director and actress Hugo and Mabel Ballin, and actress Hedda Hopper. She called Hopper "the worst cat on the screen" in a 1919 article.[10] By 1920, she wrote a new column named "West Is East" and composed more in-depth pieces and reviews. In one, Evans called Dorothy Gish "sort of a female Fairbanks who delights in performing facial gymnastics at the office."[11]

The ambitious Evans moved on to New York in 1923, writing short stories and reviews for the *New York Morning Telegraph* as well as joining *Screenland* magazine's editorial staff in October 1923. She wrote reviews and features geared to smart, young career women like herself. Her colorful, fresh analysis appealed to these modern readers. Delight wrote about Alma Rubens in that issue, calling the actress a "the little Irish girl from Frisco who looks like an Italian princess."[12]

Studios began quoting her in newspaper and magazine advertisements, realizing they indicated a stamp of quality approval to their largest audience: women. Evans became a gatekeeper of film information for independent young flappers.

Though driven, the young Evans found time to fall in love, marrying fellow film writer and publicist Herbert Crooker at New York's Little Church around the Corner on May 29, 1924. The two continually worked to better their skills and their positions throughout their careers, achieving fame without much travel to the West Coast. *Screenland* admired her work, writing that Evans "has so widely distributed laurel wreaths of praise and hurled javelins of criticism in her reviews that we are printing her picture—we are so proud of her."[13]

Thanks to popular work that increased circulation as well as advertising, the fan magazine appointed Evans head editor In December 1928, making her the first female and possibly also the youngest magazine editor in the United States at the time. They noted that *Variety* called her the "Flapper Editor." Outgoing editor Eliot Keen praised her "gentle criticism and infallible judgment, calling her modest, too self-effacing and willing to destroy work that others criticized.[14]

Evans explained her promotion this way: "I've grown up with the movies. I'm a Fan who got the breaks. . . . I know the 'low-down' and the 'high-hat.' And I'm going to pass on what I've learned about movies to you!" At the end she entreated her readers by stating, "Let's get together every month in *Screenland*."[15]

The new editor composed a monthly column highlighting important items in the industry and articles in the magazine besides her editorials, as well as giving pithy but potent reviews. Her way with words, talent, initiative, and industry promoted her to a leading position in the field of film criticism and journalism, with more than twenty stars sending telegrams praising her talents and promotion. She also discussed more progressive topics, expressing happiness at seeing more African American films made.

Her playful, chatty attitude continued at *Screenland*, with such titles and lines as "Every Lover Has His Line: They May Change Their Mamas but They Never Change Their Methods," "By his necking you shall know him," and "I Want to Be a Bad Girl." This fresh take on film attracted new readers, raising the magazine's readership and leading to a promotion for Evans as vice president in 1930.

The platform gave Evans an opportunity to promote films with social, cultural, and progressive issues as well as focusing attention on independent, successful women. Her strong female readership attracted the attention of studios, who liberally quoted from her in magazine and trade ads for their films. This position helped brand her as an industry leader and spokesperson.

Trying to spread her celebrity, Evans landed a radio show sponsored by the American Stove Company in March 1938 called *Food Secrets of the Hollywood Stars*. Reaching out to the female audience, Evans doled out film gossip while talking recipes and cooking with celebrities. The fifteen-minute show ran once a week in the morning for thirteen weeks beginning late April 1938, but it appears the show was never renewed.[16] Resigning as editor of *Screenland* in 1948, Evans stepped into the editorship of *Liberty Magazine* in 1949. The middle-aged woman could now enjoy life, after spending a large part of her life constantly on the job watching, reviewing, and talking about movies, leading the way for critics like Pauline Kael, Molly Haskell, Penelope Gilliatt, and Laura Mulvey.

Precocious, witty, and a go-getter, Evans rose quickly through the ranks writing about and reviewing films, achieving full editorship of a magazine while in her twenties. Her playful way with words attracted hip young women readers who pushed increasing female attendance at movie theaters, which rendered her one of the first entertainment influencers in print. Her joy for movies and skills in criticism increasingly brought women's values and voices into the mix in discussing and reviewing films and paved the way for other female reviewers.

Marion Jochimsen, First Studio Poster Artist

Key art was integral to the selling of motion pictures from its very beginnings. Copying circus art, pioneer companies hired lithographers to create eye-catching, colorful billboards and posters, later evolving into smaller forms of art like lobby cards and window cards advertising upcoming films. Companies like Miner Company, Morgan Lithograph Company, and ABC produced most of the first key art, before some local independent exhibitors hired designers to create advertising materials strictly for their own theaters. While women worked in conjunction with their husbands in designing posters for these local exhibitors, artist-painter Marion Jochimsen was the first woman working for a major film studio to be credited with drawing key art sold nationally to theaters across the country.

Born in Juneau, Alaska, July 4, 1894, to wealthy fur salesman and clothing manufacturer Louis Levy and his wife Leah, young Marion marched to the beat of her own drummer from a young age. The family returned to San Francisco before 1910, and gifted in art, Marion studied at the San Francisco Institute of Art and with Frank Van Sloan. She won awards in portraits and color drawing for the Saturday class at the California School of Design exhibit in 1910.[1] Stories painted her as vivacious, charming, and self-possessed, whether at art exhibits or society events.

Jochimsen continued winning awards over the next several years at various student shows for gouache and tempera (fast-drying) work that enveloped the whole canvas. Recognized for having grown up in Alaska and out of a growing respect for her talents, she and painter Maynard

Dixon contributed drawings to a book of songs from the Alaskan Native American Tlingit tribe published in San Francisco in 1915.[2]

In 1916 Jochimsen gained further acknowledgment of her budding professional reputation when the *San Francisco Examiner* depicted her and another student, posed in festive costume for the Fine Arts Ball, on the cover of the paper. She also earned critical praise later that year for exhibiting pastels as a newcomer in an exhibit of San Francisco artists at the Golden Gate Park Museum,[3] before going on to study art at the Academie Scandinave in Paris with Dufy.[4]

Jochimsen moved to Manhattan to pursue art, soon meeting former Danish master seaman Acton P. Jochimsen, a close friend of her father and sixteen years her senior. She married him August 31, 1918, and the couple lived on Central Park South. Renowned for having saved, in 1914, the starving captain Robert A. Bartlett and seven-member crew of the Canadian ship the *Kariuk* after it was crushed in ice and sank, Jochimsen was also respected as a sailing man from his days of whale, seal, and walrus hunting in the area; he earned fame for his "prowess in treacherous ice."[5] Jochimsen continued sailing materials back and forth from Seattle, Washington, to Alaska and other areas of the Arctic in the summers, while living with his wife in Manhattan.

While her husband plied the seas, Jochimsen focused on her portrait work. Somewhere in the mid-1920s, Fox Film Corporation discovered her bold, colorful paintings, hiring her as a designer for their New York commercial art department. With her long, delicate, quick strokes that evoked visceral western landscape painters Frederic Remington or Charles M. Russell, Jochimsen would create eye-catching designs for period or character-driven work for such outstanding visual directors as F. W. Murnau and Raoul Walsh, often receiving credit with her handwritten signature appearing on the corner of the key art. This makes her the first known woman to receive acknowledgment of her contribution to the artistic process in creating studio poster and lobby art.

Jochimsen appears to have first received credit for the 1926 Walsh-directed feature *What Price Glory?* starring Victor McLaglen and Edmund Lowe as a pair of World War I US Marine sergeants dealing with war in France and their fight over the innkeeper's

Sunrise (Fox, 1927) lobby card designed and signed by Marion Jochimsen. *Mike Hawks*

flirtatious daughter Charmaine (Dolores Del Rio), with Jochimsen's name prominently included on some of the film's lobby cards. Many of her designs would also be employed for theater programs, magazine ads, and other advertising material.

Jochimsen's greatest studio work promoted the first and only Academy Award–winning film for "Artistic Quality of Production": *Sunrise* (1927). Her ethereal, folk art–type designs evoked the modern folk fairy tale evidenced in German director Murnau's beautifully romantic though troubling film and art director Rochus Gliese's gently surreal sets. In 1929 Jochimsen followed up her poster art for Walsh's *What Price Glory?* when she created key art for his sequel, *The Cock-Eyed World*. She received her last-known credit for Walsh's epic western *The Big Trail* (1930), starring rising actor John Wayne. Her dramatically, powerful landscapes echoed, again, those of western masters Remington and Russell, with the artist once again given permission to acknowledge some of her wonderful works by signing them.

After her husband's unexpected death in 1931, Jochimsen dedicated herself to her watercolors. Leaving the studio, she began exhibiting in New York galleries like Ehrich-Newhouse, Inc., on Madison Avenue[6] and with the American Watercolor Society. The organization later acknowledged her as one of America's best gouache painters in landscape and portraits and accepted her as a member in 1943. Jochimsen also found time to teach students oil painting at City College of New York and later at the Pan American Art School.[7]

Living her life like the fictional character Auntie Mame, Jochimsen struck out fearlessly to seek out adventure and inspiration, living in such places as Copenhagen, Athens, Istanbul, Paris, Cairo, and Jerusalem.[8] The peripatetic artist also resided in Cuernavaca, Mexico, for several years, returning to watercolors to paint Mexican indigenous peoples and landscapes, before moving to Santa Fe, New Mexico, in 1958.[9]

Enchanted by New Mexico's arid deserts and mountains, Jochimsen focused on portraits before mixing in small sculpture and papier-mâché in the early 1960s. Restless, she resettled in Santa Cruz, California, in 1968, painting watercolors and pet portraits while devising bold landscaping outside her own home. Jochimsen died in 1996 at the age of 101 in Santa Cruz, actively creating until the end.

Independent and free thinking, Jochimsen set out to conquer new fields throughout her life. Her art demonstrated her fearless, feisty spirit, one looking to break boundaries and travel new roads. Jochimsen's poster and key art work for Fox opened the door for more women to walk through.

Woman's World

A Young Pioneer In a New Field For Women.

MISS BEULAH LIVINGSTONE.

Beulah Livingstone portrait from the column "A Woman's World," November 6, 1915, *Broad Ax.*

Beulah Livingstone, First Publicist

As MOVING PICTURE AUDIENCES SKYROCKETED IN THE 1910S DUE TO growing middle-class acceptance, studios looked to increase visibility and popularity of their films and stars. They increasingly turned to the new field of publicity to promote knowledge and interest in performers and upcoming movies, in a race to outdo one another. Beulah Livingstone, one of the first and most successful movie press agents, devised many practices and represented many of the top female stars as the first female publicist in the business.

In the first decade of the motion picture industry, small production companies copied publicity practices of the hugely popular circus field, creating dazzling eye-catching posters that they plastered around city areas to draw paying customers. These producing concerns soon employed striking illustrations and photographs in popular magazines and newspapers to reach larger audiences in the 1910s. At the same time, studios finally identified their stars by name as middle-class audiences attending movies exploded, leading to the inauguration of fan magazines and newspaper film sections for the first time, introducing the need for publicists.

The print media at this time increasingly required illustrations and information to fill their page counts, which were exploding due to paid advertising. In a quid pro quo arrangement, studios freely distributed photographic and graphic material to fill this need in exchange for credit. The film industry also inaugurated the production of information-laden pressbooks and kits stuffed with prepared background information, interviews, press releases, and even factoids for exhibitors to employ as publicity in print concerns themselves.

Moving picture stars intuitively grasped that huge popularity led to higher salaries, hiring publicists to promote upcoming shows, to plant factoids, and to land interviews in order to grow their celebrity. They turned to young entertainment professionals looking to make a mark in the newly popular field, like successful theatrical publicist Beulah Livingstone.

Beulah Livingstone Frank was born May 29, 1888, in New York City, and she attended college there before working as a kindergarten teacher on the Lower East Side, with children just learning English. First writing children's stories and then fictional work for the *New York Tribune,* Livingstone wrote plays and magazine stories like "How to Ice Cake"[1] before writing a series of newspaper stories for the *New York Sun,* conducting interviews with leading stage actresses under the title "Signed Dressing Room Chats with Well-Known Actresses" and byline "Matinee Girl."[2]

While vacationing in Europe and selling articles of her travel impressions, Livingstone met Sarah Bernhardt's leading man Lou Tellegen in Paris, and he hired Livingstone as his press representative for Bernhardt's Farewell Tour in New York. Livingstone opened a freelance publicity office upon returning to the city, quickly signing as clients prima ballerina Anna Pavlova, dancing husband and wife team Vernon and Irene Castle, and interior designer Elsie de Wolfe, among others.[3]

Personable and warm, Livingstone deftly worked a room selling a play, movie, or star without those around her realizing it. As she explained to the *Montgomery Advertiser,* "The success of a press agent depends on how cleverly he conceals the fact that he is a press agent. The story must be so skillfuly disguised that the public will not detect the fingerprints of the publicity man."[4]

Livingstone's sharp and industrious work saw her named the first female theatrical business manager in the United States, writing copy and advertisements, designing window cards and posters, budgeting, paying bills, and managing cast and crew for David Belasco in New York.[5]

Actor Granville Barker had first hired Livingstone in 1915 to negotiate his potential work in the film *Androcles and the Lion.*[6] Though the film fizzled, it sparked Livingstone's ambition for movie work. She joined with the wife of Parker Read, Thomas Ince's director, in 1916 to form the

Lillian Reed Child Players, Inc., intending to write and direct a series of films with *Civilization* toddler Lillian Reed and twenty-five other children a few months later, but funding fell short.[7]

Livingstone successfully ballyhooed Thomas Ince's mammoth anti-war picture *Civilization* that fall and found herself named head of Ince's New York publicity office. Multitasking her time, Livingstone also wrote the "Broadway in Brief" gossip column for *The Billboard* magazine in 1916, renamed the "Times Square Tattle" a few weeks later,[8] before organizing and publicizing the woman's picture *Birth* at New York's Eltinge Theatre with exclusive female-only screenings run by an all-woman staff.[9]

Press agent Livingstone turned exclusively to film work after she was hired as personal publicity director for acting diva Madame Olga Petrova's production company in 1917. Besides publicizing the actress's productions, Livingstone also arranged and publicized every aspect of a thirty-five-city, forty-stop tour across the United States in 1918 in which the star sold $487,000 in war stamps supporting the US World War I efforts.[10] She organized publicity for a few large independent film production premieres and served as eastern press representative for West Coast publicist Mabel Condon through 1918.

Livingstone's initiative, creativity, and connections impressed actress sisters Norma and Constance Talmadge. Norma hired her as general press representative for the Norma Talmadge Film Corp. in early 1919, then Constance Talmadge hired her as her Film Corp.'s press representative in May. *Wid's Daily* praised her as "the only woman in the publicity field to handle the press work of two big picture corporations."[11] Her experience and professionalism paid dividends in securing the sisters publicity in top media outlets, even better than that arranged by the publicists of the motion picture studios releasing the Talmadges' films. Livingstone's knowledge and success crowned her the doyenne of motion picture publicity.

Looking to help young women seeking employment in the working world, Livingstone crowed of opportunities and possibilities for success in movie publicity:

I think publicity is the coming game of women. I call it a "game" because it is a fascinating one. There are more possibilities in it than in newspaper work, and incidentally much more money. . . . In the old days when life was simpler and less strenuous, it was believed that so long as you had something of value to offer, the world would discover you; now, however, if you don't tell the world about it quickly and effectively, the man across the street, who has an effective town-crier, will have diverted public attention to his less worthy article, and you will be quite overlooked.[12]

Over the next eight years, Livingstone tirelessly worked promoting the Talmadges as well as their brother-in-law Buster Keaton. She toured Europe in 1921 setting up a foreign publicity office for the Talmadge Studios and then leading it once home.[13] Livingstone designed elaborate production stunts with publicity partners like department stores, sheet music companies, and makeup distributors for Talmadge films, some of the first of their kind in the business.

She continued her work when the sisters struck a producing deal with First National and when they began releasing through United Artists. Schenck elevated Livingstone to editorial director of the Reading Department in 1926 before naming her West Coast publicity director for Joseph M. Schenck Enterprises at United Artists in 1927, the only woman serving as a publicity director for a major studio.[14]

Once the Talmadges retired from filmmaking, Livingstone traveled the globe as publicity representative. She served a few years as Corinne Griffith's press agent before arranging American film premieres in London and later serving as *Variety*'s Paris gossip columnist for several years.[15] After working on the East Coast following her return from Europe, Livingstone traveled westward to serve as assistant to Paul Gulick, Universal Studios director of publicity, in 1936. She devised publicity hooks and unique stories for such titles as *Sutter's Gold* and *Show Boat*, one of the studio's largest prestige pictures in years, before heading feature publicity for two years.[16] She retired in the late 1940s.

Among the first people to arrange major movie cross-promotions with department stores and manufacturers and to design elaborate, over-the-top film premieres, Livingstone virtually created the position of film publicist. Thanks to her savvy and business smarts, publicity grew into one of the most important fields surrounding motion pictures, with women dominating the field even today.

Dorothy Hinton Maehl, First Still Photographer

PORTRAIT PHOTOGRAPHERS WERE INTEGRAL IN CREATING THE ICONIC image of film actors as movie stars. Renowned local photographers inaugurated portrait work for Hollywood films in the mid-1910s. They produced thousands of copies of each still to send to virtually every magazine and newspaper in the country in a quid pro quo arrangement, whereby the newspapers obtained free use of the photos as illustrations in exchange for merely crediting the studios.

When the Hollywood Studio System arose, studios created their own photo galleries in order to control advertising and iconography through the portraits shot by their talented photographers. Deftly employing light and shadow, these artists elegantly enhanced the beauty and personalities of the early actors, fashioning them into the stars the audience imagined them to be. Almost a decade before Ruth Harriet Louise rose to prominence as the lead portrait photographer at Metro-Goldwyn-Mayer, Dorothy Hinton Maehl served as the first Hollywood studio stills photographer.

Born in Denver, Colorado, November 29, 1883,[1] as Dorothy Isabel Smith, the young woman fell in love with the camera after marrying photographer James H. Hinton on June 25, 1903.[2] She began studying his work and assisting him with all the responsibilities of developing and finishing prints. After moving to Butte, Montana, in 1908, the couple established their own studio. Maehl mostly managed the studio and developed negatives while Hinton worked as photographer, both in the gallery and on location for special projects.

Juanita Hansen portrait for Strand-Mutual Studios 1919, where Dorothy Hinton Maehl served as head stills photographer and head of the darkroom. *Mary Mallory*

After Hinton's unexpected death during surgery in 1909,[3] Maehl struggled to pay bills while managing grief and raising three children. The young widow operated the studio for a short time before deciding to move across country to be near family in California in late 1910. Maehl purchased and abandoned two photographic studios in Sacramento and Woodside, California, before moving on to Los Angeles in 1912.[4]

While she lacked the money and prestige to attract top clients and open her own gallery in Los Angeles, Maehl's skills behind the scenes demonstrated versatility, initiative, and experience. Sometime after arriving in Los Angeles, she found employment at the Fred Hartsook Studio downtown, one of the most important photographic studios in Los Angeles and one branch of his six-studio California chain.[5] The determined woman processed, developed, and retouched the many portraits shot daily at the gallery, learning composition and artistry with each photograph she handled. During her daily routine finishing portraits in 1918, a print-drying machine exploded, igniting her clothes and causing serious burns on her body.[6]

Strong and resilient, Maehl persevered with the help of her husband Clyde, a grocer she married in 1915, returning to the photography business after a few months of recuperation. She combined her love of portraiture with her experience finishing and printing photos to lead both the stills photography and dark room divisions of two film companies, Christie Film Co., Inc., and Strand-Mutual Company, producers of comedies.[7] Showing leadership and self-confidence, Maehl became the first female photographer for any moving picture studio and also the first to supervise the all-male photography departments below her. Unfortunately, neither studio allowed name recognition for their stills photographers, so unfortunately Maehl received no official designation of her work in publicity materials.

Perhaps to be closer to their families, the Maehls returned to Sacramento in 1922, and Dorothy left Hollywood stills photography behind her. Clyde joined Southern Pacific Railroad, while Dorothy returned to photofinishing, working anonymously at a Kodak dealership until her death at the age of sixty-two in 1946. Like many of the early female pioneers, she toiled in obscurity for most of her days.

Studio Still Dept.

ANITA STEWART STUDIO
Chief Still Photographer — Hoppe Rahn.

BRUNTON STUDIO
Chief Still Photographer—J. E. Woodbury.
Dark room work by Mr. C. Graves.

CHAPLIN STUDIOS
Chief Still Photographer—Charles Levin.
Superintendent of Laboratory—Chas. Levin.

CHRISTIE STUDIOS
Still Photography and dark room work by Mrs. Maehl.

FRANCIS FORD STUDIO
Chief Still Photographer—Jerry Ashe.
Dark room work by Phil Ford.

FATTY ARBUCKLE STUDIO
Chief Still Photographer—Elgin Lessle.
Dark room work sent out.

FOX STUDIOS
Chief Still Photographer—Individual photography.
Dark room work done by Mr. Brown, Comedy; Mr. Hoffman, Drama.

FAIRBANKS STUDIOS
Chief Still Photographer—Charles Warrington.
Dark room work done under supervision of Charles Warrington.

GOLDWYN STUDIOS
Chief Still Photographers—Clarence S. Bull and Eugene Ritchie.
Dark room work done under supervision of Mr. Physioc.

GRIFFITH STUDIOS
Chief Still Photographer—Aaron Tyeko.
Dark room work by P. W. Sanders.

INCE STUDIOS
Chief Still Photographer—Carl Eadler.
Dark room work by A. Brandt.

JESSE B. HAMPTON STUDIO
Chief Still Photographer—Jimmy Dugan.
Dark room work done by Jimmy Dugan.

KATHERINE MACDONALD CORP.
Chief Still Photographer—Joe Brotherton.
Dark room work done outside of studio.

LASKY STUDIOS
Chief Still Photographer—Alvin Wyckoff.
Dark room work done by Al Palm.

LEW CODY PRODUCTIONS
Chief Still Photographer—J. A. Du Bray.
Dark room work done outside studio.

L-KO COMEDY CO.
Chief Still Photographer—June Estep.
Dark room work done by June Estep.

MARY PICKFORD CO.
Chief Still Photographer — Hoppe Rahn.
Dark room work done by Hoppe Rahn.

METRO STUDIOS
Chief Still Photographer—Mr. Clark.
Dark room work done by Tom Story.

MOROSCO STUDIOS
Chief Still Photographer—G. Post
Superintendent of dark room work—Frank Bigsy.

NATIONAL STUDIOS
Chief Still Photographer—Mr. Griffen.
Dark room work by Mrs. Corner.

ROLIN FILM COMPANY
Chief Still Photographer—J. C. Milliken.
Dark room work done outside.

RUTH ROLAND CO.
Chief Still Photographer—k. William O'Connell.
Dark room work done outside.

STRAND-MUTUAL CO.
Chief Still Photographer—Mrs. Dorothy Maehl.
Dark room work done by Mrs. Dorothy Maehl.

UNIVERSAL FILM CO.
Chief Still Photographer—Mr. L. L. Lancaster, Production; Mr. Beal, Publicity.
Dark room work done by Mr. L. L. Lancaster.

TOURNEUR FILM CO.
Chief Still Photographer—Rene Guissart.
Dark room work done under supervision of Mr. Physioc.

CAPITAL FILM CO.
Individual Photography.
Dark room work by Barney McGill.

VITAGRAPH STUDIOS
Chief Still Photographer—Individual photographers, supervised by Geigrich.
Dark room work done by J. L. Lippen.

DUG-OUT NOTES

On August 2 the Dug-Out will affiliate with the Woman's Press Club, the First Five-Hundred Club, and the Delta Rho Sorority in giving a ball for the Allied World War Veterans, at Kramers Academy.

The convalescent soldiers of the Crocker Street Hospital will be the special guests of the evening.

A few of the patronesses are Mrs. Josiah Evans Cowles, Mary Clough Watson, President of The Woman's Press Club of America; Dora Oliphant Coe, Vice-President; Bertha Lincoln Heustin and Mr. and Mrs. Charles Winsel, the Belgian consul and his wife. All the Allied consuls will assist.

Among the guests will be Meredith Woodsworth, Florence Porter Parks, Meriam Meredith, Mildred Richer, Edith Roberts and Neal Burns will give an exhibition dance.

MOTION PICTURE PATENTS

Apparatus for taking photographs for the stereoscopic projection of motion-pictures. Sidney N. Baruch, San Francisco, Cal. Filed August 9, 1918. Serial No. 249,102. 5 claims.

1. An apparatus for taking photographs for the stereoscopic projection of motion-pictures, comprising two adjacent reflecting prisms arranged to reflect images into a motion-picture camera, two spaced prisms arranged to reflect images to said reflecting prisms and means for moving said reflecting prisms to reflect images from either and both of said spaced prisms simultaneously into said camera.

5. A motion-picture film containing pictures of subjects alternating with pictures consisting of two partial views of the same subject taken from different view points.

Motion-Picture Apparatus. Samuel F. Stein, Williamsport, Pa. Filed July 17, 1918. Serial No. 245,283. 2 claims.

1. The combination of a picture projecting machine, a phonograph for producing sounds pertinent to the pictures projected from the projecting machine, a plurality of telephone receivers, seats with which the receivers are respectively associated for the individual use of seat occupants, and means for transmitting sounds from the phonograph to the receivers comprising a circuit acted upon by the phonograph with which circuit the telephone receivers are connected in parallel, the receivers bing detachable.

Moving-Picture Machine. James A. Cameron, Brooklyn, N. Y. Filed Jan. 3, 1916. Serial No. 69,731. Received Nov. 9, 1918. Serial No. 261,934. 3 claims.

1. The combination with the casing of a moving-picture machine, of a fire shield spaced a distance from said casing to provide a ventilating space between the shield and the casing, and a radiating shield interposed in said ventilating space, the said shields and casings having an alignment for the passage of light.

Dorothy Hinton Maehl credited as Christie Comedies and Strand-Mutual head stills photographer and in charge of the darkroom, August 16, 1919. *Camera! magazine*

Though unknown until recently, Hinton Maehl's portraiture work demonstrated that women could both create striking images, shaping a public image, while also finishing them in the lab, opening the opportunity for other women to succeed in Hollywood still photography.

BE NATURAL--DON'T LOOK AT CAMERA

Only Instructions New Movie Actress Is Given

J. WARREN KERRIGAN, "EXTRA GIRL" AND DIRECTOR JACCARD, AND PAY CARD

Film critic Gertrude Price posing with J. Warren Kerrigan on the set of *Smouldering Fires* (Universal Feature Play Manufacturing Co., 1915), from the January 20, 1915, *Los Angeles Evening Post-Record*

Gertrude Price, First Film Critic

For its first decade of existence, moving pictures were virtually ignored by the mainstream press. Seen as a novelty directed toward immigrants and the working class, movies only received major publicity after accidents, court cases, or other out-of-the-ordinary events. Growing acceptance by the middle class finally led newspapers to add movie reviews and departments as early as 1909, following the inauguration of the first fan magazine in 1910. Just two years later, assertive feature writer Gertrude M. Price became the first female movie reviewer when critiquing moving pictures for the Scripps-McRae newspaper chain and the Newspaper Enterprise Association.

Calling Price their "movie" expert after her hiring by the midlevel chain in October 1912, the *Chicago Day Book* praised her investigative and interviewing skills for her "personality sketches" of the stars, illustrated by movie stills and original sketches.[1] Besides her thoughtful features focusing largely on ethnic, children, and physical female performers, the daring young woman actively participated in the difficult and sometimes dangerous process of making motion pictures to accurately report on them. She eagerly joined the syndicate in November 1912 to educate growing female audiences on the industry, one that offered promise to industrious, ambitious young women.

Curious about the actual filmmaking process, the self-possessed Price embedded herself in Universal Pictures' western film *Smouldering Fires*, starring J. Warren Kerrigan, after she was hired as a movie extra. Price's report on her experiences ran a few days later, describing walking from present day into the historic past, understanding the expectations for extras, and performing a little rehearsal before hearing the word, "Picture":

> Out of 1915 civilization into a typical old-time frontier street, I walked
> in the space of three minutes, and with less than 50 steps. What a trans-
> formation. I found myself in a quaint, but rough-looking, street lined
> with little adobe houses. Indian baskets stood, carelessly, on deep win-
> dow sills. A dozen saddled, bridled horses champed and stamped at the
> wooden rail outside an honest-to-goodness looking saloon. . . . Right
> into the midst of this scene we walked. Everyone stopped and stared.
> Director Jaccard came up with his script. Kerrigan turned suddenly to
> me. And then and there I received my first and only instructions in
> "movie" acting. These were: "BE NATURAL. DON'T LOOK INTO
> THE CAMERA."[2]

Price intuitively understood that the new moving pictures industry offered a plethora of opportunities for young women looking to leave a mark on the world. Exploding in popularity, the business needed women to help produce movies to keep up with growing demand, as indepen-dent, educated females fought at the same time to be accepted as equals. Both needed each other.

She wrote, "The mental market place of the nations has been thrown open to the woman with wares to sell. Her originality and her perse-verance and her brains are coming to be recognized on the same plane as man's. And there's nowhere that you can find this hap-up [*sic*] new equality of originality and ability as in the wonderful field which the moving pictures has opened. The movie 'world' is the great new woman's field!"[3] In May 1915, the Los Angeles paper bragged of Price's work, calling her the "woman who has written more about the movies than any one in the United States."[4]

Appreciating Price's insightful and objective reporting, the *Los Ange-les Evening Post-Record* had hired her away from the Scripps organization in early 1914 to serve as a combination feature writer–film critic, though the syndicate would occasionally publish her work.[5] Price's warm, per-sonal style built rapport with readers looking for progressive changes and imagining hopeful new possibilities for the future, whether in moving pictures or in the business world. Price provided in-depth reviews and investigations of female issues, promoting women's opportunities in the workplace, living wages, and suffrage. In recognition of her laudatory work, the paper named Price editor of the daily page "Woman's Life—Here—There—Everywhere" later that month, further reducing her film work.

Taking on more responsibilities, Price also began writing an advice column under the name Cynthia Grey which advocated for justice issues like feeding the hungry and housing the homeless. She also penned daily stories about life and character issues, besides answering readers' questions in print or in personal letters sent their way. Once a week, Price even met in person with readers for three hours to hear their concerns on top of selecting local and national stories for the page.[6]

Price tried to open the eyes of her readers to how they themselves could better society, recognizing similarities with others rather than tearing them down, and working to bring change by demonstrating charity rather than just complaining. In a story demonstrating the similarities between rich and poor and those struggling with financial as well as personal issues, Price wrote, "Wealth and want, living and dying side by side in a crowded city, each desperate for the aid the other might have given; yet total strangers. There never was a time in the history of the world, perhaps, when the rich and the poor needed each other more. The rich can help the poor by aleviating [sic] their condition. The poor can help the RICH by giving them SOMETHING TO DO! Real happiness in this world must be earned."[7]

By the 1920s, Price turned her focus almost exclusively to women's issues, particularly those demonstrating growing political participation by women looking to improve and advance society. Assertive and proactive herself, Price personally called out her husband William H. Bradshaw for emotional and physical abuse when she divorced him in 1919 after four years of marriage, an example to female readers that they were of worth and deserved better treatment.[8]

In time, Price joined the Southern California Women's Press Club, working to raise the quality of writing in her field as well as to educate new entrants to journalism. *The Record* later promoted Price to editor of their "Club" page. Respected in newspaper circles, the *Los Angeles Daily News* hired her as their female editor in 1942, where she worked steadily until retiring in the 1950s.[9]

While only serving a few years as movie critic, Price's inquisitive mind and cogent thoughts educated as well as entertained readers about the wildly popular moving picture industry. Price's drive and excellent writing skills paved the way for many future female film critics to inform movie lovers on the changing industry and the many films it produced.

Producer Fanchon Royer portrait, circa 1932. *Margaret Herrick Library*

Fanchon Royer, First Trade Magazine Editor

In motion pictures' earliest decades, most public outreach and advertising occurred through magazines and newspapers, since virtually everyone in the United States read one or the other. Studios and actors employed fan magazines to reach average audiences enthralled with the movies, while they employed trade journals to reach theater owners and other entertainment professionals to assist them in selling product to the moviegoing public. One of the first trade journals introduced in 1907, *Moving Picture World* led the way for documenting technology changes, the introduction and rise of the star system, the transition from short films to features, and the evolution of independent production companies into massive film studios. As audiences and industry revenues exploded, so did journals.

In 1920 Fanchon Royer became the first woman to edit a trade magazine, shaping the industry outlook on attracting audiences to their films, before going on to practice her principles as an independent movie producer. Ambitious and driven, Royer demonstrated leadership talents that led her to succeed while always selling the movies in one form or another.

The daughter of self-made man Elwood Royer, Fanchon Royer was born in Des Moines, Iowa, January 21, 1902, a go-getter organizing and producing entertainment from a young age. In high school she organized an "aesthetic dancing" performance by two schoolmates, which "delighted the audience."[1] The headstrong and driven young woman immediately struck out for Hollywood in 1918 after graduating high school early, determined to be a star.

After a year attending the University of Southern California and of constant auditioning and begging for extra parts, she joined *Camera!* magazine as society editor in 1919, at the age of eighteen, at the urging of its publisher, her future husband Raymond Cannon. Rising quickly at the magazine, Royer was named assistant editor in early 1920, later rising to full-time managing editor in 1921.[2]

Unlike many of the other editors of trade magazines, Royer often focused on reporting and reviewing more esoteric and even ethnic productions. Perhaps for this reason, first-time producer-director James B. Leong purchased an ad promoting the premiere of his film, *Lotus Blossom*, the first Chinese American film produced and filmed in Hollywood, along with two small photographs of himself and actress Etta Lee in the November 26, 1921 issue.[3]

Royer's editorials, which often took a "pointed, snappy, and slightly sarcastic style,"[4] also confronted topics others ignored, including arguing against master showman Sid Grauman's overly long and lavish prologues before features, which often forced patrons to wait almost an hour, sometimes in the rain, for the actual start time of the film: "The famous Grauman showmanship standard is the greatest loser. Neither its popularity nor the public's good nature should be put to too tiresome a test."[5] She also examined odd and conflicting film censorship choices by neighboring cities. She described the work of most of the local censors thus: "He would seem to be inconsistent to the point of mental questionability, a strange combination of impurity and guilelessness of mind . . . his sentiment is often times both unpleasantly sticky and contradictory."[6]

Many readers wrote in praising her work, acknowledging how her honest columns often offered wise words on bettering film practices while also opening thoughtful dialogue regarding them within the industry. For example: "The fact that your editorials have been repeatedly reprinted by such standard and sterling journals as 'The Literary Digest' and magazines of that type prove your justification and sets the seal of merit upon the splendid work you have performed."[7]

After a few years of publication and ready to put their knowledge and thoughts about production into action, the Cannons joined with production company Protean Arts in 1922 to film one-reel novelties directed by

Cannon and written by Royer on current topics of the day.[8] Watching, asking questions, and learning on the job had inspired her to lean forward and ask for increasing responsibility. While nothing really came of the venture, it whetted her appetite to make more films.

Over the next few years, Royer employed her creative writing skills after Cannon sold *Camera!* She served as film critic at the *Story World and Photodramatist*, replacing future screenwriter Robert Sherwood.[9] After two years, Royer turned publicity and literary agent, turning out copy promoting her clients and keeping their names in front of the public. She was also elected secretary of the Women's Association of Screen Publicists in 1925, working to better women's participation and respect in the industry. While Royer pushed her own clientele, the savvy professional recognized star quality in many she met,[10] discovering new talent and guiding them toward fame. On the side, the industrious, energetic young woman composed screenplays.

Tired of agenting, Royer determined to enter independent production, convincing her husband to make their first feature film, *Life's Like That*, in 1928, off an idea she conceived while waiting for him for dinner at a restaurant. The film starred actors Wade Boteler and Grant Withers and was shot without a script, as actors ad-libbed comic action and a story as they went along. Royer obtained financing from the family's personal banker, who told her, "Miss Royer, I have watched you for years and feel that you can put this over. Go ahead and we'll back you."[11]

An early female version of Roger Corman, Royer entered independent production full-time in 1931 under the name Fanchon Royer Productions, understanding the filmmaking game and its machinations as well as anyone. She claimed she was answering women's clubs calls for more stories from a woman's angle.[12] A savvy risk-taker, she financed pictures with her own money, making "action epics with abbreviated budgets and shooting schedules," hiring young actors rising out of obscurity or stars descending the fame ladder, shooting a feature film in one to two weeks for less than $20,000.[13] Royer specialized in "he-man dramas" that crackled with action, melodrama, and energy,[14] the ones popular as the bottom part of double bills or as the lead in more rural theater locations.

Grace Kingsley of the *Los Angeles Times* called her "the only woman producer of pictures in the world."[15]

Over the next ten years, Royer produced her action-filled, sensationalistic pictures while mothering five children, learning to juggle projects as well as family activities. Her penny-pinching, speedy ways continually brought profits that she rolled over into new productions, aided by sometimes asking crew members to work double positions. In just two years, she produced ten pictures with such titles as *Cannonball Express* (1932), *Alimony Madness* (1933), and *Her Resale Value* (1933), both in English and Spanish, all of which received favorable reviews.

Royer completed seventeen features by 1938, with her last a fictional spoof exposé of seances and charlatans called *Religious Racketeers*. Royer's film inspired Harry Houdini's widow to combine with the filmmaker to produce an actual exposé of spiritualism called *The Mystic Circle Mystery*, released through states' rights in 1940.[16]

Originally an agnostic who considered religion hypocrisy, meetings to discuss spirituality with Catholic monsignor Edward R. Kirk at St. Basil's Church in Los Angeles led Royer to a dramatic conversion and the birth of a deeply felt Catholic faith.[17] Royer gave up producing Hollywood product to focus on creating nontheatrical inspirational and religious pictures particularly of Mexico and Central America. She produced travelogues for Pan American Airways as well as *Boys of Atitlán* in 1941 through Way of Life Films, revealing "native life in some of the small Indian villages of Guatemala."[18] Royer became a leader of the Catholic Film and Radio Guild in 1944; at the same time, she served as a producer for the Office of the Coordinator of Inter-American Affairs.

Royer blended her faith and love of Mexico by writing books and producing films in Central and South America highlighting a country's sights, praising religious leaders, and celebrating Catholicism for the rest of her life. In 1946 she wrote and directed the film the *Bell Ringer of Antigua*, shot in Guatemala, and in 1956 produced the color film *Day of Guadalupe*, which documented the formal ceremony celebrating Our Lady of Guadalupe in Mexico on her festal day, narrated by Mexican American actor José Crespo.[19]

The first woman to serve as editor of a Hollywood trade magazine, the multitalented Fanchon Royer also served as Hollywood's first female film producer in the 1930s, more than a decade after most were pushed out and Wall Street money turned film studios into international conglomerates. Disciplined and industrious, Royer succeeded both in creating Hollywood entertainment and spiritual and inspirational films, reaching audiences of all persuasions throughout her career.

EXECUTIVES

Agnes Egan Cobb, First Distribution Sales Executive

As THE MOVING PICTURE INDUSTRY BOOMED IN THE 1910S AFTER THE Motion Picture Trust Corporation dissolved and movie audience numbers exploded, salesmen sold a company's moving pictures to states' rights distributors looking to fill the country's movie theaters and trying to drive demand for a particular brand or studio. The liaison between producers and buyers, salespeople were truly the embodiment of a flourishing new field. During this same period, women themselves found the film industry a thriving location to chase dreams and move beyond administrative assistant jobs. At a time when men dominated the sales profession, Agnes Egan Cobb won fame as the first woman to serve as a distribution sales executive, leading the women for more female executives to come.

Born Agnes Egan, October 19, 1877, in Brooklyn, New York, to Irish immigrants, young Egan Cobb demonstrated initiative and ambition in bettering herself. She graduated from high school and attended Mount Holyoke Seminary for over two years before the unexpected death of her father forced her to seek work. Just three years after marrying William Hoffman in 1898 and giving birth to a daughter, Egan Cobb found herself a young widow after Hoffman died unexpectedly. She returned to the workforce, looking for a way to support her family. Eager for work, she joined the Cieneguita Copper Company as secretary to its president, getting the opportunity to live in Sonora, Mexico, for a time before returning to New York. Once back in the United States, she worked as a stenographer for the Fire Insurance Company.[1]

Recognizing the growing popularity of films and sensing an opportunity to get in on the ground floor, Egan moved quickly. *Motion Picture News* called her the "pioneer lady exchange proprietor" in a 1912 story, noting she opened and operated the Joselyn Exchange before selling her interest and joining P. A. Powers to help sell Buffalo Bill pictures for the Sales Company. She also assisted Frank Winch write the life stories of western celebrities Pawnee Bill and Buffalo Bill.[2]

Reliance president Adam Kessel Jr. then hired her as his assistant before he moved on to California just a few months later. Looking for a challenge, she served as secretary to Frederick A. Cook at the Morgan Lithograph Company, becoming the first woman to sell the striking lithographs to film companies.[3] Observant and a quick learner, Egan gained an intimate knowledge of the selling and marketing of films, which turned her into a sales professional.

B. F. Clements, head of the National Film Distributing Company, hired Cobb as his private secretary in 1911. Demonstrating her competence, she managed sales on top of her administrative duties, with *Motion Picture News* stating that "she traveled over 5,000 miles showing the National Program" as she promoted its product. R. Prieur of the Lux Company hired her as secretary for its Los Angeles office, through which she met Charles Lang Cobb Jr. and married him February 5, 1912. Cobb rose quickly, too, working for Edison and Vitagraph before helping organize the Associated Motion Picture Company, leaving in fall 1911 to organize the Consolidated Motion Picture Supplies Company. Not long after their marriage, Cobb became a traveling salesman for Reliance, with Egan Cobb succeeding him as general manager at the company.[4]

Egan found her passion in distribution, beginning a sales career buying and selling both foreign and domestic films, the only woman working in the field. In 1912 Egan Cobb gained recognition when she became sales agent and general office manager for Itala Film Company of America, with *Moving Picture World* praising her thus: "One of the best known young women in the film business . . . Miss Egan possesses several years' experience, a good personality and a vast acquaintance in the trade, which makes her a valuable asset."[5] Many stories praised her charming and outgoing personality, with the *Brooklyn Daily Eagle* in

1914 proclaiming her "a very charming little lady with a winsome smile, soft, pleasing voice, pretty eyes and a sense of humor that enables her to make the best of many vexatious situations."[6]

Ambitious to lead, Egan Cobb convinced her husband to found the Cobb Motion Picture Bureau in late May 1913 to serve as a feature film brokerage. While Cobb was president, he retained his position in charge of publicity and sales for Ramo Films, with Egan Cobb the actual active head of the self-named concern.[7] Due to her deep knowledge and experience, she also managed the office. A trade paper described the policies of the company as follows: "To buy and sell film; to procure and establish a market for new film; to place features on a territorial basis and to supply feature film manufacturers with a ready and substantial market."[8] Egan Cobb also managed sales and distribution for Union and Ideal features for the Eclair Parisian Office, acknowledged in trade stories as the "only woman sales manager."[9] In love with their work and each other, the couple traveled the country together selling their entertainment wares.

Unusual for her time, Egan Cobb admitted to the press she preferred the working world to housewife duties, acknowledging her ambitions and drive. In an interview, she saluted housewives and mothers while stating her own love of challenging work. Egan Cobb described a home as "what makes life worth while," but emphasized her abhorrence of housewifely duties. "I can cook things fit for a king to eat, but I despise the kitchen. I can sew, make clothes, do fancy work, anything a woman can do, but I would rather not. I do not enjoy it and it makes me nervous; but I do love to be in business solving its problems. With all my business ambition I am every inch a woman, and always hope to be."[10] She astutely acknowledged the permanence of the motion picture industry, thanks to Wall Street investment expanding the field.[11]

Egan Cobb's professional success and expert decisions drew business her way. By the summer of 1914, she also served as the general manager for Leading Players Corporation in New York, selling their films across the country while also handling publicity materials like posters, heralds, and the like. Thanks to her experience selling Eclair's foreign produced films, Egan Cobb gained additional European clients that fall, serving as selling agent in the United States for the London company Clarenden and the Swedish company Filmfabriken through Leading Players.[12] Egan Cobb and other distributors were now realizing both the entertainment and monetary value of purchasing rights to show foreign films in the American market, expanding revenues and drawing in new audiences.

In 1915 Egan Cobb took over management of the Egan Film Company, her brother Charles Egan's company, when he fell ill. The industrious agent dissolved her other companies to focus her attention on keeping the company afloat while also adding the selling of educational product to her list of accomplishments. *Motion Picture News* also proclaimed her the first person to serve as an "advisor" in the moving picture business, serving as what we would now call a consultant, offering advice on strategy, finance, and policies, which she had been offering free to friends for years.[13] After her brother's recovery, Egan Cobb joined Claridge Films, Inc., in 1916 as vice president and general manager, in charge of sales for its film productions.

Perhaps strain or a breakdown from too much work also overcame Egan Cobb in 1917, as trades announced her two-month recuperation at home for "nervous prostration."[14] Whatever happened during this time, whether physical or emotional, her life would never be the same, alternating between work and health issues. For two years Egan Cobb appears to have retreated from moving pictures, until a 1919 announcement of her appointment as sales manager for Schomer-Ross Productions on the states' rights market.[15]

Change came quickly for her over the next several years: short stops as sales manager at a variety of companies as well as possible separation from her husband, as they appear to take up different addresses. In 1922 Egan Cobb worked for a variety of companies as distributor and sales manager, ending the year by signing a deal to distribute two-reel animal shorts created by filmmaker Nell Shipman.[16] Just like Shipman, her career was winding down, sliding into obscurity after years at the top. Wall Street money and the changing industry pushed out veterans in favor of younger and male replacements.

Innovative and insightful, Agnes Egan Cobb introduced new practices to the field of distribution which last to this day, such as hiring expert consultants to plan and organize projects and events and thus save money. She challenged perceptions of women as salespeople, demonstrating great success as the industry's first woman sales executive, setting the stage for more.

Peggy Coleman, First Nurse

Making movies is often dangerous. Stunts go wrong, accidents happen, people get ill, and medical attention is required. In its early decades, the film industry skimped on safety procedures or left it to cast and crew to fend for themselves. In the late 1920s, studios began establishing a medical office to manage health issues. MGM hired experienced war nurse Peggy Coleman in the mid-1920s to provide medical assistance on the lot, thus making her the first official nurse to serve in the motion picture industry.

Metro Studios, Goldwyn Studios, and Louis B. Mayer Productions merged to form Metro-Goldwyn-Mayer Studios in 1924, creating one of the largest film conglomerates in the world. Realizing the value of their stars, they hired veteran nurse Coleman in 1925 to head their studio hospital and provide medical assistance to any who needed it. They chose well, hiring an experienced nurse who had graduated from college, provided emergency service to injured American troops during World War I, and served in a variety of roles in major hospitals.

Born in 1892, Coleman spent her life dreaming of serving others as a nurse. She graduated from Philadelphia's University of Pennsylvania before receiving additional training in surgery in New York City and working in some of the city's largest hospitals. Coleman enlisted in the American Expeditionary Forces after the United States entered World War I, and she received a commission for Field Hospital Service. As such, she served at the front, undergoing a poisonous gas attack.

After returning to the United States, Coleman worked for the Federal Immigration Service, where she helped examine anywhere from three thousand to six thousand immigrants per shift for any ailments or afflictions that might affect their acceptance for several years. She then worked at various hospitals across the country before arriving in California.[1]

Coleman was not only MGM's head nurse but she also served as the lead medical officer for the whole studio. Coleman often handled, on an average day, thirty-five to eighty-five patients sporting a variety of simple, miscellaneous injuries like cuts, bruises, and burns along with more serious ones that occurred during construction or while completing special effects or performing stunts. She sometimes managed flu or other epidemics, which required the use of masks when not on camera. She even provided treatment for serious injuries that occurred to Culver City residents immediately adjacent to the lot until a city ambulance arrived.

Her professional medical facility topped many small-town doctors' offices. The well-equipped studio hospital stood adjacent to Stage 18, at the north end of the MGM dressing rooms. Patients walked in to a spotless reception room lined with chairs and a desk holding the sign-in register at the front. A professional dispensary, treatment room, and up-to-date emergency room also completed the hospital.

Studio workers often approached Coleman to approve the authenticity of medical treatment depicted onscreen. She would often visit sets to place equipment properly and demonstrate the actual use and practice of equipment and supplies, while also occasionally offering quick lessons on working as a doctor or surgeon. She even occasionally went on location during the filming of dangerous sequences, in case of injury. Coleman was such an expert, that virtually everyone on the lot who suffered an injury was told, "You better see Peggy."[2]

Coleman learned patience and tact in dealing with MGM's major stars and executives, which wasn't always easy. Most appreciated the care and ministrations they received, but others, like Lionel Barrymore, resented the help or care provided to them. Many stars' reactions to their pain and care reflected their onscreen personas, as relayed by Coleman. "William Powell likes to joke and belittle anything that may be the matter with him. Joan Crawford doesn't like to take medicine and would rather 'wear out' a headache. We have to use persuasion."[3]

The nurse also relayed to the press some humorous moments surrounding her medical work on the lot. Frank Morgan woke one day after being desperately ill to hear Coleman call a Culver City undertaker, and he took a fright. She explained to him that any ambulances required by the studio were dispatched from the local funeral parlor. Ethel Barrymore refused treatment for an eye infection because she heard the nurse call Dr. Blind. Coleman told on herself as well, revealing that as she was being carried away to the hospital suffering from appendicitis, she opened her eyes to see John Barrymore standing beside her wearing a blue military coat, but no pants.[4]

Coleman retired from studio service in 1938 at the age of forty-six, after serious surgery the previous year. As war tensions rose and then exploded between Germany and future US allies Canada and England, she volunteered her nursing services once again, joining the Hospital and Medical Supply Division of the British War Relief Association in Los Angeles in 1941, serving as "sergeant in charge of supplies."[5] By that October, Coleman joined the Aerial Nurses Corps, nursing those seriously injured across the state who required immediate transfer by plane to a Los Angeles hospital.[6] She continued serving as a nurse through the end of World War II, before permanently retiring from service.

Medical personnel provided professional health care to studio employees for minor ailments and major injuries during the Classic Hollywood system and continue to do so to this day. Most studios during the Golden Age of Hollywood employed a man to head medical units, but glamorous MGM appointed experienced nurse Peggy Coleman to manage and provide all medical care for its staff for its first decade, thus making her the first official nurse in motion picture history.

Lillian Greenberger, First Business Manager

THROUGHOUT THE SILENT-FILM INDUSTRY, WOMEN TOOK AN ACTIVE part in production, gaining the most positions and power that women would occupy until now. Besides serving in administrative jobs, they served in creative behind-the-scenes positions, providing the labor and creative equity required to produce movies. As Alice Eyton wrote in an article titled "Unknown Women of the Films" in the March 1923 issue of the *Story World and the Photodramatist*, "These women belong to various departments of the moving picture industry, and their work therein—it is as important, just as creative, and sometimes, more self-developing than the work of the stars, writers, supervisors, and directors. . . . These silent workers form the real background of the profession."[1]

While women served in executive positions in writing and development, few served in actual business executive positions managing budgets, organizing assets, or investing money. In the late 1910s, Lillian Greenberger supervised the daily working of a studio as the industry's first female business manager, demonstrating that women possessed excellent skills in budgeting, maintaining buildings, and making deals.

Born in New York, May 14, 1891, Greenberger would attend high school through her freshman year before beginning to work. How she landed in Hollywood is unclear, but in 1916, Greenberger was serving as Eastern Representative for the L-KO Company, looking for and acquiring talent.[2] Obviously talented and intelligent, acclaimed director Lois Weber recognized her skills, hiring her as business manager for her independent Lois Weber Productions in 1917, when she organized her own private studio at 4350 Santa Monica Boulevard. At the time, Greenberger was the only female business manager in Hollywood.

Contributing what she could to the United States' war cause during World War I, Greenberger served as purchasing agent for the Committee on Women's War Work of the Women's Motion Picture War Service in 1918, finding products, negotiating prices, and purchasing equipment on behalf of the group.[3] In effect, she would serve in the same capacity as she did at the Weber Studio. That same year, Greenberger married Spencer Valentine, purchasing agent and later business manager for the Thomas Ince Studio.

Looking for further opportunity at a major studio, Greenberger departed the Weber Studio late in April 1919 to join Universal Film Manufacturing Company as casting directress,[4] at a time when women were coming to dominate the field. Her job of interviewing and hiring the casts of films turned her into one of the starmakers of the industry. At any one time, fifteen companies were often shooting, giving Greenberger trade publicity for her busy work. Perhaps looking to move into producing, Greenberger wrote a two-reel western melodrama called *A Voice in the Night*, which was purchased by the studio.[5] Later, she also wrote other works, including the 1921 *Adventures of Tarzan* serial, under her married name of Lillian Valentine.[6]

Recognizing her business acumen and sharp intellect, general manager Irving Thalberg hired her as his assistant in 1921. This position was not a secretarial one but one that relayed information to and from department heads and directors on the executive's behalf. Greenberger had achieved a feat few if any other women had by obtaining this position, one that often led to producing films or becoming a major executive at a studio.

For at least one year, Greenberger served in her position, only for trades to announce on April 4, 1922, that Julius Bernstein would replace her.[7] At that point, Greenberger's film career goes cold, at a time when multiple forces are ushering in foreboding practices for women that would soon force many of them from the industry. *Close Up* magazine published an uncredited story in its December 5, 1922, issue that indirectly commented on women being forgotten, noting that producers recognized Greenberger's "bright intellect and business acumen, especially her knowledge of vital statistics regarding moving pictures and its colony, yet here she is resting and squandering her valuable time, when she should be placed at the head of a department in which her talents could be utilized to great advantage by the producing company or unit. Why let her rest?"[8]

For the next several years, Greenberger remained a Beverly Hills housewife to husband Spencer Valentine. Finally, in 1926 she became head of Columbia's casting department, but it lasted only a short time. She was forced to resign and head to New York to care for her ailing mother.[9] At the same time, Greenberger began investing in a number of companies involved in the motion picture industry in a variety of ways, from agenting to exhibition, under her maiden name. She joined with colleagues William M. Brown and Sara Goldberg in 1928 to organize the William M. Brown & Company, Inc., in New York for $50,000, but not much appears to have happened with the concern.[10] Greenberger joined with Julius Rubin and Sara Goldberg in 1930 to fund Studio of Sister Arts, Inc., which would "offer ways to perform, singing, acting, dancing."[11] In 1936 she joined with Goldberg and Victor R. Volder to incorporate the Allied Artists Opera Company, but once again, nothing appears to have actually succeeded.[12] Her attempts at establishing her own business and becoming an executive never succeeded.

In the 1920s, much would change for women as the industry evolved into the motion picture factory system working in vertical integration, controlling production, distribution, and exhibition. As Wall Street money began flowing in to complete financial takeovers, studios began releasing women, with the formation of unions at the end of the decade forcing out many more. While Greenberger only served for a short time as studio business manager and assistant to Thalberg, she demonstrated that women possessed strong business and leadership skills for running a studio. She opened a door that other women would later walk through.

One advantage of being a youthful celebrity is that visiting grown-up celebrities take notice of you. The great Pavlowa does not think it beneath her dignity to give Jackie dancing lessons.

Victor Herbert teaching Jackie the rudiments of the 'cello. This internationally known director and composer was once solo 'cellist with the Metropolitan Opera Company.

Jackie Coogan and his tutor, Mrs. Kora Newell, who has taught many child stars of stage and screen.

Jackie enjoys some special coaching in chess from "Sammy", the famous little Polish wizard of the chess-board.

Teacher Kora Newell posing with her superstar pupil Jackie Coogan, *Visual Education,* 1923.

Kora Newell, First Studio Teacher

CHILD STARS GAINED EDUCATION OF ALL KINDS WORKING ON MOVIE sets, from the art of acting to the art of pleasing others. While working longer hours in harsher conditions than today's kid performers, they also received on-set tutoring from local teachers hired to coordinate their school education. Longtime teacher Kora Newell served as on-set teacher to child actors Wesley Barry and superstar Jackie Coogan in the early 1920s, making her the first known woman to serve in such a capacity.

Child labor laws in the early 1920s required that children in the acting field maintain the same pace of learning as those their own age attending public school.[1] Studios hired credentialed public school teachers to educate these young actors during setups, breaks, and downtime from filming. Besides their school training, these tutors required enormous patience and tact in managing the daily chaos of filmmaking, which occurred at all hours, in town or on location. Actress Constance Talmadge wrote in an article extolling opportunities for women in moving pictures that a preferable candidate should be a "more mature woman, whose nature has been mellowed by experience, and who is possessed of a motherly love of children."[2]

Kora Newell fit all requirements. Born Kora McKee in Syracuse, Nebraska, in 1872, she was a veteran teacher with experience working in Colorado, Nebraska, and California schools. Marrying Fred Newell in Buffalo, Nebraska, in 1898, she served as a music teacher and taught various grades in Colorado before the couple and their daughter returned to her native Nebraska. During 1913, she first served as a principal in Beatrice before splitting her time as a teacher and monitor of young children during playground activities after the family transferred to Lincoln during the summer.[3] After becoming a widow in 1917, Newell moved west to be near her young adult daughter and taught in Los Angeles public schools. Health issues soon required a step back from full-time education, and Newell searched out new possibilities. To ease her stress and workload, Newell turned to the moving picture industry to instruct the growing number of young child stars, like freckled Wesley Barry and eventual child superstar Jackie Coogan.

In 1922 Newell gained her greatest recognition as a movie teacher after the Coogan family hired her to serve as young Jackie's private tutor following the giant success of his appearance opposite Charlie Chaplin in *The Kid* (1921). The family breadwinner since the age of two, seven-year-old megastar Jackie possessed little actual education but a strong desire to learn. During setups or between scenes, Newell schooled Coogan in everything from penmanship to reading and what Constance Talmadge in a newspaper article called "refinement without undue prudishness," just as she had for Wesley Barry before him.[4]

Illustrated World called Newell "the most popular and certainly the most successful of the movie teachers," and noted, "Not only has she won the hearts of her talented pupils, but she has permitted her work to undergo examination by the authorities and has been given the highest commendation for the results she has obtained."[5] Other journalists even called her "the presiding goddess in the temple of 'Reading, Riting and Rithmetic.'"[6]

When Coogan toured Europe in 1924, Newell accompanied her young ward and his parents across the continent, a chaperone as well as teacher. As they visited such countries as England, France, Germany, Italy, Switzerland, and Greece, she provided instruction on etiquette, art, history, and geography, while also suggesting he keep a diary for personal growth and perhaps publicity use.[7]

Thanks to Coogan's huge celebrity as the most famous child star of the period, Newell enjoyed greater opportunities and publicity than other teachers during her time as his tutor. After Coogan began attending a real school, Newell spent less time instructing him, turning to work with other young movie children, like Priscilla Moran. Studios opened their own schoolhouses on the lot, further reducing hours for individual tutors like Newell, forcing her into housekeeping work on the side in order to pay bills. While finding little support after concluding her service as a child star tutor, Newell's leadership and example as Coogan's private teacher paved the way for movie children to receive steady and professional education throughout their performing careers.

Edna Williams, First International Distribution Sales Executive

IT WAS IN THE DECADE OF THE 1910S THAT THE GROWING POPULARITY of motion pictures saw the introduction of salespeople trying to promote and differentiate a company's product to states' rights distributors through all the swelling clutter. Traveling from office to office, they explained product, offered demonstrations, and provided supplemental information, trying to sell merchandise through sometimes aggressive tactics or persuasion and wily charm. Though very few women served as traveling salespeople in any profession at the time, the film industry provided more opportunities to serve in unusual positions like this. Taking a risk, Edna Williams saw a wide-open opportunity for someone with finesse and knowledge. Pioneering trailblazer Williams followed her ambitions and successfully sold American films to foreign distributors in Europe and Asia for over a decade, the first woman to hold such a position.

Born in St. Louis, Missouri, March 12, 1887, Williams moved to Los Angeles as a teenager in 1904 in order to live with her mother, Caroline "Carrie" Williams, and pursue a music career. She wrote verses and composed songs, becoming popular around the city and finally getting a hit. Thanks to that success, Williams and her mother spent a year in New York visiting sheet music publishers off Broadway, hoping to get her noticed and hired. Joseph W. Stern & Company, one of the largest Tin Pan Alley publishing concerns, signed her as one of their stable of writers.[1]

On January 2, 1909, *Billboard* described the talented and friendly Williams as "one of the brilliant feminine writers on the staff" of the company, "whose works bear the stamp of high genius." Besides composing, "she attends to the wants and secures the services of all the leading professional singers for the house."[2] Though Williams and a few other women composed songs for Stern & Company, very few operated in the heart of Tin Pan Alley at all, a competitive field dominated by assertive and loud men.

Over the next few years, Williams quickly turned out lyrics and sometimes music by herself or with a writing partner on novelty or wordplay songs, many of which became hits. Most of these were amusing, tongue-in-cheek songs with such titles as "If the Wind Had Only Blown the Other Way"; "Big Swamp Boogie-Man"; "Mr. Gollywood, Good-Night"; "I Looked Just Once and What I Saw Was Quite Enough for Me"; "Did You Advertise for Some Dreamy Eyes"; "I'd Like to Build a Fence around You"; "Don't Go Up in That Big Balloon, Dad"; "Mr. Editor, How Do You Know?"; "Let Me Have a Kiss until Tomorrow"; "Epidemic Rag"; "June Rose"; "You've Made a Home Run with Me"; "Subway Glide"; "Exceeding the Speed Limit"; "My Turkish Opal from Constantinople"; "Over the Great Divide"; "Maid of My Heart"; and "Old Erin, the Shamrock, and You."

Williams didn't merely pen songs on her own; sometimes she was commissioned to write tunes for vaudeville acts or even performers like stage star Carter De Haven. Thanks to all her hard work, she earned a promotion to head of the professional song department, working to keep talent happy as well as befriending and entertaining song pluggers who sold their tunes to bars, stages, musical acts, and anyone who required new and funny music. She was learning the game of salesmanship.

The Billboard reported on Williams's new position: "She has achieved the distinction of being the only, genuine, female business manager for a music publishing house." Even better, she succeeded in finding plagiarists and song stealers for litigation purposes as well as all necessary witnesses better than any detective. At the same time, the magazine perhaps employed coded language in its writeup to suggest her sexuality. The magazine noted her accomplishments by stating, "She is a GIRL. A girl? Yes, a girl! And a regular, all-round good fellow (we mean sweet, young lady), at that!"[3] Not only a pioneer in the songwriting field but in life as well, Williams broke boundaries by dressing in a more masculine style with tie and men's hat, along with shorter hair, "out" at least in dress.

The successful songwriter bucked trends by serving as the music industry's first female business manager, hunting down plagiarists and pirates, enforcing copyrights and trademarks, developing new business, and schmoozing potential new composers. Williams looked forward to applications of music for new technology rather than remaining stuck in old practices, while learning the importance of the courts.

Perhaps tired of the grinding business of churning out songs or looking for new challenges, Williams entered the booming motion picture field just a few years later. She began purchasing films for exhibition in Australia and South America, expanding their reach in the world. She became secretary of Bishop, Pessers and Lorimore, Inc., in 1916, which served as a foreign clearinghouse for selling American movies in Great Britain, Japan, and South America, continuing her successful sales work with Frank J. Seng and Frank G. Hall's U.S. Exhibitors Booking Corporation.[4] Williams gained so much experience by late December 1917 that Robertson-Cole hired her as a trade representative, to market American film territorial rights to foreign buyers for themselves as well as the US Exhibitors' Booking Corporation.[5]

Impressed with her talent, *Exhibitors Herald* devoted a half page to her in 1918, noting that "feminism is advancing in the motion picture industry," as she and many others moved into groundbreaking fields in that industry. The story demonstrated her farsightedness in growing new audiences and box office receipts. In just three months, Williams had expanded Robertson-Cole's business of distributing special film productions overseas, recognizing the importance of building relationships and landing deals by setting up offices in major international cities instead of conducting business by telephone and telegram. Heading the new division out of the Times Building in New York City, "this energetic young woman . . . directs virtually single-handed one of the largest enterprises now operating in the recognized American films' growing popularity around the world," predicting that even Russia would buy American product after the conclusion of World War I.[6]

Williams's efforts were so successful that Robertson-Cole moved into larger, elaborate headquarters at 1600 Broadway in the fall of 1918. The offices featured projection rooms as well as individual departments managing the sale, exploitation, and delivery of their films overseas. Entertainment trades and newspapers turned to Williams, a recognized expert and professional, for information and description of selling foreign rights to American films. She also employed her composing skills to help market Robertson-Cole films with the song "That Beloved Cheater of Mine," written in conjunction with L. Wolfe Gilbert for the movie *The Beloved Cheater*.[7]

Meeting with overwhelming success, Film Booking Office (FBO) stole Williams away from Robertson-Cole in 1922, allowing her to set up foreign distribution offices around the globe to sell their product. For six months of 1923, she toured the European continent and also made plans for establishing offices in Mexico City, Havana, and a few South American countries.[8] Over the next few years, Williams would spend months at a time visiting the outlying offices and drumming up purchases of the company's output as well as opening offices in Asia and Eastern Europe.[9]

After achieving all her goals and gaining enormous respect, Williams struck out on her own in 1926, establishing Ednella Export with her life partner, actress Nella Walker, handling foreign distribution of American films throughout the world. Besides running her New York office, she established other branches in London, Paris, and Berlin. Ads in *Moving Picture World* show that she also handled sales for such companies as Preferred Pictures, Gotham Productions, and William Fairbanks Productions, and stories also mentioned work for Columbia Pictures.[10] Virtually everyone considered her the top professional in the field.

Just a year and a half later, Williams closed Ednella Export. Perhaps tired of all the traveling and ready to settle down, Williams moved west to Los Angeles, making her relationship with vaudeville/stage actress Nella Walker permanent. Possibly a couple as early as 1926, when ship records show them returning from England together and then taking subsequent foreign trips, the women became a bona fide couple when Walker began landing film roles in Hollywood. The 1930 Census listed Williams as a guest with Walker, while the 1940 Census called her

Walker's lodger.[11] Both women are buried together at Forest Lawn, in Glendale, California.

Pushing boundaries and expectations, Williams demonstrated that women possessed the brains and assertiveness to make deals and sell movies, reaching new audiences in the process. Following her own beat and heart, Williams became the first female international distribution sales executive, drafting business plans and sales as deftly as she did lyrics.

ACKNOWLEDGMENTS

It took a virtual village to create this book. So many people contributed to the completion of it, whether they know it or not. I thank scholars and writers for their many insights in their books on early women in film, which pointed me to potential firsts as well as connections and references. Without many of them working over the last few decades to acknowledge the contributions of women to the motion picture industry over its early years, these women would be forgotten. The Columbia University's Women Film Pioneers Project, led by Jane Gaines, is a wonderful source for collecting the stories of female film pioneers and making them more visible to the public.

Thanks go to scholars like Richard Abel, Donald Crafton, Jane Gaines, Anthony Slide, Arthur Dong, Mindy Johnson, and others for all their work in acknowledging and expanding on the contributions and importance of early female film pioneers. Thanks go to Robert Israel, Rodney Sauer, Dwight Cleveland, Mike Hawks, Donna Hill, Dan Strebin, Vicki Callahan, Michael Blake, John Hillman, Angela Schneider, Eric Lynxwiler, and Marc Wanamaker of Bison Archives for all their help in completing the book.

The Margaret Herrick Library and its staff have been very helpful in locating photos, suggesting reference sources, and making photocopies. The library is a wonderful resource for film writers and scholars. The Media History Digital Library Project is an unbelievable free resource that offers greater access to vintage trade and fan magazines that help document more fully the little-known contributions and even existence of women during film's early decades.

Finally, thanks go to Eugene Brissie and Lyons Press for allowing me the pleasure of writing this book.

Notes

Introduction

1. "50 Odd Jobs for Invisible Stars of the Movies," *Courier Journal*, May 6, 1923, 90.

2. Ruth Clifford, *The Silent Feminists: America's First Women Directors* (London: Rowman & Littlefield, 1996), 42.

3. Robert Grau, "Women's Conquest in Filmdom," *Motion Picture Supplement*, September 1915, 41.

Tsuru Aoki, First Asian Star

1. "Round and Round the World: The Romance of Travel," *The Observer*, May 7, 1892, 5; "Want Their Scenery," *San Francisco Call and Post*, July 2, 1899, 18.

2. "A Star from Lotus Land," *Picture-Play Magazine*, May 1920, 54–55.

3. "Asiatic Invasion a Failure," *San Francisco Dramatic Review*, September 9, 1899, 3.

4. "Story of Tsuru Aoki," *Los Angeles Times*, March 13, 1919, 15.

5. Cari Beauchamp, *Without Lying Down: Frances Marion and the Powerful Women of Early Hollywood* (Berkeley: University of California Press, 1997), 31.

6. "2 Artists Guests at Tea," *Oxnard Daily Courier*, January 3, 1913, 5.

7. "Recital at Majestic by Egan Students," *Los Angeles Evening Express*, January 15, 1913, 23.

8. "Doings at Los Angeles," *Moving Picture World*, June 14, 1913, 11.

9. "New York Motion Picture Corp.," *Reel Life*, January 31, 1914, 3.

10. Ibid.

11. "Eleventh Knickerbocker Triangle Program," *Motion Picture News*, December 25, 1915, 119.

12. "Triangle Program at Knickerbocker Theater," *The Billboard*, December 18, 1915, 132.

13. "The Beckoning Flame," *El Paso Herald*, January 24, 1916, 17.

14. "A Star from Lotus Land," *Picture-Play Magazine*, May 1920, 54.

Theda Bara, First Vamp

1. "The Rising Tide," *Cincinnati Post*, November 19, 1891, 1.

2. "The Big Feast," *Cincinnati Post*, December 22, 1891, 5.

3. "Music," *Cincinnati Enquirer*, June 7, 1896, 27.

4. "Stage and the Movies," *Atchison Daily Globe*, January 8, 1916, 7.

5. "The Expressions of Theda Bara," *Picture Show*, March 19, 1921, 7.

6. "Theda Bara Is an American," *Birmingham News*, May 9, 1915, 26.

7. "Theda Bara Not a Real Vampire," *Daily Times*, August 7, 1915, 4.

8. "Stage and the Movies," *Atchison Daily Globe*, January 8, 1916, 7.

9. Delight Evans, "Does Theda Bara Believe Her Own Press Agent?," *Photoplay*, 1918.

10. "Theda Bara's Life Romance," *Movie Weekly*, December 31, 1921, 27.

CLARA BOW, FIRST SEX SYMBOL

1. "Fame and Fortune Contest" ad, *Motion Picture Magazine*, May 1921, 4.

2. David Stenn, *Runnin' Wild* (New York: Doubleday, 1988), 16.

3. Stenn, *Runnin' Wild*, 18.

4. Ibid., 25.

5. "The New Star," *Motion Picture Magazine*, January 1922, 55.

6. Stenn, *Runnin' Wild*, 37.

7. Clara Bow and Adela Rogers St. Johns, ed., "My Life, by Clara Bow," *Photoplay*, February, March, and April, 1928.

8. "Black Oxen at the Rialto Again Today," *Hamilton Evening Journal*, March 5, 1924, 11.

9. Alma Whitaker, "A Dangerous Little Devil Is Clara, Impish, Appealing, but Oh, How She Can Act," *Los Angeles Times*, September 7, 1924, 45.

10. David Gill and Kevin Brownlow, "Star Treatment," in *Hollywood: A Celebration of the American Silent Film* (London: Thames Television, March 25, 1980).

11. Adela Rogers St. Johns, "Clara Bow's Tempestuous Success," *American Weekly*, December 24, 1950, 6–7.

12. "The Shadow Stage: A Review of the New Picture Mantrap," *Photoplay*, August 26, 1926, 54.

13. Elisabeth Goldbeck, "The Real Clara Bow," *Motion Picture Classic*, September 1930, 108.

MARIE ELINE, FIRST CHILD STAR

1. "Thanhouser Kid" ad, *Daily Register*, October 1, 1913, 15.

2. "Marie Eline," *1931 Motion Picture Almanac*, 422.

3. "Thanhouser Kid at Empire," *Daily Register*, October 1, 1913, 9.

4. "Motion Picture Notes," *Burlington Daily News*, May 13, 1913, 6.

5. "David Copperfield," *Moving Picture News*, September 23, 1911, 23.

6. "The Judge's Story," *Moving Picture World*, August 19, 1911, 466.

7. *The Governor's Daughter* ad, *Great Falls Leader*, July 19, 1910, 5.

8. "From Our Western Correspondent," *Moving Picture News*, August 12, 1911, 17.

9. "Kid to Hold Reception," *The Journal*, June 9, 1913, 3.

10. "'Thanhouser Kid' No Longer," *Reel Life*, Mutual Film Corporation, December 6, 1913, 1.

11. "Tom's Cabin Is in the Movies Now," *Daily Oklahoman,* August 28, 1914, 12.

12. "The Thanhouser Kid at the Empress," *Des Moines Register*, May 9, 1915, 20.

13. "Two Excellent Acts on Piedmont Program," *News and Record*, June 4, 1915, 2.

14. "Clara's Latest Is Now at Indiana," *Indianapolis Times*, March 30, 1929, 8.

15. "Girl Show at Loew's Next Week," *Portsmouth Star*, October 2, 1929, 5.

MYRTLE GONZALEZ, FIRST HISPANIC STAR

1. "Spanish Dinner a Success," *Los Angeles Evening Post-Record*, September 30, 1898, 8.

2. "Big Mexican Holiday Will Be Celebrated," *Los Angeles Evening Post-Record*, September 13, 1905, 5.

3. "Booming Guns, Waving Flags," *Los Angeles Times*, April 1, 1906, 5.

4. "Beauty to Devote Her Life to Song," *Los Angeles Times*, September 15, 1907, 73.

5. "Passion Play to Be Impressive," *Los Angeles Herald*, February 4, 1910, 8.

6. Mary H. O'Connor, "Myrtle Gonzalez, of the Vitagraph Company," *Motion Picture Story Magazine*, 105–6; "Myrtle Gonzalez, Leads, Universal," *Motion Picture News*, January 29, 1916, 121.

7. "Missy," *Motion Picture News*, January 8, 1916, 105.

8. "Myrtle Gonzalez Dead," *Los Angeles Times*, October 23, 1918, 11.

9. "Myrtle Gonzalez to Ride in Flower Auto at Pasadena," *Motion Picture News*, January 8, 1916, 15.

10. "Myrtle Gonzalez Ill," *Motion Picture News*, October 14, 1916, 2372.

11. Ibid.

ELSIE JANIS, FIRST PERSON TO VISIT THE TROOPS

1. "Miss Elsie Janis," *New York Clipper*, February 20, 1904, 1249.

2. "Elsie Janis Opens in Vanderbilt Cup," *The Billboard*, August 11, 1906, 10.

3. David S. Shields, https://broadway.library.sc.edu/content/elsie-janis.html.

4. "Elsie Janis Makes Big Score in London's Palace Musical Revue," *Variety*, April 24, 1914, 4.

5. "Miss Janis to Sing in War Hospitals," *Boston Globe*, February 10, 1918, 41.

6. "Elsie Janis to Sing for Soldiers in France," *Morning Call*, April 2, 1918, 12.

7. "In the Service," *Variety*, May 10, 1918, 8.

8. Elsie Janis, *The Big Show: My Six Months with the American Expeditionary Force* (New York: Cosmopolitan Book Corporation, 1919), 81.

9. "Elsie Janis Sees Yankee Wounded," *Birmingham News*, June 16, 1918, 19.

10. Ibid.

11. "The 'Y' and the War," YMCA ad, *Moving Picture World,* September 2, 1918, 634.

12. "Playgirl of the Western Front Is Elsie Janis," *Los Angeles Express Tribune*, July 21, 1918, 6.

13. Ibid.

14. *Atlantic News Telegraph*, August 10, 1918, 10.

15. "In and Out of the Service," *Variety*, February 7, 1919, 8.

Evelyn Preer, First African American Star
1. "Evelyn Preer Dead, Was Most Famous Dramatic Actress," *Twin City Herald*, November 26, 1932, 1.
2. Frank J. Calvin, "Evelyn Preer Ranks First as Stage and Movie Star," *New Pittsburgh Courier*, April 16, 1927, 13.
3. Evelyn Preer, "Evelyn Preer Nearly Drowned in Realistic Movie Scene," *New Pittsburgh Courier*, June 11, 1927, 13.
4. "Reopening of the Avenue Theater," *Broad Ax*, February 1, 1923, 2.
5. "An Electric Salome," *Washington Times*, April 18, 1923, 24.
6. Harry S. McAlpin, "Footlights," *Washington Tribune*, January 27, 1928, 8.
7. Floyd J. Calvin, "Evelyn Preer Ranks First as Stage and Movie Star," *Pittsburgh Courier*, April 16, 1927, 13.
8. "Bancroft Pulls Capacity Business in Rialto Talkie," *Motion Picture News*, February 2, 1929, 364.

Lilian St. Cyr/Red Wing, First Native American Star
1. Angela Aleiss, *Hollywood's Native Americans: Stories of Identify and Resistance* (Santa Barbara, CA: Praeger, 2022), 8.
2. Ibid.
3. "Vitagraph Films: *Red Wing's Gratitude*," *Moving Picture World*, October 16, 1909, 545.
4. Aleiss, *Hollywood's Native Americans*, 8.
5. "Los Angeles Home of Three Film Concerns," *Moving Picture World*, February 19, 1910, 256.
6. "The Red Girl's Romance," *Moving Picture World*, January 22, 1910, 92.
7. Linda M. Waggoner, *Starring Princess Red Wing: The Incredible Career of Lilian St. Cyr, the First Native American Film Star* (Lincoln: University of Nebraska Press, 2019), 215.
8. "'Squaw Man' at the Lyric," *Star Tribune*, March 25, 1914, 12.
9. "Plays and Players," *Salt Lake Tribune*, March 8, 1914, 48.

Gloria Swanson, First Fashion Icon
1. Stephen Michael Shearer, *Gloria Swanson: The Ultimate Star* (New York: St. Martin's Press, 2015), 9.
2. Ibid., 13–14.
3. Lawrence J. Quirk, *The Films of Gloria Swanson* (Secaucus, NJ: Citadel, 1973).
4. Mack Sennett, *King of Comedy* (San Francisco: Mercury House, 1990), 171.
5. Shearer, *Gloria Swanson*, 30.
6. Larry Carr, *Four Fabulous Faces* (New York: Galahad, 1970), 42.
7. Jeanine Basinger, *Silent Stars* (New York: Alfred A. Knopf, 1999), 208–9.
8. Shearer, *Gloria Swanson*, 52.
9. Maurice Zolotow, *Billy Wilder in Hollywood* (New York: G. P. Putnam's Sons, 1977), 248–49.

Anna May Wong, First Chinese American Star

1. Shirley Jennifer Lim, *Anna May Wong: Performing the Modern* (Philadelphia: Temple University Press, 2019), 32.
2. Betty Willis, "Famous Oriental Stars Return to the Screen," *Motion Picture Magazine*, October 1931, 45.
3. Ibid.
4. Graham Russell Gao Hodges, *Anna May Wong: From Laundryman's Daughter to Hollywood Legend* (New York: Palgrave Macmillan, 2004), 23.
5. Willis, "Famous Oriental Stars," 44.
6. Lim, *Anna May Wong*, 25.
7. Hodges, *Anna May Wong*, 52.

Alice Guy-Blaché, First Filmmaker

1. Alice Guy-Blaché, *The Memoirs of Alice Guy Blaché*, ed. Anthony Slide (Metuchen, NJ: Scarecrow Press, 1986), 6–9.
2. Ibid., 10.
3. Ibid., 11.
4. Ibid., 14–16, 21–24.
5. Ibid., 32–33, 39.
6. "Madame Alice Blaché," *Moving Picture News*, June 17, 1911, 9.
7. "Solax to Have New Plant—Splendid Beginning of Monthly Special Releases," *Moving Picture News*, December 9, 1911, 16.
8. "The Violin Maker of Nuremberg," *Moving Picture World*, December 9, 1911, 800.
9. Guy-Blaché, *Memoirs*, 69.
10. Louis Reeves Harrison, "Studio Saunterings," *Moving Picture World*, June 15, 1912, 1007.
11. Alice Guy-Blaché, "Woman's Place in Photoplay Production," *Moving Picture World*, Cinematography special edition, July 4, 1914, 194.
12. Erven Malakaj and Laura L. S. Bauer, eds., "Alice Guy-Blaché," in *Hollywood Heroines: The Most Influential Women in Film History* (Santa Barbara, CA: Greenwood, 2018), 155.
13. "Madame Olga Petrova, A Remembrance," in Guy-Blaché, *Memoirs*, 101–2.

Zora Neale Hurston, First African American Filmmaker

1. "Prize-Winning Plays," *The Billboard*, May 16, 1925, 48.
2. Valerie Boyd, *Wrapped in Rainbow: The Life of Zora Neale Hurston* (Los Angeles: Scribner, 2003), 205–6.
3. Zora Neale Hurston, *Mules and Men* (Philadelphia: J. B. Lippincott, 1935), 65.
4. "Ambling about Amusement Artists," *Washington Tribune*, November 17, 1934, 34.
5. John Selby, "The Literary Guidepost," *Sandusky Register*, October 11, 1935, 4.
6. Franz Boas, preface to *Mules and Men* (Philadelphia: J. B. Lippincott, 1935).

Beatriz Michelena, First Hispanic Filmmaker

1. *Princess Chic* ad, *Waco Times-Herald*, November 7, 1902, 6.
2. "Beatriz Michelena, Noted Prima Donna, to Act for California Motion Picture Corporation," *Motion Picture News*, February 28, 1914, 38.
3. "Beatriz Michelena Will Sing at Mechanics' Fair," *San Francisco Examiner*, September 14, 1913, 20.
4. "Noted Singer in Vaudeville," *San Francsico Call*, October 8, 1912, 7.
5. "Beatriz Michelena Will Sing," 20.
6. "Moving Pictures for Today," *Quincy Journal*, November 11, 1914, 11.
7. "A Closeup of Beatriz Michelena," *Moving Picture World*, September 4, 1915, 1656.
8. Beatriz Michelena, "Talks with Screen-Struck Girls," *Jersey Observer and Jersey Journal*, June 3, 1916, 9.
9. Michelena, "Talks," 9.
10. "Silents Destroyed in Frisco Studio Fire," *Motion Picture Daily*, July 10, 1931, 2.
11. *The Flame of Hellgate* ad, *South Bend News-Times*, August 22, 1920, 5.
12. "Rialto Today," *Monett Weekly Times*, September 17, 1920, 2.

Mary Pickford, First Major Studio Founder, Actress-Producer

1. Christel Smith, "Father of the Family: Mary Pickford's Journey from Breadwinner to Businesswoman," in *Mary Pickford: Queen of the Movies* (Washington, DC: Library of Congress, 2012), 48.
2. "Burlesque," *The Billboard*, June 28, 1903, 4.
3. "Third Avenue Theatre," *New York Clipper*, March 21, 1903, 94.
4. Eileen Whitfield, "The Natural: Transitions in Mary Pickford's Acting from the Footlights to Her Greatest Role in Film," in *Mary Pickford: Queen of the Movies*, ed. Christel Schmidt (Washington, DC: Library of Congress, 2012), 9.
5. Christel Schmidt, "Crown of Glory: The Rise and Fall of the Mary Pickford Curls," in *Mary Pickford: Queen of the Movies*, 170.
6. Schmidt, "Father of the Family: Mary Pickford's Journey from Breadwinner to Businesswoman," in *Mary Pickford: Queen of the Movies*, 55–56.
7. Alison Trope, "Little Mary: Formidable Philanthropist," in Schmidt, ed., *Mary Pickford: Queen of the Movies*, 81, 83.

Marion E. Wong, First Chinese American Filmmaker

1. *Midnight Frisco* ad, *Stockton Evening and Sunday Record*, September 16, 1916, 6.
2. "Pretty Marion Wong Is Annexed by the Columbia Theater," *Oakland Tribune*, November 21, 1916.
3. "Columbia," *Oakland Enquirer*, November 18, 1916, 5.
4. "Chinese Girl Is Film Star in Her Own Drama," *Oakland Tribune*, July 22, 1917, 15.
5. Ibid.
6. Ibid.
7. Ibid.

8. Ibid.

9. Mara Math, "Marion Wong: Chinese Film Pioneer," 2, clipping from *The Curse* file at Margaret Herrick Library.

10. "The Curse of Quon Gwon," *Moving Picture World*, July 7, 1917, 113.

11. Math, "Marion Wong," 5.

MABEL NORMAND, FIRST COMEDY DIRECTOR

1. Mabel Normand, "Motion Picture Actresses Talk about Themselves," *New York World*, November 1, 1918, 18.

2. Steve Massa, *Slapstick Divas: The Women of Silent Media* (Albany, GA: BearManor Media, 2017), 32.

3. "Career in Pictures," *Los Angeles Times*, October 1, 1916, 45.

4. George D. Proctor, "It's an Interesting Life!" *Motion Picture News*, December 13, 1913, 17.

5. "Mabel Normand Seriously Ill," *Moving Picture World*, October 9, 1915, 274.

6. Massa, *Slapstick Divas*, 41.

LOIS WEBER, FIRST AMERICAN-BORN DIRECTOR-PRODUCER

1. "The Screen's First Woman Director," *Motion Picture Director*, January 1926, 62.

2. "For Non-Church-Going Men," *Yonkers Statesman*, November 8, 1900, 4.

3. "Religious and Charitable," *Pittsburgh Press*, April 9, 1902, 9.

4. Elizabeth Peltret, "On the Lot with Lois Weber," *Photoplay*, October 1917, 89.

5. "Screen's First Woman Director," 62.

6. "Grand Opera House," *Morning Journal-Courier*, January 11, 1904, 7.

7. "Two Clever Favorites," *Moving Picture News*, October 12, 1912, 12.

8. Alice Guy-Blaché, *The Memoirs of Alice Guy Blaché*, ed. Anthony Slide (Metuchen, NJ: Scarecrow Press, Inc., 1986), 73.

9. Jennifer A. Zale and Laura L. S. Bauer, eds., "Lois Weber," in *Hollywood Heroines: The Most Influential Woman in Film History* (Santa Barbara, CA: Greenwood, 2019).

10. "Lois Weber—Mrs. Phillips Smalley," *Universal Weekly*, October 4, 1913.

11. Peltret, "On the Lot with Lois Weber," 89.

12. Ibid.

13. Elizabeth McGaffey, "The Hollywood Studio Club," *Photoplay*, September 1917, 85.

GENE GAUNTIER, FIRST SCREENWRITER

1. "In Society," *Kansas City Times*, June 4, 1899, 10.

2. "The Opera at Fairmont," *Kansas City Star*, June 25, 1898, 10.

3. "Some People of the Stage," *Kansas City Star*, January 7, 1905, 45.

4. Gene Gaunter, "Blazing the Trail," *Woman's Home Companion*, October 1928, 1.

5. Ibid., 183.

6. Ibid.

7. Ibid., 184.

8. Frederick James Smith, "Unwept, Unhonored, and Unfilmed," *Photoplay*, October 1924, 67, 106.

9. "Gene Gauntier, Movie Pioneer, Writes a Novel," *Kansas City Star*, September 25, 1929, 14.

NELLIE BLY BAKER, FIRST PROJECTIONIST

1. "O'Brien-Baker," *Modern Light*, March 30, 1916, 7; Todd Watkins, "Taboose," *Mono Herald and Bridgeport Chronicle-Union*, June 3, 1976, 2.

2. "Miss Baker Wins Scenario Contest," *Tulsa World*, February 28, 1915, 1.

3. "Gather at Topeka," *Columbus Daily Advocate*, January 25, 1916, 1.

4. Watkins, "Taboose," 2.

5. "Woman Gets License," *Los Angeles Times*, October 3, 1918, 17.

6. Ibid.

7. "First Girl Operator in L.A.," *Moving Picture World*, October 26, 1918, 498.

8. Grace Kingsley, "The Women Lend a Hand," *Picture-Play Magazine*, March 1919, 79–80.

9. "Green Room Jottings," *Motion Picture Magazine*, January 1919, 94.

10. "Chaplin's Clerk Grasps Career," *Washington Times*, March 31, 1924, 22.

11. Watkins, "Taboose," 2.

12. "The Hollywood Boulevardier Chats," *Motion Picture Classic*, June 1924, 64.

13. "Chaplin Aide in Talmadge Film," *Camera!* December 29, 1923, 21.

14. "Chaplin's Clerk Grasps Career," *Washington Times*, March 31, 1924, 22.

15. "Our Reporter's Notebook," *Motion Picture Magazine*, July 1924, 84.

16. *Standard Casting Directory*, February–June 1925, 155.

17. "Metropolitan-Breakfast at Sunrise," *Evening Star*, October 23, 1927, 3.

KATHERINE RUSSELL BLEECKER, FIRST DOCUMENTARIAN

1. "She Will Be Social Secretary of the Nation," *Buffalo Times*, August 28, 1931, 17.

2. "Society Acts for 'Movies,'" *Kansas City Times*, April 9, 1915, 7.

3. "Fair Author and Some Characters in Unique 'Movie,'" *Pittsburgh Post-Gazette*, August 29, 1915, 22.

4. "Amateur Movies—A New Form of Entertainment," *Hartford Courant*, April 18, 1915, 25.

5. "Great Pittsburg [*sic*] Press Movie Is Being Made," *Pittsburgh Press*, August 15, 1916, 1.

6. "Local People to Appear in Movies," *Asbury Park Press*, October 18, 1915, 1.

7. "She Will Be Social Secretary of the Nation," 17.

8. "Prison Moving Pictures Taken by a Girl," *New York Times Magazine*, November 21, 1915, 65.

9. "Rosenberg Leaves," *Variety*, December 28, 1917, 256; "These Women Pioneers Find Men's Shoes Just Fit Them!" *Press and Sun-Bulletin*, January 3, 1918, 9.

10. "Emily Post—Social Advice by Wire Will Be Latest," *Cincinnati Post*, August 20, 1931, 17.

11. "New York Woman to Solve Social Problems of Nations," *Evening Courier*, August 29, 1931, 6.

12. Walter Winchell, "On Broadway," *Scranton Republican*, November 12, 1932, 5.

13. "Finds Money in Manners," *Star Weekly*, November 20, 1937, 44.

14. "Social Registerite to Talk," *South Bend Tribune*, May 30, 1938, 9.

HELEN GIBSON, FIRST STUNTPERSON

1. "Clever Press Agent," *Dayton Herald*, April 27, 1910, 5.

2. Larry Telles, *Helen Gibson: Silent Serial Queen* (Hayden, ID: Bitterroot Mountain, LLC, 2013), 2.

3. "101 Ranch Show Today," *St. Louis Republic*, April 16, 1910, 5.

4. Michael Wallis, *The Real Wild West* (New York: St. Martin's Griffin, 1998), 362; Mike Kornick, "In Very Early Days," *Films in Review*, January 1968, 28.

5. "Cupid Ropes Ed 'Hoot' Gibson," *East Oregonian*, September 8, 1913, 1.

6. Kornick, "In Very Early Days," 29–30; Shirley Freitas, "The Two Helen's: Action Women in Films," Bitterroot Mountain Publishing, Inc., June 2011, 4.

7. "Kalem Has a New 'Helen,'" Kalem Kalendar, September 1915, 16.

8. Kornick, "In Very Early Days," 31.

9. Ibid., 31–32.

10. Ibid., 34.

11. Frances Miles, "The Story of a Stunt Girl," *Silver Screen*, July 1938, 31.

WINIFRED LAURANCE, FIRST ASSISTANT DIRECTOR

1. "Girl of Many Nations Works in Hollywood," *Butte Standard*, October 18, 1931, 122.

2. "The Film Shop: Intimate Glimpses behind the Silver Screen," *Tyrone Daily Herald*, 5.

3. "Around the Movies," *Kingston Daily Gleaner*, September 25, 1926, 28.

4. "Girl of Many Nations," 122.

5. "Enter the First Woman Assistant Director," *Hollywood Filmograph*, April 5, 1930, 7.

6. "Sights, Sounds in Hollywood," *Daily Herald*, July 23, 1936, 3.

7. "Studio Scraps," *Detroit Free Press*, November 6, 1938, 15.

8. Louella Parsons, "Garbo's Maid Spills Dope on Marital Plans," *San Antonio Light*, February 11, 1938, 12.

9. "Films to Be Seen," *Beaudesert Times*, January 23, 1948, 6.

10. "British-Russian-American in WAACS," *Lowell Sun*, May 22, 1943, 36.

VIOLA LAWRENCE, FIRST EDITOR

1. "Forthcoming," *Anaconda Standard*, September 28, 1919, 21.

2. "Women Are Creating a New Field and Succeeding as Film Editors," *Omaha Bee*, May 1, 1919, 11.

3. "The Feminine Film Editor," *Indianapolis Star*, May 11, 1919, 58.

4. "Behind the Films: Woman's Part in Film-Making," *Picture Show*, June 28, 1919, 25.

5. "Film Editor's Job Is Like a Surgeon's," *Valley Times*, July 5, 1946, 18.

6. "Star Says Women Should Stay in Front of Camera," *Los Angeles Times*, April 28, 1943, 19.

7. *"Only Angels Have Wings," The Movies . . . and the People Who Make Them* (New Haven, CT: Theatre Patrons, Inc., 1939), 213.

8. Harold Hefferman, "Film Cutters Last Long in Hollywood," *Baltimore Evening Sun*, October 4, 1960, 15.

9. Viola Lawrence letter to Karol Reisz, November 22, 1949, Viola Lawrence Collection, Pollak Library, Special Collections, California State University Fullerton.

NELL SHIPMAN, FIRST ANIMAL TRAINER

1. "Paul Gilmore Secures New Target for His Oscillatory Broadsides," *Evening Statesman*, March 6, 1907, 1.

2. "'The Barrier,' Rex Beach's Great Play," *Daily Capitol Journal*, January 7, 1911, 2.

3. "Strange 'Co-incidents' in Scenario Contest," *Moving Picture World*, November 30, 1912, 870.

4. "Nell Shipman, Photoplaywright," *The Bioscope*, January 23, 1913, iv.

5. "Notes from All Over," *Motography*, November 27, 1915, 1154.

6. "God's Country and the Woman," *Moving Picture World*, May 6, 1916, 985.

7. "Two Episode Story with Bad Spots Helped by Players," *Wid's*, September 28, 1916, 999.

8. Nell Shipman, in *The Silent Screen and My Talking Heart*, ed. Barry Shipman (Boise, ID: Boise State University, 1988), i.

9. "Barees Aid to Red Cross Movie Dogs Do Their Bit," *Dayton Forum*, September 6, 1918, 1.

10. Joseph and Juanita Walker, "Danger in God's Country," *American Cinematographer*, May 1985, 38.

11. "Nell Shipman Heads New Company," *Moving Picture World*, September 4, 1920, 89.

12. "Shipman Films Go through Selznick," *Exhibitors Herald*, July 19, 1924, 39.

13. "Don't Be Chinese Women!" *Camera!* October 15, 1921, 20.

JULIA HERON, FIRST SET DECORATOR

1. 1910 US Census.

2. "A Truly Big Task," *Paramount Pep*, June 26, 1922, 12.

3. "Pathé DeMille Studios Listing," *Film Daily Year Book 1928*, 411.

4. "Gush over 'It' Girl," *Los Angeles Evening Post-Record*, November 14, 1930, 15.

5. *Secrets* Pressbook, United Artists, 1933, 22.

6. "Inside Hollywood News and Gossip," *Movie Mirror*, January 1935, 77.

7. Lowell E. Redelings, "The Hollywood Scene," *Hollywood Citizen-News*, November 13, 1950, 13.

8. Howard Barnes, "Bits of Perfection," *Silver Screen*, November 1937, 22, 76.

9. "Relief Fund Dedicates New Hollywood Country House," *Motion Picture Herald*, October 2, 1942, 32.

10. "Film Furniture Styles Displayed," *Los Angeles Times*, October 16, 1941, 30.

11. Kay Campbell, "Julie Heron's Rules for Amateurs," *American Home*, April 1946, Julia Heron clipping file, Margaret Herrick Library, Academy of Motion Picture Arts and Sciences.

ELSA LOPEZ, FIRST ART DIRECTOR

1. Frances L. Garside, "Elsa Lopez Makes Movies Look Right," *El Paso Herald*, September 30, 1920, 6; "Introducing Miss Elsa Lopez, Triangle Research Director," *Motion Picture News*, March 3, 1917, 1408.

2. "Introducing Miss Elsa Lopez," 1408.

3. "Newslets for Your Program," *Motography*, November 27, 1917, 1103.

4. "Edwards Stages Venetian Scene," *Moving Picture World*, December 1, 1917, 1311.

5. "Louise Glaum, Noted Star, Being Filmed in Desert Scenes," *Oxnard Courier*, December 3, 1918, 1.

6. "Random Reels," *Des Moines Register*, February 2, 1919, 21.

7. Garside, "Elsa Lopez Makes Movies Look Right," 6.

8. Ibid.

9. "Norma Talmadge in *The New Moon*," *Anaconda Standard*, May 18, 1919, 24.

10. "Big Scenes Being Made at Bennett Studio for 'Mysteries of Paris,'" *Exhibitors Herald,* August 26, 1922, 77.

11. Open market ad, *Motion Picture News*, July 8, 1922, 154.

12. *Fair Lady* ad, *Motion Picture News*, August 22, 1922, 985.

13. "Vaudeville Placements," *The Billboard*, May 9, 1923, 17.

CLARE WEST, FIRST COSTUME DESIGNER

1. Madame Theres Lavoisier, "The Latest Fashions in Moving Pictures," *Motion Picture Magazine*, July 1915, 117.

2. "Fairy Godmothering Fairy-ellas," *Buffalo Courier Express*, October 31, 1920, 35.

3. Louise Williams, "A Painter in Fabrics," *Picture Play*, February 1920, 43.

4. "Andalusia Airings," *Rock Island Argus*, April 26, 1899, 4.

5. "Sifted from the Studios," *Motography*, March 11, 1916, 600.

6. Williams, "Painter in Fabrics," 43.

7. "Madame West in Charge of Costume Department," *Motion Picture News*, March 11, 1916, 1471.

8. Williams, "Painter in Fabrics," 43.

9. "Plan for Stanley Opening," *Motion Picture News*, January 29, 1921, 1047.

10. Williams, "Painter in Fabrics," 43; "Up the Wooden Stairs," *Buffalo Courier Express*, June 12, 1921, 29.

11. "Fads and Fancies," *Daily Nonpareil*, November 26, 1921, 5.

12. Drake Stutesman, "Clare West," in *Women Film Pioneers Project*, ed. Jane Gaines, Radha Vatsal, and Monica Dall'Asta (New York: Columbia University Libraries, 2013).

13. "Dress Genius Gauges Changes of Fashion to Keep Movies 'Young,'" *South Bend News-Times*, December 18, 1921, 24.

14. "The Movies May Save Short Skirts," *Times Herald*, December 3, 1922, 49.
15. "Costume Designer Signed for Talmadges," *Motion Picture News*, September 15, 1923, 1309.
16. "Gown Window Showed Original Sketches," *Exhibitors Trade Review*, August 16, 1924, 74.
17. "Los Angeles," *Variety*, December 9, 1925, 56.

MARGARET WHISTLER, FIRST PROPERTY MASTER
1. "Margaret Whistler," *Motion Picture*, October 21, 1916, 240.
2. "Margaret Whistler," 240.
3. "Film Flickers," *York Gazette*, August 15, 1916, 3.
4. "Vitagraph Reception Keeps Them Talking," *Motion Picture News*, September 26, 1918, 7; Grace Kingsley, "The Women Lend a Hand," *Picture Play*, March 1919, 78–79.
5. Kingsley, "Women Lend a Hand," 78.
6. "The Queen of Sheba," *Camera!* October 15, 1921, 17.
7. "One of Betty Blythe's Gowns Cost $6,200," *Los Angeles Evening Express*, September 28, 1921, 27.
8. "Wardrobe of Wondrous Beauty," *Moving Picture World*, August 7, 1920, 753.
9. Fine Arts Studios ad, *Camera!* April 15, 1922, 17.
10. Cinema Mercantile Company ad, *Camera!* July 15, 1922, 2.
11. "Troupers Entertain at Dinner, Program," *Hollywood Evening Citizen News*, June 19, 1933, 5.

LILLIAN ROSINE, FIRST MAKEUP ARTIST
1. Jack Jungmeyer, "Old or Young, Ruddy, Pale, Fat or Thin, Miss Rosini Can Make You That Way," *Freeport Journal-Standard*, May 11, 1926, 5; Jerry Asher, "A Maker of Faces," *Film Weekly*, October 3, 1931, 10.
2. Jack Jungmeyer, "Beauty Builders Make Up Pretty Faces for Camera," *Canton Daily News*, May 9, 1926, 49.
3. Ibid.
4. "The Screen Test at Hollywood and How It Felt—and Looked," *St. Louis Post-Dispatch*, October 31, 1928, 41.
5. "Monte Carlo Next Week," *Santa Rosa Republican*, August 23, 1926, 9.
6. "The Girls behind the Stars," *Screenland*, May 1930, 120.
7. Jack Jungmeyer, "Beauty Builders Make Up Pretty Faces for Camera," 49.
8. "A Maker of Faces," *Film Weekly*, October 8, 1931, 10.
9. "Ladies Only," *Talking Screen*, July 1930, 38.
10. "Through the Looking Glass," *Chicago Tribune*, July 4, 1935, 11.
11. "Tomorrow," *Hollywood Citizen News*, September 27, 1938, 16.
12. "Metro-Goldwyn-Mayer Listing, Studio Personnel," *1936 Film Daily Year Book of Motion Pictures*, 712.
13. Pat Nation, "Linger," *Los Angeles Times*, February 10, 1978, 159.

Hattie Wilson Tabourne, First Hairdresser

1. 1890 US Census.

2. "Mrs. Hattie Wilson Tabourne, Madame Hattie Wilson Tabourne," *California Eagle*, December 19, 1915, 1.

3. Ibid.

4. "Gorgeous Head Dresses of Film Stars Created by Art of Negro Woman," *Los Angeles Times*, April 26, 1925, 39.

5. Ibid.

6. "Abrams Plans to Sign Big Stars as Contracts Expire," *Exhibitors Herald*, April 18, 1925, 30.

7. "Madam Hattie Tabourne Laid to Rest," *California Eagle*, April 10, 1925, 1.

8. "Bobbed Hair Proves Too Much for Movie Star's Hairdresser," *Pasadena Post*, May 21, 1925, 9.

9. "She Hated Bobbed Hair," *Los Angeles Times*, April 26, 1925, 39.

10. Harrison Carroll, "Gorgeous Head Dresses of Film Stars Created by Art of Negro Woman," *Los Angeles Times*, April 26, 1925, 39.

11. "Hollywood Worker Leaves $25,000," *Afro American*, April 11, 1925, 5.

12. Ibid.; "Filmland's Popular Hairdresser Dies Following an Operation," *The Monitor*, April 10, 1925, 1.

Edith Lang, First Composer-Accompanist

1. "The Oracle," *Transcript-Telegram*, February 3, 1920, 12.

2. "Reviews of Latest Musical Compositions," *Motion Picture News*, May 5, 1920, 4056.

3. Edith Lang and George West, *Musical Accompaniment of Moving Pictures* (Boston: Boston Music Co., 1920), 1.

4. "Books: News and Reviews," *The Billboard*, June 19, 1920, 9.

5. "Music for Pictures," *Daily Telegraph*, June 26, 1920, 4.

6. "Motion Picture Music Notes," *The Billboard*, March 5, 1923, 31.

7. Edith Lang, "Out Or In?," *The Billboard*, May 23, 1925, 30.

8. Charles D. Isaacson, "Sense of Humor Essential to Movie-Musical Success," *Motion Picture News*, May 18, 1921, 3304.

9. "Organ Recital for Women Players," *Boston Globe*, January 4, 1927, 11.

10. Ibid.

Helena Smith Dayton, First Stop-Motion Animator

1. *Cartoons Magazine* ad, *Oak Leaves*, March 25, 1916, 44.

2. "Helena Smith Dayton Caricatures Real Art and Makes New Toys for Grownup Friends," *New York Sun*, June 21, 1914, 43.

3. "Woman's Place," *New York Tribune*, December 17, 1916, 114.

4. "Woman Trails the Laughs Walking the Streets of City with Lump of Clay for Notebook," *New York Sun*, June 21, 1914, 43.

5. Ibid.

6. Ibid.

7. "Statues That Dance, Act, Jump, and Fight," *Brooklyn Daily Eagle*, January 21, 1917, 61.

8. Ibid.

9. "Written on the Screen," *New York Times*, March 18, 1917, 92.

10. *Motography*, March 17, 1917, 562.

11. "Helena Smith Dayton, Sculptress," *The Billboard*, March 10, 1917, 58.

12. "'Split Reel' Notes for Theater Men," *Motography*, April 7, 1917, 718.

13. "Another 'Romeo and Juliet,'" *Moving Picture World*, September 22, 1917, 1845.

14. "Prominent Sculptor in Film," *Moving Picture World*, November 24, 1917, 1164.

15. "Argus Pictorial, December 16, Shows Five Subjects," *Motion Picture News*, December 22, 1917, 4378.

16. 1918 US Passport, Helena Smith Dayton.

17. *"New York in Seven Days*, Helena Dayton," *New York Tribune*, November 15, 1925, 74.

BESSIE MAY KELLEY, FIRST ANIMATOR

1. Jonaki Mehta, "Her Work as a Pioneering Animator Was Lost to History—Until Now," NPR, December 24, 2022.

2. Ibid.

3. "Special Thanksgiving Attractions, with Picture, at Auditorium," *Brattleboro Reformer,* November 25, 1925, 4; "Stage Near Set for Chautauqua Wednesday," *Reading Times*, June 13, 1927, 10; "Animated Cartoonist to Explain Her Art," *Daily Local News*, July 20, 1927, 2.

4. Mehta, "Her Work as a Pioneering Animator."

5. "Bessie May Kelley Tells of Her Work," *Portland Press Herald*, May 12, 1931, 6.

6. "Special Thanksgiving," 4.

7. "New Members of Woman's Club Are Reception Guests," *Fitchburg Sentinel,* January 20, 1927, 2.

8. Chautauqua ad, *Putnam Patriot*, July 1, 1927, 6.

9. "Chautauqua Assn. Comes into Being," *New Britain Daily Herald*, July 11, 1927, 2.

10. "Randolph," *Barre Daily Times*, December 15, 1928, 6.

11. "Entertainment Course, 1927–1928," *United Opinion*, February 30, 1927, 1.

M. J. WINKLER, FIRST ANIMATION DISTRIBUTOR

1. "Distributor as a Woman Proves Surprise," *Exhibitors Herald,* December 30, 1922, 90.

2. 1920 US Federal Census.

3. "Distributor as a Woman Proves Surprise," 90.

4. Leonard Maltin, *Of Mice and Magic: A History of American Animated Cartoons* (New York: Penguin Books, 1987), 22–23.

5. "Woman in Film Business," *Kentucky Post*, April 23, 1924, 14.

6. Mindy Johnson, *Ink & Paint: The Women of Walt Disney's Animation* (Glendale, CA: Disney Editions, 2017), 40.

7. "Margaret Winkler: First Female Film Distributor," *Disney Family Museum Blog*, March 3, 2023.

8. "The Life of the Program, a Feature in One Reel," *Film Daily*, May 11, 1924, 28.

9. "Margaret Winkler: First Female Film Distributor."

10. "Incorporations," *Film Daily*, November 8, 1923, 2.

11. Ibid.

IRIS BARRY, FIRST ARCHIVIST

1. Robert Sitton, *Lady in the Dark: Iris Barry and the Art of Film* (New York: Columbia University Press, 2014), 11.

2. Tony Slide, Iris Barry letter to Slide, *Silent Pictures* 26, no. 6 (Spring 1970): 16.

3. Michael Binder, *A Light Affliction: A History of Film Preservation and Restoration*, Lulu.com, 2014, 23.

4. Ibid.

5. "The Pictures," *Manchester Guardian*, January 20, 1927, 7.

6. Slide, Iris Barry letter, 16.

7. Iris Barry, "The Motion Picture," in *Art in America in Modern Times*, ed. Holger Cahill and Alfred Barr Jr. (New York: Reynal & Hitchcock, 1934), 91–93.

8. "The Screen Acquires a Family Tree," *New York Times*, June 30, 1935, X3.

9. Sitton, *Lady in the Dark*, 245.

ELIZABETH MCGAFFEY, FIRST REFERENCE LIBRARIAN

1. H. G. Percey, "Problems of a Motion Picture Research Library," *Journal of the Society of Motion Picture Engineers* 26, no. 3 (March 1936): 253.

2. Ibid.

3. "The F.P.-Lasky Studio," *Motion Picture News*, June 8, 1918, 3450.

4. "Additions Made at the Hollywood Studios," *Motion Picture News*, February 14, 1920, 1687.

5. "Money Drive Starts," *Camera!* March 10, 1923, 10.

6. "Great Bible Being Used for Data in DeMille Film," *The Journal*, May 19, 1923, 1.

7. "Research Department Head Signed by Cecil B. DeMille," *Moving Picture World*, May 9, 1923, 225.

8. "*The King of Kings* Half Complete," *Motion Picture News*, November 6, 1926, 1758e.

9. Dorothea Hawley Cartwright, "Their Business Is Looking Up," *Talking Screen*, July 1930, 66.

10. "Screen Oddities," *Washington, D.C. Evening Star*, June 4, 1932, A-11.

11. Ruth Tildesley, "What? Why? When? Where? How?" *Screenland*, July 1933, 28.

12. "The Smartest Gals in Hollywood," *Washington, D.C. Evening Star*, October 28, 1931, 4.

13. "Advisory Library Board Appointed by Academy," *Motion Picture Herald*, September 21, 1940, 27.

Delight Evans, First Fan Magazine Editor

1. "Let's Talk about You!" *Screenland*, November 1929, 112.
2. "Miss Evans Enters Contest," *Fort Wayne Daily News*, November 23, 1915, 4.
3. "A Local High School Student Enters *Photoplay* 'Brains and Beauty' Contest," *Fort Wayne Daily News*, November 26, 1915, 1.
4. "Society," *Fort Wayne Weekly Sentinel*, September 8, 1917, 3.
5. "Society," *Fort Wayne Daily News*, September 17, 1917, 8.
6. "Society," *Fort Wayne Sentinel*, November 27, 1917, 6.
7. "Hoosier Girl in Early Twenties Edits Magazine," *Muncie Evening Press*, December 5, 1928, 1.
8. Delight Evans, "Does Theda Bara Believe Her Own Press Agent?" *Photoplay*, May 1918, 62–63.
9. Ibid.
10. Delight Evans, "Learn about Vampires from Her," *Photoplay*, November 1919, 58.
11. Delight Evans, "Seriously Speaking," *Photoplay*, 57.
12. Delight Evans, "Mia Rubens' Gal," *Screenland*, December 1923, 51.
13. "Delight Evans' Reviews," *Screenland*, December 1927, 42.
14. Eliot Klein, "She's a Friend of Yours!" *Screenland*, December 1928, 15, 79.
15. Delight Evans editorial, *Screenland*, January 1929, 14.
16. "American Stove Series Presents Movie Editor," *Radio Daily*, March 2, 1938, 1.

Marion Jochimsen, First Studio Poster Artist

1. "Pupils Show Work at Art Institute," *San Francisco Call and Post*, May 14, 1910, 5.
2. "SHI-YE DU-SHI," *San Francisco Bulletin*, August 28, 1915, 10.
3. "Museum Art Exhibit Is Extremely Popular," *San Francisco Chronicle*, February 13, 1916, 29.
4. "Santa Fe Will Substitute If Mexico Gets Difficult," *Santa Fe New Mexican*, February 22, 1959, 23.
5. "Famous Arctic Ice Pilot Passes Away," *Sun Journal*, January 9, 1931, 10.
6. Ehrich-Newhouse, Inc., ad, *Brooklyn Daily Eagle*, April 28, 1935, 33.
7. "Santa Fe Will Substitute If Mexico Gets Difficult," *Santa Fe New Mexican*, February 22, 1959, 23.
8. "Pet Portraits Her Pet Project," *Santa Cruz Sentinel*, December 9, 1973, 19.
9. "Santa Fe Will Substitute If Mexico Gets Difficult," 23.

Beulah Livingstone, First Publicist

1. Scottie McKenzie Frazier, "Beulah Livingstone, a Southern Girl, Tells the Secrets of the Press Agent," *Montgomery Advertiser*, September 12, 1915, 19.
2. Constance Talmadge, "Opportunities for Women in Motion Pictures: VI: Publicity Writer," *Brownsville Herald*, May 38, 1922, 6; "Beulah Livingstone Promoted," *Moving Picture World*, April 17, 1926, 489.
3. Frazier, "Beulah Livingstone, a Southern Girl," 19.
4. Ibid.

5. "Woman's World: A Young Pioneer in a New Field for Women," *Broad Ax*, November 6, 1915, 6.
6. "Willing to Negotiate," *The Billboard*, November 15, 1915, 54.
7. "Ince Signs Baby Star," *Motography*, September 2, 1916, 554.
8. "Broadway in Brief," *The Billboard*, September 9, 1916, 10.
9. "Flashes from Cinema and Footlights," *The Sun*, April 15, 1917, 6.
10. "See What Beulah Landed," *Moving Picture World*, September 7, 1918, 1420.
11. "Beulah Livingstone Promoted," *Wid's Daily*, May 7, 1919, 2.
12. Constance Talmadge, "Opportunities for Women," 6.
13. "Livingstone to Go Abroad," *New York Tribune*, May 15, 1921, 77.
14. "Girl Publicity Chief," *Exhibitors Daily Review*, May 20, 1927, 1.
15. "Paris," *Variety*, March 21, 1933, 52.
16. E. de S. Melcher, "Bogart Joins Ranks of Screen's Tough Guys, *Evening Star*, February 14, 1936, C6.

DOROTHY HINTON MAEHL, FIRST STILL PHOTOGRAPHER

1. California death record.
2. Smith-Hinton 1903 marriage certificate, Denver, Colorado.
3. "Don't Want to Pay Him," *Anaconda Standard*, July 24, 1909, 4.
4. "Studio Closed, Artist Is Gone," *Sacramento Bee*, April 7, 1911, 5; "Photographess Leaves without Settling Claims," *Woodland Daily Democrat*, March 15, 1912, 1.
5. 1913 Los Angeles *City Directory*, 920.
6. "Treated for Burns," *Los Angeles Evening Express*, June 12, 1918, 10.
7. "Studio Still Dept.," *Camera!* July 20, 1919, 14.

GERTRUDE PRICE, FIRST FILM CRITIC

1. "The Movies," *Day Book*, November 11, 1912, 11.
2. Gertrude M. Price, "Be Natural—Don't Look at the Camera," *Los Angeles Evening Post-Record*, January 20, 1915, 1, 8.
3. "Movie World Offers Great New Field for Women Workers," *Sacramento Star*, April 14, 1914, 2.
4. Newspaper ad, *Los Angeles Evening Post-Record*, May 28, 1915, 1.
5. "200,000 Women to Cast First Vote in Chicago," *Los Angeles Evening Post-Record*, February 9, 1914, 5.
6. "Cynthia Grey and Everyone's Page," *Los Angeles Evening Post-Record*, January 1, 1913, 5.
7. "The Parallel," *Los Angeles Evening Post-Record*, December 9, 1914, 3.
8. "Divorces Man Who Tore Up Dress," *Los Angeles Evening Post-Record*, December 5, 1919, 7.
9. "The Catholic Women's Club Increases Red Cross Work," *Los Angeles Daily News*, January 1, 1942, 10.

Fanchon Royer, First Trade Magazine Editor
1. "The Dancers," *Des Moines 1917 High School Year Book.*
2. Masthead, *Camera!* October 22, 1921, 1.
3. *Lotus Blossom* ad and photographs, *Camera!* November 26, 1921, 4–5, 15.
4. "Letter to the Editor," *Camera!* March 18, 1922, 18.
5. "Degree of Showmanship," *Camera!* December 24, 1921, 3.
6. "The Censors Differentiate," *Camera!* December 3, 1921, 3.
7. "Don Marq Hix, Letter to the Editor," *Camera!* June 4, 1921, 3.
8. "Film Capital Production Notes," *Camera!* August 19, 1922, 4.
9. Blurb, *Camera!* June 16, 1923, 13.
10. "The Girl Producer," *Screenland*, 1933, 101.
11. "The Girl Producer," 101.
12. "Woman Enters Cinema Field," *Los Angeles Times*, October 8, 1931, 29.
13. "Two Score Success as Movie Producers," *Waterbury Democrat*, September 8, 1933, 14.
14. "People in the Films," *New York Times*, May 15, 1938, 151.
15. Grace Kingsley, "Ten Films, Four Babies to Woman Producer's Credit," *Los Angeles Times*, February 5, 1933, A1.
16. "Get Houdini Film," *Boxoffice*, March 16, 1940, 65.
17. Fanchon Royer, http://www.catholicauthors.com/royer.html.
18. "*Boys of Atitlán* listing," *Home Movies*, October 1941, 480.
19. "Day of Guadalupe," *1956–1957 Film Incorporated Catalog*, 72.

Agnes Egan Cobb, First Distribution Sales Executive
1. "Brooklynite Occupies Unique Post in Motion Picture Business Circles," *Brooklyn Daily Eagle*, July 19, 1914, 16.
2. "Wedding Bells," *Motion Picture News*, February 17, 1912, 31.
3. Ibid.
4. Ibid.
5. "Flickers," *Moving Picture World*, September 28, 1912, 1283.
6. "Brooklynite Occupies Unique Post in Motion Picture Business Fields," *Brooklyn Eagle*, July 19, 1914, 16.
7. "Cobb Joins Reliance," *Moving Picture World*, April 28, 1912, 218; "The Cobb Motion Picture Bureau," *Motography*, May 31, 1913, 413.
8. "Cobb Motion Picture Bureau," *Motion Picture News*, June 7, 1913, 10.
9. "A Successful Woman Sales Manager," *Moving Picture World*, December 20, 1913, 1414.
10. "Mrs. Cobb Favors Sensible Censorship," *Motion Picture News*, August 8, 1914, 65.
11. Ibid.
12. "Live News of the Field," *Motion Picture News*, July 11, 1914, 85.
13. "Resigns from Position," *Motography*, February 20, 1915, 270; "Mrs. Cobb Creates New Profession in Filmdom," *Motion Picture News*, May 29, 1915, 37.
14. "Mrs. Cobb Recuperating," *The Billboard*, January 27, 1917, 66.

15. "Agnes Cobb Made Sales Head for Schomer-Ross," *Moving Picture World*, December 20, 1919, 946.

16. "New Series Coming," *Film Daily*, December 18, 1922, 2.

PEGGY COLEMAN, FIRST NURSE

1. "Better See Peggy," *Motion Picture Studio Insider,* May 1936, 19.

2. Ibid., 58.

3. Robbin Coons, "When It Comes to Pain . . . Nurse's Secrets," *News-Pilot*, January 2, 1936, 6.

4. "Studio Nurse," *Photoplay*, April 1938, 70.

5. "Appointments Made," *The Los Angeles Times*, March 23, 1941, 22.

6. "In and About the Bay District," *West Los Angeles Independent*, October 3, 1941, 8.

LILLIAN GREENBERGER, FIRST BUSINESS MANAGER

1. Alice Eyton, "'Unknown Women' of the Films," *Story World and the Photodramatist*, April 1923, 37; March 1923, 45.

2. "Miss Gertrude Shelby Praises Alice Howell," *Moving Picture Weekly,* June 24, 1926, 14.

3. "Women's War Work Committee Meets," *The Moving Picture World*, July 20, 1918, 368.

4. "She's Gone to Universal," *Exhibitor's Trade Review*, April 5, 1919, 1356.

5. "Lillian Greenberger, Casting Director," *Camera!* August 2, 1919, 12.

6. "'The Adventures of Tarzan' Serial," *Motion Picture News*, August 27, 1921, 1090.

7. "Bernheimer to Replace Greenberger," *Camera!* April 4, 1922, 17.

8. "Why Let Her Rest?" *Close Up*, December 5, 1922, 6.

9. "Mrs. Valentine in New Columbia Post, Lytell to Star in 'Obey Law,'" *Exhibitors Herald*, August 28, 1926, 30; "Columbia Signs Casting Director," *Film Daily*, November 12, 1926, 11.

10. "6 New Companies Enter Industry in N.Y. State," *Motion Picture News*, December 8, 1928, 1752.

11. "Studio of Sister Arts, Inc.," *Variety*, February 18, 1930, 41.

12. "Four Form Companies," *Motion Picture Daily*, April 21, 1936, 12.

KORA NEWELL, FIRST STUDIO TEACHER

1. Constance Talmadge, "Opportunities for Women in Motion Pictures," *Fall River Globe*, July 6, 1922, 12.

2. Ibid.

3. "Program for May Festival," *Beatrice Daily Sun*, April 27, 1913, 4.

4. "Former Syracuse Girl Instructs Jackie Coogan," *Syracuse Journal-Democrat*, August 14, 1925, 1.

5. E. Leslie Gilliam, "Will Woman Leadership Change the Movies?," *Illustrated World*, February 1923, 861.

6. "50 Odd Jobs for the Invisible Stars of the Movies," *Fort Worth Star-Telegram*, May 6, 1923, 54.

7. "Jackie Arrives in London Tomorrow," *Los Angeles Times*, September 11, 1924, 25.

EDNA WILLIAMS, FIRST INTERNATIONAL DISTRIBUTION SALES EXECUTIVE

1. "Edna Williams, Film Executive," *Exhibitors Herald*, February 23, 1918, 28.

2. "Jos. W. Stern Notes," *The Billboard*, January 2, 1909, 11.

3. "In Right Writers—No. 4." *The Billboard*, May 10, 1913, 9.

4. "Alec Lorimore Active in Two Companies," *Motion Picture News*, December 26, 1914, 48; Donald Crafton, "Edna Williams," in *Women Film Pioneers Project*, ed. Jane Gaines, Radha Vatsal, and Monica Dall'Asta (New York: Columbia University Libraries, 2018).

5. "Edna Williams, Film Executive," 28.

6. Ibid.

7. "Miss Williams Heads Company," *Motion Picture News*, February 9, 1918, 878.

8. "F.B.O. to Have Branches in London, Paris, Berlin," *Motion Picture News*, June 16, 1923, 2860.

9. "F.B.O. to Have Branches in London, Paris, Berlin," *Motion Picture News*, February 16, 1923, 2660.

10. "Ednella Corp. Formed," *Film Daily*, October 6, 1926, 4; Crafton, "Edna Williams."

11. 1930 US Federal Census; 1940 US Federal Census.

Index